Icarus Restrained

Icarus Restrained

An Intellectual History of Nuclear Arms Control, 1945–1960

Jennifer E. Sims

Westview Press
BOULDER • SAN FRANCISCO • OXFORD

Studies in Global Security

Published in 1990 in the United States of America by Westview Press, Inc., 5500 Central Avenue, Boulder, Colorado 80301, and in the United Kingdom by Westview Press, 36 Lonsdale Road, Summertown, Oxford OX2 7EW

Library of Congress Cataloging-in-Publication Data
Sims, Jennifer E.
  Icarus restrained : an intellectual history of nuclear arms control, 1945–1960 / Jennifer E. Sims.
     p. cm.—(Studies in global security)
  Includes bibliographical references (p.   ) and index.
  ISBN 0-8133-7750-1
  1. Nuclear arms control—United States—History. I. Title.
II. Series.
JX1974.7.S4767 1990
327.1′74′0973—dc20

90-13041
CIP

Printed and bound in the United States of America

The paper used in this publication meets the requirements of the American National Standard for Permanence of Paper for Printed Library Materials Z39.48-1984.

10   9   8   7   6   5   4   3   2   1

To my parents, Ruth and Albert G. Sims

Contents

Part Three: Arms Control as Security Instrument

Preface

I was first inspired to write an intellectual history of arms control during my graduate studies at the Johns Hopkins School of Advanced International Studies (SAIS). Listening to the SALT ratification debates, studying the evolution of national security policy, and holding an internship at the U.S. Arms Control and Disarmament Agency inspired an interest in understanding the origins of the postwar arms control community and its set of shared beliefs.

The original manuscript was mostly researched and written between 1979 and 1985 as a doctoral dissertation for The Johns Hopkins School of Advanced International Studies. Partial financial support for the dissertation came from a Hubert H. Humphrey Arms Control and Disarmament fellowship administered by the United States Arms Control and Disarmament Agency.

I will be forever grateful for the guidance, encouragement, and insights offered by my thesis adviser, Dr. Robert Osgood. I have missed him. Among others who have read the manuscript in whole or in part and have taken the time to provide helpful comments and criticisms are Robert L. Gallucci, Robert W. Tucker, David Alan Rosenberg, David Calleo, Charles Doran, James Rosenau, G. Allen Greb, Lawrence Freedman, George Quester, Uwe Nerlich, and Ruth and Albert Sims.

Among those who patiently listened to my evolving ideas on the subject, I especially wish to mention William T.R. Fox, Lawrence Weiler, Richard Burt, Lewis Dunn, Catherine Kelleher, Marc Trachtenberg, Donald Brennan, Charles Van Doran, Charles Henkin, Lucas Fischer, Ned Sabrosky, Ivo Daalder, and Milton Leitenberg.

I owe an intellectual debt of enormous magnitude to Professor Craig MacLean (formerly of Oberlin College). Most scholars have at least one teacher who challenged them to be more than they ever thought they could be; I was fortunate to have one who also took the time to show me how. He taught me to think analytically and, more importantly, how to persevere. Someday I hope to be able to meet his standards and at least in some measure to follow his example.

A manuscript cannot become a dissertation or a book without a great deal of editing and line-in/line-out advice. For his patience with detail as well as substantive advice I would like to thank David Rodgers, without whom this book would never have gone to press. Others who contributed time and energy to production of the final version include Christopher Weuve, Sean McCormack and Derek Freda. The original manuscript was produced by Elizabeth Izawa in Rome, Italy. Her excellent secretarial skills were critical to the preparation of the dissertation.

My husband, Bob Gallucci, never doubted me. My two children, Jessica and Nicholas, never let me lose perspective. For their years of patience and encouragement, mere thanks would never be enough.

Of course I take full responsibility for the final product.

Jennifer E. Sims
College Park, MD

PART ONE

Delimiting the Approach

If one behaves in a particular way, in anticipation of the other's reciprocation, there is a need to make clear precisely how one is behaving, with what mutual purpose in mind... (I)f the idea behind what we think we are doing is not perceived by our partner (enemy), what we expect of him ... may be too dimly perceived to be the basis for genuine reciprocation.
—Thomas C. Schelling
"Reciprocal Measures for Arms Stabilization," in Brennan, *Arms Control*, 178.

(T)he very fact that we transmit such concepts to the Soviets serves to indicate that, in our estimation, the differences between us do not necessarily imply the issue of social extinction. Such an attitude may, in the long run, reduce the likelihood of any large-scale military conflict between us.
—Thomas C. Schelling
"The State of the Arms Race," in Dougherty and Lehman, eds., *The Prospects for Arms Control*, 55.

1

Introduction

The Case for an Intellectual History

Ideas on how to achieve security have greater impact on this society than does any other set of ideas. More of our public money is spent on them than on any other area of national life. The peace of mind of our people depends on them. Yet we do not examine where we get the ideas, nor, after almost forty years, do we stop to test them.[1]

This commentary by a well-known defense policy critic has a special truth today as the nation struggles with its nuclear policies. From weapons procurement decisions to arms control policy, controversy and confusion over our nuclear premises and objectives are manifest. Logic would suggest that history, in its most intimate, intellectual form, could give us insight into the origins of our ideas and myths about nuclear weapons. Especially in the field of nuclear arms control, which is wrapped in a thick cloak of rhetoric and political grand-standing, intellectual history can help us understand the fiber, weave and texture of our current thinking.

However the notion of writing about the intellectual history of nuclear arms control is frequently met with boredom, skepticism or astonishment even by those who have been engaged in the process of developing policies in the area. Such reactions are at first startling and then sobering: How is it that in matters of such importance many of those concerned can be unaware of their premises and, more importantly, uncertain of the value of researching the history behind them? The lack of enthusiasm for intellectual history has even extended to academics in the nuclear field, reflecting both a weariness with theorizing about deterrence and a fascination with the data, gradually being released, on the history of weapons arsenals and targeting plans themselves. No longer is it necessary to consider only what we thought or said we would do with nuclear weapons; the facts themselves regarding procurement, deployment and options for the Single Integrated Operations Plan (SIOP) are being disclosed through Freedom of Information Act Requests and routine declassification processes. This flow of information has turned nuclear history into an attractive field for military historians as well as political scientists, persuading many in the field to turn from discussion of shifting paradigms and the evolution of strategic theories to exploration of where precisely weapons were, how many, what kind and why.

The availability of data for the study of the nuclear era is, of course, a tremendous help in distinguishing fact from myth in this important field. Yet the data or "hard information" must not be mistaken for "nuclear reality." Facts concerning hardware will not tell us very much about the evolution of ideas about how best to deter war, what was believed to be available in our arsenals by decision-makers, or what was deemed politically possible by national leadership. If the "reality" an analyst is striving to explain involves what policy-makers thought their options were and how they chose to refine these—ignorant though they may have been regarding what was actually available—the circulation of ideas and enduring myths become as integral an aspect of nuclear reality as the evolution of the hardware or the Strategic Air Command's (SAC's) targeting plans. That the contents of arsenals may be documented and ideas and intellectual trends may not be, only makes the task more difficult for the scholar of intellectual history. It does not make it irrelevant.

Nuclear "reality" might best be considered a combination of myth, political paradigm and military fact. If we are learning much more now than we were previously about the facts of arsenal evolution and targeting plans, this ultimately highlights the importance of myth and political processes for an understanding of American nuclear history. Juxtaposing myth and fact exposes the great disjuncture between declaratory policies, presidential preferences and SIOP options. It lends perspective to analyses of such critical junctures as the Cuban Missile Crisis, when nuclear myth and images in the heads of decision-makers may have played as telling a role as the facts regarding each side's capabilities.[2]

If one accepts the importance of studying the history of our ideas, then it is not such a great leap to accept the value of studying intellectual trends, not only to know "nuclear reality" but also to deepen understanding of ourselves. Intellectual history involves, after all, both the study of ideas and of how and why ideas took hold. As such, it involves an attempt to grasp the elusive concept known as "strategic culture"—that national soup of ideals, interests, and propensities upon which decision-makers have been nourished as professionals and as citizens. For knowledge of strategic culture helps us, among other things, to understand why particular solutions to strategic problems win, why they sometimes fail abroad, and why, though discredited, they nevertheless tend to reappear, albeit in slightly altered forms.

Indeed, intellectual history is particularly satisfying when it exposes commonalities among policies which, at first blush, appear to be reversals. The arms control record of the 1980s is rich in such unifying concepts and is therefore worth a brief review. It offers a solid case both for examining the history of our ideas about nuclear restraints and for seeking to understand their patterns.

SALT, START and SDI: The Intellectual Links

The end of the 1970s witnessed the strange, aborted debate which brought the Strategic Arms Limitation Treaty (SALT) era to a close. Critics of the SALT II treaty lacked consensus on its flaws and on whom or what to blame for them. Some conservative politicians argued that the whole SALT decade had been dangerous, given the obviously opportunistic orientation of the Soviet leadership and the super-secretive society which it purported to represent. In their view, a new SALT accord would have only further obscured Western security interests, thereby tempting continued complacency.

Several conservative strategic analysts such as Edward Luttwak, William Hyland, Helmut Sonnenfeldt and Richard Burt argued that the agreement exemplified the tendency for weapons management and security policy to be dictated by a deleterious arms control ethic.[3] According to this view, the United States had allowed its goals to become infused with impossible political purposes such as teaching "stabilizing" strategic concepts to the enemy, or facilitating doctrinal convergence and detente through the ongoing contact offered by negotiations. Sometimes one heard that these ill-conceived ideas had skewed our thinking about defense planning only recently. On other occasions the ideas were traced to the early 1960s. Arms control preoccupations were blamed for the development of the US's allegedly inferior nuclear force structure and for the failure subsequently to do anything to correct it by treaty.[4] Such conservative critics found themselves in an uncomfortable tactical alliance with those on the political left who opposed SALT II for a different reason: it seemed tacitly to ratify and legitimize the arms race. From both perspectives SALT II, while certainly an effort at nuclear management, was not "real" arms control.[5]

Unfortunately, the dispute over premises never became explicit during the SALT II ratification debate. It was unclear whether the critics' primary objective was the defeat of a particular treaty, the negotiating process, or the arms control establishment more generally. SALT II advocates in the Carter Administration had to defend their position across a broad front, including theoretical areas where their footing as practitioners was sometimes uncertain. The result was confusion and obfuscation: official moderation in characterizing treaty objectives merged with appeals for support for this "first step to disarmament"; official embrace of both strategic stability and reductions was juxtaposed with aggressive pursuit of major new weapons programs to assure conservatives of the Administration's realism and resolve in the arms competition. Whether or not SALT should have been killed is not the point; there was no clear, widespread understanding about what the SALT process was trying to achieve. The American arms control establishment was left politically rootless.[6] To a large segment of the general public the whole affair must have seemed an undecipherable charade.

From one perspective, the Soviet Union's invasion of Afghanistan and the subsequent tabling of SALT II provided a merciful end to a debate going nowhere. In another and more important sense, it prevented a much needed dialogue about our collective purpose with respect to nuclear arms control and thus temporarily foreclosed the possibility of achieving renewed consensus in this field. The country became split by the fear of communist advance on the one hand and unrestrained nuclear competition on the other. In a vivid reflection of this anxiety, it elected a new administration simultaneously committed to anti-communist rhetoric, the greatest peacetime defense build-up of the Cold War, and "significant" nuclear reductions in a strategic arms agreement.

Yet in spite of the apparent contradictions in public attitude there in fact existed a certain consistency; one sensed more a popular yearning for simplicity—a common sense approach to national security issues—than a wholesale rejection of either deterrence or arms control *per se*. There was an exasperation with the record of the SALT era during which ever more complex agreements were displayed against a backdrop of ever more complex and redundant strategic arsenals. But there was also an exasperation with the esoteric and politically unpalatable "solutions" to security problems proposed by the new negotiators (e.g., the Mx/Dense Pack "bargaining chip"). Thus the paradox: establishment arms controllers found little political support in a public clearly interested in serious weapons restraint.

In this context the public's attraction to bold initiatives in the new Strategic Arms Reduction Talks (START) and the concept behind President Reagan's Strategic Defense Initiative (SDI) was understandable. SDI seemed to be a technologically neat, fast track to reduced vulnerability and strengthened nuclear stability—perhaps even the safety of nuclear superiority. Its built-in arms control logic embraced a "negotiated transition" and limited disarmament. This cooperative element softened the program's impact as a weapons building initiative. The Reagan Administration proposed the nuclear shield less as a new way to shore up deterrence in the near-term than as a way to render ballistic missiles "impotent and obsolete" in the long run.

SDI's critics, who largely represented the orthodox arms control approach of the SALT era, which was symbolized by the Anti Ballistic Missile (ABM) Treaty, pointed out that the disarmament aspects of the formula seemed to have more meaning for the public than for the policy-makers. They noted the lack of government planning for a cooperative or negotiated transition to a world organized around defenses against ballistic missiles.[7] SDI advocates responded that the Soviets would be compelled to follow the American lead. Marginal cost considerations would force each side to choose less expensive increments of defense over relatively costly offensive measures. In effect, the technological race, which the U.S. would lead, would compel the opposition to develop strategic defenses out of economic necessity. The critics replied that compellance could not be expected to bring with it the exquisite timing and deliberate pace that a non-provocative deployment of defenses would require. They noted that it would be difficult to determine ideal ballistic missile levels and basing modes unless one had a fairly good idea of the defenses which might be arrayed against them. Such predictability would be unlikely in a non-cooperative, defensive arms race—economically unavoidable though it might be. Indeed the lack of planning regarding future requirements in a vastly altered strategic world made talk of U.S. interest in negotiating deep cuts in ballistic missiles seem suspect.

Without delving too deeply into the debate over SDI, one critical point can be grasped: The Reagan Administration identified the dominant arms control ideas of the SALT years, publicly rejected them, and then adopted a new approach whose central elements were strikingly similar to the old. To the extent that advocates of SDI argued that stability could be assured through a cooperative transition to a world of strategic defenses, the case for SDI rested once again on teaching a particular strategic model and abstract concepts of stability to the Soviets. If a cooperative transition were to be seriously entertained, then arms control would once again be central to defining the strategic relationship with the Soviet Union. Perhaps most significantly, fundamental instruments would remain unchanged: "education" of the Soviets would be pursued simultaneously by means of tacit bargaining and American example.

In any case a stable transition would, we were assured, happen almost automatically. Faith that the US could control the technological race, preserve defense dominance and compel the Soviets to behave rationally and without regard to minor technological leads and lags was remarkably like the faith that had suffused the McNamara years when rational models and technological superiority were expected to preserve offensive dominance, influence the Soviets, and possibly cinch American advantage. That the Soviets might be forced to calculate as we would, and that they would not take political or military advantage of incremental leads, were almost taken as givens—though few SDI advocates had accepted such premises in their previous roles as SALT critics.

In policy circles, the tendency to compartmentalize strategic planning continued, with SDI negotiated at one table and ballistic missile reductions negotiated more swiftly at another. It was the United States, not the Soviet Union, that sought to de-link negotiations on strategic reductions (START) from discussion of SDI. The Reagan Administration left office without an integrated security design in place. In an era when cooperative transitions could prove possible, SDI seems irrelevant and obsolete.

A brief look at the SALT and SDI debates strengthens the impression that U.S. arms control policy has been laced with enduring themes as well as recurring disputes. The ideas that join and divide us, perhaps because they are derived from our formative strategic culture, are not carefully considered in the process of policy debate. It may be understandable that in discussions so urgent and emotionally charged, advocates fail to focus on deeper premises and objectives and instead question the motives or sophistication of their adversaries. It is less understandable that the historical existence of such differences and their importance to current affairs goes unexamined by scholars. Precious time is wasted by trampling old ground and choosing paths previously explored.

During this period of rapid change in the international system and improved prospects for political accommodation with former adversaries, it is crucial to consider the prerequisites for disarmament and to probe the linkages between these conditions and those stability formulas with which we have become so comfortable over the years. The vanity of neglecting history in such an effort could indeed be costly.

The Historiography of Arms Control

The general literature maintains that the major theoretical foundation for modern nuclear arms management was laid in the late 1950s and early 1960s after disarmament efforts had proven unproductive. The central publications and intellectual momentum behind the theory are generally associated with work then underway in Cambridge Massachusetts.[8] Interest in the juncture between military strategy and arms control was explicitly recognized and underscored in 1960 as academics and former policy-makers sought to review the arms control record and to explore future options in preparation for the start of a new administration. The Harvard-Massachusetts Institute of Technology (MIT) Faculty seminars on arms control, the American Academy of Arts and Sciences (AAAS) Summer (1960) Study on Arms Control and the separate AAAS conference on the 1960 *Daedalus* volume concerning arms control, are ascribed particular importance in the synergistic development of arms control thought at this time.[9]

These seminal fora and the publications they inspired by Donald Frisch, Arthur Hadley, Thomas Schelling, Morton Halperin and others, led to a basic framework for arms control and a common denominator of concepts.[10] Brennan first outlined the framework in his chapter "The Setting and Goals of Arms Control" in *Arms Control, Disarmament and National Security*, a classic arms control volume based on the special issue of the AAAS journal *Daedalus*.[11] Others, such as George W. Rathjens, Michael Sheehan, and the author have since described the framework in more elaborate terms.[12] The central concepts were discussed, developed and expanded by many authors of diverse backgrounds such as Bernard T. Feld, Paul M. Doty, Victor Weisskopf, Jerome Wiesner, Arthur Hadley, Robert A. Levine, Morton Halperin, Herbert York, and Harvard economist Thomas Schelling.[13]

The arms control approach which developed out of these efforts of the early 1960s is widely viewed as having influenced the nuclear weapons policies of the Kennedy and Johnson Administrations, no doubt because participants or associates such as Herbert York, Jerome Wiesner, Thomas Schelling, Robert Bowie, McGeorge Bundy, and John McNaughton went on to have significant roles in the nuclear and foreign policy establishment. Central to the approach was the belief that international stability—which meant, essentially, minimizing the risks of nuclear war—should be the principle objective of arms control policy. Stability would best be assured by reinforcing mutual deterrence through manipulation of technological capabilities. Defined broadly, this arms control approach continues to have substantial support within and outside government.

So important were the meetings held in Cambridge in 1960, that subsequent descriptions of the origin of American nuclear arms control thought often have begun with them.[14] Yet this view of the roots of our arms control thinking is misleading in some important respects. For example, ascribing such importance to these seminars implies that ideas about arms control—as opposed to disarmament (that is, the general reduction or abolition of weapons)—were generated in the late 1950s because disarmament ideas and efforts had not born fruit. This is a misleading view, perhaps based on a lack of appreciation of the close relationship between the histories of arms control and strategic thought. Arms control theorists embraced deterrence theory. Their work became almost indistinguishable from modern strategic literature in range, preoccupation and sometimes even prescription.

In fact, the history of nuclear arms control thought as it came to be known in the 1960s, extends back to the earliest days of the postwar period and is more closely allied with strategic than with disarmament theory. As one analyst has justly written:

> ... any intellectual history of arms control theory ... must survey the evolution of American thinking on deterrence, strategic war, limited war, and arms control, so as to emphasize that all four sets of analyses really consisted of logical deductions from a single set of hypotheses about technology and stability.[15]

Once the close association between nuclear arms control and strategic theory is recognized, one can begin to appreciate that arms control's component concepts began to be developed much earlier than generally believed.

Arms control thought similar to the Cambridge Approach and intellectually distinct from disarmament, began to develop with the formulation of the Acheson Lilienthal Report, precursor to the Baruch Plan of 1946. Indeed, among the framers of the Baruch Plan were those who considered their task less one of achieving effective disarmament (which was then associated with abolition of all nationally operated sensitive nuclear facilities) than one of seeking enhanced stability by mitigating the dangers of surprise attack.[16] A limitationist approach to arms control thought was sustained by critics of the Truman and Eisenhower Administrations who saw danger in the disjointed pursuit of nuclear advantage and disarmament. The rapid development of a relatively coherent arms control community after

1957 suggests the significant theoretical groundwork that had previously been laid.

The arms controllers of the 1940s and 1950s were not unanimous in their views. Their instrumentalist attitudes toward nuclear weapons and their concern with stability above all else, left them with little company in a country intermittently rallying behind proposals for large scale reductions and new defense commitments or weapons build-ups. And while it is important to understand that arms control concepts were being explored at the earliest stages of the Cold War, the catalytic work which consolidated the approach was left to the theoreticians of the late 1950s and early 1960s. Any reference to the importance of the earliest nuclear arms control theorists must readily acknowledge that the period 1958–1965 is correctly identified as the "golden age" of arms control. The eventual popularity of the "new" arms control thinking followed in large part from its practical appeal: by stressing neither disarmament nor the limitless pursuit of a nuclear arms race, but rather the benefits of a rational, balanced and limitationist approach to arms management, it offered a middle ground for frustrated disarmers, as well as for budget managers and competing military services.

Another common and imprecise critique is that American nuclear arms control thought lacked political content and that its highly technological, "game-theoretic" bent was its central problem. Robin Ranger has argued that the dismal postwar record for arms control (as judged by the small number of agreements reached and the small number of weapons programs restrained) has been due to an arms control approach uninformed by political purpose.[17] Philip Green laments the assumption in arms control theory of excessive rationality in the control of force by states as well as its ahistorical and apolitical orientation.[18]

Yet it is hardly fair to judge theory on the basis of policy outcomes derived from its application. Theory should be heuristic and thus imperfectly fitted to reality. Otherwise it would merely be description. It is necessary to distinguish weaknesses in arms control theory from weaknesses in its practice. If policy-makers or negotiators used arms control theory without sensitivity to political context, the policy results must be laid at the feet of the practitioners not the theoreticians.

In any case, to the extent that arms control theorists attempted to bridge the gap between theory and policy—which, like the rest of the strategic community, they often did attempt—they actually based many of their propositions and prescriptions on political premises. They also often entertained political objectives that can only be appreciated by setting the ideas of the "golden age" in historical context. Whether the political premises and objectives were right or wrong is another question.

There is a further point to be made here: contrary to the implications of the conventional wisdom so far cited, arms control policy with a distinct political purpose was tried prior to 1957. The failure and then obsolescence of the approach increased the attractiveness of ideas related to technical stability which had been explored only superficially before and relegated political purposes to a secondary status. Insofar as arms control literature became technically biased in its prescriptions, this was more a reflection of practical lessons learned than a naive projection of theory.

What is suggested here is not that arms control thought has been unexceptionable, but rather that many critiques of it have been flawed. For example, if arms control's central purpose was technical stability and not, as Ranger asserts, agreements for purposes of economy or political effect, then surely success ought to be measured more by the absence of nuclear war than by the number of agreements reached or the number of weapons systems cancelled. In fact, the arms control literature of the later 1950s and 1960s de-emphasizes written accords in favor of tacit understandings, improved communications and stabilizing force deployment decisions. The most prominent arms control thinkers repeatedly affirmed that nothing *in theory* required that either defense expenditures or numbers of nuclear weapons be reduced in the near-term if their approach was adopted.

This study ends in 1960 though it is fair to say that the arms control approach which it describes continued to develop over the course of the next two decades. Though certain concepts hung on and aspects of the framework remained at the center of defense debates, the Cambridge Approach never achieved the status of an arms control "school" or "dogma."

The arms control community's cohesiveness diminished radically in the late 1960s and 1970s. Changes in military technology, the superpowers' arsenals, the international economy and political structure, and the moral self-confidence of the American public after Vietnam and Watergate, made arms control both more complex and urgent than it had been in the years of nuclear superiority, strategic consensus and public complacency. At the same time the compromises and flexibilities which arms control and disarmament groups and the military had been willing to make during an era of American dominance and moral hubris became untenable in the new age of American retreat and uncertainty. The neat, rational formulas for stability which had been so attractive when the modern world was believed to be understood and manageable seemed simplistic in the new post-dollar, post-Keynesian, post-Cold War environment.

Thus, at the very time that arms control finally became institutionalized as an ongoing international effort, its domestic base was cracking under the weight of a broader public introspection regarding the country's international purposes. While there continued to be strong public desire for arms control, neither SALT nor its supportive institutions represented a single "ethic" about how it ought to be pursued.

Finally, the persistence of arms control concepts in the postwar American approach to national security policy may not be adequately explained by reference solely to the strength of theory, the role of scientists, or the development of an arms control bureaucracy. Of greater importance may have been the belief among government officials that there were limits to public tolerance of extremism either in disarmament or weapons building. It was almost as if there were an implicit political "contract" between government and people regarding the relationship between nuclear controls and defense expenditures. Repeatedly, government officials seemed to calculate that the morally sensitive, isolationist, and fiscally conservative American public would support the maintenance of a nuclear arsenal so long as: (a) the communist adversary remained a greater threat to the American way of life than did the existence of nuclear weapons themselves, and (b) the Government made credible efforts to limit the development of the superpowers' nuclear arsenals, thereby mitigating the moral cost of their possession.[19]

An argument can thus be made that the persistence of arms control concepts since the early 1960s has been due less to the invidious intellectual preoccupations of experts and newly influential scientists than to the public's insistence on military self-restraint. Since American administrations in the 1940s and 1950s found it difficult to increase nuclear arsenals without simultaneous pursuit of weapons restraint, it is not surprising that a body of thought which suggested that one could do both at the same time should prove desirable and long lasting.

This point is important enough to deserve repetition, since an awareness of the domestic context of arms control thought serves to relieve the theory itself of the kind of definitiveness which otherwise would be required to explain its historical salience. What the Cambridge approach to arms control policy did was to provide an intellectual basis for rearmament in the late 1950s and early 1960s, when the United States thought it might be losing ground in the nuclear competition. It offered a neat recipe for the pursuit of both responsible arms control and weapons modernization. As such it appealed to security analysts, the military, government officials, and scientific experts eager for a logical and coherent model on which to base policy.

Such hypotheses about the persistence of arms control ideas and the particular longevity of the Cambridge framework are attractive. If tested they might be compelling. This study does not take on this task because it is primarily concerned with the origins of the Cambridge Approach—not the reasons for its acceptability in the 1960s or for its eventual demise.

Methodology

Any analysis, as an intellectual history, must answer some basic questions: how is the subject delimited; how are the "intellects" chosen; and why is the history bounded by the dates specified?

In response to the first question, "arms control" is here defined as any cooperative international effort to reduce the likelihood or destructiveness of war, or the cost of an adequate defense. An intellectual history of arms control involves the exploration of the origins and development of ideas relating to this effort. However, this particular study is further narrowed by the previously stated assumption that one particular approach to arms control came to dominate in the early 1960s and was characterized by a central preoccupation with the maintenance of nuclear stability. Although it is the development of this approach that is the focus of the following analysis, contending ideas about arms control objectives and how to achieve them will be discussed intermittently and for purposes of contrast.

Arms control thought includes ideas generated both by the elaboration of theory and by policy analysis. Therefore, the intellectual history traced here will include contributions from academics, politicians and policy-makers. Anyone whose ideas significantly affected the development of the dominant postwar approach may be included in the study. Not everyone who fits this description can be mentioned; only the best known or most important contributors will be identified and discussed.

Evaluating the importance of people's ideas for this study may have little to do with their proximity to policymaking. Previously classified reports such as NSC 68, Robert Bowie's reflections on disarmament plans while heading the Policy Planning Staff at the State Department, or Harold Stassen's first ambitious disarmament plan of the mid 1950s, though historically important, had little impact on the public marketplace of arms control ideas. And in that marketplace only those ideas which presaged concepts developed within the Cambridge Approach are of interest here.

Given the foregoing delimitation, it should be clear that the history which will emerge from the analysis will not be a history of negotiations or agreements. It will not even be a comprehensive history of arms control thought insofar as this could be conceived as including ideas about disarmament and the development of international institutions for conflict management. Rather, it is a study of the nature and origins of the dominant postwar approach to strategic nuclear arms control in an attempt to clarify it, distinguish it from others, and begin to explain the qualities which made it so attractive and eventually so widely accepted. The study ends with the early 1960s by which time the central theoretical features of the approach had achieved cohesiveness and stature.

The study is divided into several parts. Part One, of which this is the first chapter, serves to introduce the subject. Chapter II discusses the central premises and objectives of the dominant postwar arms control school—hereafter referred to as the Cambridge Approach in recognition of the historical importance of the 1960 seminars and associated work conducted at Harvard and MIT from 1959 to 1961.

Parts Two and Three are historical sections which will discuss the roots of the ideas which later comprised the Cambridge Approach. The concluding chapter will briefly examine the crystallization of these ideas into a coherent body of thought and discuss the weaknesses of the resulting approach to nuclear controls.

Notes

1. Richard Barnet, "When Will We Ever Wage Peace?" *Washington Post* (26 December 1982): E1.

2. Important work in this area has been undertaken at Harvard's Center for Science and International Affairs under the direction of Joseph Nye and James Blight. Interest in the psychological effects of crises on policy-makers has led to important insights on the Cuban Missile Crisis. See, James Blight, "The Shattered Crystal Ball."

3. For examples of these views see Richard Burt, ed., *Arms Control and Defense Postures in the 1980s* (Boulder: Westview Press, 1982), esp. pp. 1–21.

4. Conservative strategists discussed the uses and prospects for arms control in an important series of seminars on the subject at the Washington Center for Foreign Policy Research at The Johns Hopkins School of Advanced International Studies during the fall of 1979. The seminars were funded by the Ford Foundation and organized by Richard Burt, then with the New York Times. For representative views see Richard Burt, *Arms Control and Defense Postures in the 1980s*, esp. pp. 1–21.

5. For a broad critique of the SALT era's approach to arms control see Edward Luttwak, "Why Arms Control Has Failed," *Commentary*, 65 (January 1978): 19–28; also Fritz W. Ermarth, "Contrasts in American and Soviet Strategic Thought," *International Security*, Vol. 3, No. 2 (Fall 1978): 138–155.

6. Roger Molander's project, "Ground Zero" was originally intended as a national educational effort, seeking to fill the gap in public understanding of the subject. (Address by Roger Molander, Seminar on National Security Policy, Washington, D.C., Session 1, 1980, personal notes.) However, despite Molander's initial insistence on neutrality with respect to prescription, Ground Zero became absorbed by the nuclear freeze movement.

7. At a conference organized by the International Institute for Strategic Studies at Windsor Park in February 1987, representatives from the Defense Department and its SDI Office admitted that work on the arms control implications of a cooperative transition from offense to defense dominance had not yet begun. Some of the best work on the strategic implications of a transition to defenses has been done at RAND. See Dean Wilkening, Kenneth Watman, Michael Kennedy and Richard Darilek, "Strategic Defenses and First Strike Stability," *Survival* (March/April 1987): 137–165.

8. Here it should be emphasized that catalytic work in Cambridge drew upon resources in part developed elsewhere. For example, John Phelps, who contributed data and analysis on the vulnerability of missiles, worked in collaboration with Ohio's Mershon Center. See the Mershon National Security Program (Columbus Ohio: Ohio State University); RP 1 Phelps, Foye, Howland, "Some Calculations on Counterforce Strategies in a General Nuclear War"; RP-4, Phelps, "Strategy and Arms Controls"; RP-6, Cummins, *et al.*, "Accidental War: Some Dangers in the 1960s."

9. Leaders in the preparation of the *Daedalus* volume included: Gerald Holton, Professor of Physics at Harvard University and Editor-in-Chief of the AAAS, who initiated and organized the effort; and Jerome Wiesner, Director of the Research Laboratory of Electronics at MIT and member (later to be Chairman) of the President's Science Advisory Committee, who served as Chairman of the guest Editorial Board. Other key participants included: Robert R. Bowie, Director of the Center for International Affairs, Harvard; Donald G. Brennan, Guest Editor of the *Daedalus* volume; John T. Edsall, Professor of Biology at Harvard and Chairman of the Committee on the Technical Problems of Arms Limitation of the American Academy; Bernard T. Feld, Professor of Physics, MIT, and Chairman of the Operating Committee on the Technical Problems of Arms LImitation of the Academy; William T.R. Fox, Director of the Institute of War and Peace Studies, Columbia University; Stephen R.

Graubard, Historian at Harvard and Managing Editor of *Daedalus*; Henry A. Kissinger, Director of the Harvard Defense Studies Program; Louis B. Sohn, Professor of International Law, Harvard.

Key participants (Steering Committee members) in the AAAS Summer Study on Arms Control, which was an endeavor separate in organization and initiation from the *Daedalus* one, included: Bernard T. Feld, Chairman; Donald G. Brennan, MIT; Paul M. Doty, Harvard; Donald H. Frisch, MIT; and Jerome B. Wiesner, MIT. Other participants who delivered papers or made presentations included: Marvin Kalkstein, Hans A. Bethe, Arthur Barber, Frank Bothwell, John Phelps, John Mullen, Winthrop Smith, Morton Halperin, Max Singer, Jay Orear, Thomas Schelling, H. Roberts Coward, Marvin Gewirtz, Arthur Hadley, Joseph Kubis, Joseph Salerno, Louis Sohn, and Roger Fisher. For a more complete list refer to Chapter 2, note 3.

10. Schelling's books include *The Strategy of Conflict* (Oxford: Oxford University Press, 1963); *Arms and Influence* (New Haven: Yale University Press, 1966); and, with Morton Halperin, *Strategy and Arms Control* (New York: The Twentieth Century Fund, 1961). Morton Halperin did considerable work on nuclear restraints in war. See *Limited War in the Nuclear Age* (New York: John Wiley and Sons, 1966). Also see Arthur Hadley, *The Nation's Safety and Arms Control* (New York: Viking Press Inc., 1961) and Arthur Herzog, *The War-Peace Establishment* (New York: Harper and Row, 1963).

11. Donald G. Brennan, ed., *Arms Control, Disarmament and National Security* (New York: George Braziller, 1961).

12. George W. Rathjens, "Changing Perspectives on Arms Control," in *Arms, Defense Policy and Arms Control*, a special issue of *Daedalus*, Journal of the American Academy of Arts and Sciences, Vol. 104, No. 3 (Summer 1975): 201–214. Jennifer Sims, *An Intellectual History of American Arms Control Thought, 1945–1960*, a Ph.D. dissertation submitted to the Johns Hopkins University, Baltimore Maryland, 1985. Michael J. Sheehan, *Arms Control Theory and Practice* (Oxford: Basil Blackwell Ltd., 1988). For a somewhat different approach, see Robert Levine, *The Arms Debate* (Cambridge: Harvard University Press, 1963).

13. The records of the important and seminal discussions held by the American Academy of Arts and Sciences at MIT were edited by Gary Quinn and Karin Plaskett and published in limited number by the American Academy of Arts and Sciences as the *Collected Papers: Summer Study on Arms Control* (Boston, 1961). Hereinafter referred to as *Collected Papers*. This contains an interesting bibliography as well as an informal account of the discussions. The author located the Collected Papers with the assistance of Robert Osgood. Copies may be found at the National Security Archive, Washington, D.C, and at the library of The Johns Hopkins School for Advanced International Studies, Washington, D.C.

14. This may in part be attributable to the participants in the AAAS meetings themselves. Comments were often made about the revolutionary qualities of the work underway in 1959 and 1960. See Arthur Barber, "Arms Control: A Search for Policy," in *Collected Papers*, pp. 11–15.

15. Robin Ranger, *Arms and Politics 1958–1978* (Toronto: The MacMallian Company of Canada, Limited, 1979), p. 20.

16. See Part Two, Chapters 3 and 4.

17. Ranger, *Arms and Politics*, p. 3–9.

18. Philip Green, *Deadly Logic: The Theory of Nuclear Deterrence* (New York: Schocken Books, 1968), esp. pp. 157–252 on rationality and deterrence theory, and pp. 255–264 on the non-political character of deterrence theory.

19. For example, there was considerable opposition in the first Eisenhower Administration to "Operation Candor"—a proposed effort to share more information on the nuclear dilemma with the American people—for fear that such knowledge would jeopardize rearmament plans. Interestingly, according to a recent analysis of the history of public attitudes towards nuclear weapons, roughly 86% of American people in 1945 approved of the use of the atomic bomb against Japan. Support for using the weapons was highest during the Cold War, peaking during the Korean War. Support for use in a world war went from 76% in favor (1950) to a slight plurality opposed in 1955. See Thomas W. Graham, "American Public Opinion on NATO, Extended Deterrence, and Use of Nuclear Weapons: Future Fission?" (Cambridge: Center for Science and International Affairs, 1989).

2

The Cambridge Approach

Introduction

In 1960, the American Academy of Arts and Sciences (AAAS) organized two projects to explore the "state of the art" in arms control theory. Although a number of participants took part in both projects and both were conducted in the same general location, the projects were independent. One, initiated by Gerald Holton, Editor-in-Chief of the Academy and a professor of physics at Harvard University, produced a special issue of *Daedalus* devoted entirely to the subject.[1] Shortly thereafter Donald Brennan edited the book version, *Arms Control, Disarmament, and National Security*, which has been referred to as the "bible" of arms control.[2]

Bernard T. Feld of the Massachusetts Institute of Technology (MIT) organized the second effort, the Summer Study on Arms Control,[3] which led to the publication of:

- *Strategy and Arms Control* by Thomas C. Schelling and Morton H. Halperin;
- *Arms Reduction: Program and Issues*, edited by D.H. Frisch;
- the record of seminar discussions, papers and notes published as a limited edition compendium by the Academy; and
- a short set of papers on "psychological inspection."[4]

These publications recorded a revolution in the conception and practice of national security and nuclear strategy. Within months the revolution and the debate which it swept forward was known worldwide.[5] Decades later 1960 was seen as a turning point; "The Golden Age" of nuclear arms control had begun.

The purpose of this chapter is to present the central premises, concepts, and objectives of this dominant postwar American approach to nuclear arms control, which, for convenience, has been termed the Cambridge Approach.[6] Although not all the contributors to this body of thought subscribed to the entire approach as set forth below, most accepted the majority of its features and recognized the remainder to be at least plausible.[7] What is described below should, therefore, be considered an ideal-typical arms control paradigm—that is, more suggestive of a dominant orientation towards the problem than descriptive of a creed or dogma. The utility of attempting to generalize in this way is that it allows one to identify the most salient ideas and themes of modern arms control thought and to proceed with a tracing of their history. It allows one to distinguish those strategists who contributed to the approach from those who did not, and to understand the sources of those debates which portended divisions, both within the arms control community and between that community and the broader public. The following should therefore be considered a simplified outline, presented with a bias toward clarity, simplicity, and conciseness as opposed to detail and completeness.

Premises

The Cambridge Approach to arms control incorporated basic assumptions about the international system, the nature of politics, and the implications of modern weapons technology. These assumptions provided usually implicit building blocks for the arguments and policy recommendations of its adherents.[8] Some were believed to be immutable principles, others were simply judgments about the conditions prevailing just over a decade after the last World War. If there was frequent failure to distinguish between the two, it may perhaps be attributable to the policy orientation of much of this body of thought.

The Threshold and the Firebreak

The most salient aspect of the Cambridge Approach was its concentration of effort on the nuclear dilemma. This focus was not particularly surprising. Nuclear weapons seemed categorically different from conventional types in their potential for destructiveness. Not only did they offer an unprecedented magnitude of deliverable force but their spectacular use on Hiroshima and Nagasaki during the war demonstrated that they could be quick, indiscriminate and, under the right circumstances, decisive in their effects.[9]

The unique implications of nuclear weapons for modern management of force became ever more impressive as nuclear and related delivery technologies matured. By the mid-1950s military analysts were still trying to digest the worst: either side could be defeated before having mobilized or tested its military forces against those of its opponent. Nuclear weapons had introduced an era in which national survival could be gambled away on the basis of one hand of cards and only a couple of plays; the stakes of conflict and the implications of misjudgment seemed unprecedented.

Yet the problem for strategists was not so much the new qualities of the technology but the old: While nuclear weapons increased the stakes by introducing a new and powerful suit to the military deck, their effects seemed to fit within the rules of the game and therefore tempted governments to gamble.[10] Nuclear weapons were, in short, militarily meaningful. Unlike exotic biological and chemical means, they incorporated explosive effects which were, at least initially, an extension of the kind of warfare to which armed forces were already geared.[11] Therefore, nuclear capabilities could be easily integrated into war plans and methods.[12] This combination of devastating potential and military attractiveness put nuclear weapons in a unique category, the distinctiveness of which was enhanced by the revolutionary qualities of the technology from a scientific point of view.

The interplay of these factors led to an important conclusion: given that general nuclear war would incur costs unlikely to be met by any equal or greater political gain and that the technical characteristics which separated nuclear from conventional weapons offered the only clear limit on force during conflict, then the way to avoid nuclear devastation was to reinforce the perception of a conventional/nuclear threshold and to raise it so that the initiation of hostilities would be unlikely to cause it to be crossed.[13] Establishing the mutual recognition of separate levels of warfare became critical to establishing the perception of common interests which both sides had in the avoidance of nuclear war. The Cambridge arms controllers thus became absorbed with the problem of preserving the nuclear stigma. They sought to raise the threshold by assuring adequate conventional capabilities and by opposing the "cleansing" of nuclear arms.[14] The assumption was that once any nuclear weapons were used, the atomic escalator might have no natural stopping place and might well proceed to general use.[15]

The need to maintain a high threshold for nuclear employment, which in turn enhanced the conventional-nuclear "firebreak" in time of war, became conceptually linked to the need to prevent first use of nuclear weapons anywhere.[16] If the United States had to resort to first use in Europe, it was meant to be as premeditated, controlled, and clear an act as possible in order to signal the adversary that an important escalatory step had been taken. to the extent the firebreak could be made this discreet, the "signal" implied by non-use would be enhanced.

Thus, the theorists of the Cambridge Approach came to identify two escalatory problems: the one implicit in the diversification and miniaturization of nuclear weapons within the superpowers' arsenals; and the other attending the potential spread of nuclear weapons technology to third parties.[17] The opposition to nuclear proliferation was based on the notion that the more nuclear players there are the more likely is first use and a catalytic war between East and West.[18] The first use by any state would break a precedent and make subsequent use more likely.[19] If this first use were by an ally, the likelihood that the bipolar nuclear threshold would be breached would be high. But even use by a non-ally could lead at the very least to the first slipped stitch in the fabric of psychological constraints against nuclear exchanges.

Both the threshold and the firebreak were implicitly conservative concepts in three respects. First, they biased the Cambridge arms controllers against technical innovations which reduce the effects of nuclear weapons and thereby blur the boundary between them and more conventional types. Second, since the technology for peaceful nuclear uses and weapons is the same, technological advances which make the safeguarding of these separate uses more difficult were discouraged. Third, by reinforcing nonproliferation policies, the threshold and firebreak concepts worked in favor of preserving the bipolarity of the international system. It is arguable that this last feature compounded the politically conservative bias of the Cambridge arms control paradigm.[20]

Nevertheless, there is no necessary implication of technological pessimism in the concepts of the threshold or the firebreak. Arms controllers of the Cambridge Approach did not believe that all advances in nuclear technology were necessarily bad. While modern weapons had unusually dangerous and destabilizing features, technological change could be positive if it improved those features of the weapons that made them less likely to be used or those features of power generation that made diversion to weapons use less feasible. This view contrasted sharply with those held by more traditional disarmers who found nuclear weapons inherently evil and those who were opposed to peaceful nuclear power generation of any kind for similar reasons.[21]

The unique implications of nuclear weapons for modern force management became impressive only after the technology and related delivery capabilities had matured.   Identifying the problems associated with first use and the limitation of war required the realization of both the possibility of nuclear proliferation and the stakes that other actual or potential nuclear weapons states had in the status quo. Although these conditions were not generally evident until the late 1950s, this study will demonstrate that some astute analysts recognized the trends and developed the threshold and firebreak ideas much earlier than this.

Rationalism and the Origins of War

Both recognition of man's capacity for technological innovation (which arose not only with the American nuclear breakthrough but after duplication of that breakthrough in other states) and the clarity with which the nuclear dilemma presented itself, led postwar American arms controllers to a rationalist orientation to the nuclear question.

By the late 1950s and early 1960s, arms controllers were lamenting the emotionalism that had gripped the American public after the Soviet nuclear test of 1949, the bomber overflight in Moscow in 1956, and the launch of Sputnik in 1957. The call to arms control at the end of the Eisenhower administration was wrapped in the appeal for logic, reason and a sense of measure in our arms policies. Implicit in the rationalist approach was a wariness of politicizing the process of formulating and implementing defense policies. Drawing on strategic theory, the Cambridge arms controllers sought to disassociate their near-term objectives from those of the broader disarmament community. In 1959 and 1960, when the theoretical framework of the approach was being assembled in Cambridge, a number of the arms control theorists were reluctant to back disarmers in support of a nuclear test ban for fear of giving credence to environmental and health considerations not thoroughly grounded in factual analysis.[22]

This new preoccupation—indeed faith—in reason, which was reflected more generally in the surge of academic behavioralism in the 1950s, lent arms control a scientific bias. It was assumed that once the facts of nuclear warfare were known, and the common interest which all states shared in avoiding such a war was understood, certain formulas might be derived for making such a war unlikely.[23]

Implicit here was a faith that political and ideological differences between societies need not interfere with cooperative action when mutual interests presented themselves. The only requirement was

that leaders understand the facts and so perceive their national
interests clearly. Passion could then be overcome by reason and
peace be made more solid. In other words, what was missing in
Rousseau's famous fable about the stag and the hare was adequate
education of the hungry hunters to the nature of their plight, and
communication among them. Given such improvements in
information, the cooperative efforts to capture the stag could have
prevailed even in the event of a crisis prompted by one hunter's
sighting of a hare.

Stability

The fearsome qualities of nuclear weapons and faith in man's
ability to reduce international tension through the exercise of reason
made international stability the primary concern of the Cambridge
Approach to arms control. Decreasing the destructiveness of war
was deemed less important—especially when one considered that the
avoidance of nuclear war depended upon the perception of its
inevitable horror.[24] Indeed, lessening apparent risks associated with
use of these weapons seemed in certain cases positively undesirable;
the escalatory ladder so integral to extended deterrence had to be
easily and surely climbed *even though* a gap between conventional
and nuclear rungs offered a prearranged opportunity for mutual
reflection. And the greater the horror reflected upon, the better from
the standpoint of intrawar deterrence.[25] As far as reducing the costs
of an adequate defense was concerned, this goal was eclipsed by the
perceived requirements of national survival, which could actually
involve increased expenditures on new forces and special equipment
for monitoring compliance with agreements.

In the effort to present an approach to stability, two more
assumptions were evident in the Cambridge Approach: first, the
international system would be characterized by sovereign states with
conflicting and overlapping interests for the indefinite future; second,
the correlation of forces between those states could best be
engineered or controlled by their governors. Not only could men
theoretically devise formulas for stability and a balance of military
power, it was better to attempt to implement them than it was to let
interstate competition create a balance via some form of "invisible
hand."

Central to these arms controllers' prescription for nuclear peace
was what we shall call the "weapons-stability nexus." This was the
belief that the existence of nuclear weapons would be—at least for

the foreseeable future—necessary to ensure their non-use. Reductions could enhance stability, but they also might damage it.[26] Certainly complete nuclear disarmament would tend to be unstable or at best dangerous since all the advantages of first-strike capability would accrue to the side which proved best able to evade whatever controls were in place. Moreover, each side's expectation that the other might be cheating would make the balance at zero all the more volatile.[27]

This point exposes another aspect of the Cambridge paradigm: it was believed that one of arms control's most important roles concerned its potential contribution to a psychology of peace.[28] In conformity with its somewhat behavioralist orientation, the approach described methods by which state actors, singly or in unison, could change each other's attitudes and expectations through communication, education, and demonstrations of intent.[29] Moreover, by suggesting the necessity of merging arms control with defense policy and of assuring their complementarity, it implied that this was not only an element of a sound peace policy but in fact a critical part of security policy more generally. This focus on intentions and perceptions of the strategic equation was perhaps not surprising given that modern military strategy turned on the concept of deterrence—itself a concept with a strong psychological component.

Although it was concerned with stability "formulas," the Cambridge Approach, it must be emphasized, did not assume that the military balance was the sole determinant of war or that international political structure itself had nothing to do with the stability of the system. Rather, it was assumed that, given the bipolar structure of power, the status quo orientation of the major powers and the salience of nuclear weapons in the balance of power system, implementation of certain stability formulas could reduce the risk of war. But this was not to say that in other political situations with different international structural conditions, these arms control solutions would necessarily work. In fact, the contrary view has been most evident in the attitude of many Cambridge thinkers to the proliferation issue. Most have resisted, if not opposed, the transfer of stability formulas and assumptions from the strategic or East-West context to regional ones.

Again, a certain conservative bias is evident. The Cambridge Approach implicitly placed a positive value on maintenance of the political, technical, and international structural conditions on which its policy recommendations became based. With the diffusion of power in the international system that occurred during the 1960s and

1970s, the conflicts between arms control and alliance or Third World policies became increasingly apparent.

Comparative Risk and Arms Control Outcomes

The Cambridge Approach to arms control assumed that competitive arms acquisition in the nuclear age tends to be destabilizing because it aggravates tensions between adversaries and alters calculations about the likelihood of war and the potential gains to be derived from it. The notion that unfettered international arms competition would, in general, be more destabilizing than cooperative security measures taken in the common interest, accounts for the risk assessments implicit in the Cambridge Approach. The Cambridge theorists assumed that both parties in the bipolar contest shared a substantial interest in the status quo and the avoidance of nuclear war. Therefore the risks associated with reaching agreements in nuclear arms *could be* less than the risks associated with open competition, even with imperfect verification.

According to this approach, the calculation of risk associated with any particular arms accord involves both political and technical considerations. So long as both states wish to avoid general war, they will avoid abrogating equitable arms control agreements for fear of provoking a renewed weapons competition that might lead to conflict or even preemptive attack. For any agreement then, each side determines whether the other's stake in the status quo (including the entire network of previous understandings, whether tacit or explicit) would be greater than the gains which might be available to it through cheating on that accord. The first calculation is a political one. The second is a complicated, technical one: How wide would be the intelligence gap? What technical advantage might the opponent acquire through cheating? What would be the risks of getting caught (e.g., as a result of a breakthrough in verification capabilities by the other side)? What would be lost if the cheating were to be discovered (i.e., how threatening to the other side would the exposure of cheating be)?

Although for any particular accord, arms controllers of the Cambridge Approach have differed over the answers to such questions and therefore over the limits of adequate verification, they nonetheless have distinguished themselves by giving political considerations significant weight and by emphasizing the dangers of the alternative prospect of unrestrained competition.[30] Cambridge theorists have generally considered technological leads to be difficult to gain in practice and so potentially destabilizing to attain as to be clearly undesirable for either side.

Summary

Before moving from premises to a discussion of the central objectives of the Cambridge Approach, it will be useful to summarize the points made so far. The following statements would be affirmed by most past and present adherents of this approach:

- *Nuclear weapons* are different from all others due to a combination of: the surfeit of force they offer, relative to any conceivable political objective; the instabilities they introduce to military competition because of the speed with which they can be delivered and the potential decisiveness of a first strike; the attractiveness they nonetheless hold for military establishments due to the relatively orthodox form of their primary effects (explosions) and their compatibility with traditional delivery systems.
- The *international system* is composed of sovereign states with conflicting and overlapping interests and will be for the foreseeable future.
- The *structure of the system* is bipolar and is likely to remain so; as fundamental hostility between East and West coexists with mutual interests in avoiding nuclear war.
- The *leaders* of the major powers can recognize the above truths and reduce the likelihood of war by acting on their common interest in controlling or avoiding technical instabilities while observing the constraints of the system.
- Critical to the success of arms control efforts is recognition of the *"weapons-stability nexus"*—that is, the importance of the existence of nuclear weapons for security against their use and the delicate relationship between the pace and nature of changes in nuclear arsenals (up or down) and the likelihood of nuclear war.

Further clarity may be achieved by stressing what the original approach was not. First, it was not apolitical: the existence of political conflict and ideological hostility was assumed. As the arms controllers discussed the issue at the end of the Eisenhower administration, it seemed to them that neither the government nor the disarmament community had taken adequate account of the political instabilities which their respective positions portended.   The government was engaged in distributing tactical nuclear weapons in Europe and the disarmers were suggesting the emergence of a global community of trust at the height of the Cold War. The Cambridge theorists were convinced that political realism required a middle ground and that they were claiming it.   Thomas Schelling stressed in 1960 that a distinction had to be made "between the political conditions which an arms control agreement would require and those which it would create." Arms control could not be pursued in a system ripe for dramatic political change; yet the implementation of arms control would have to continually adapt to the political changes it itself would bring about.[31]   The importance of political calculations was also emphasized in such concepts as "comparative risk" as a measure of verification capability.

Second, the Approach did not rest on the assumption that disarmament would necessarily bring peace.   During seminar discussions in Cambridge in 1960 there were lively exchanges between participants on this matter.   Harry Rowen, Donald Brennan and Thomas Schelling emphasized the need to manage the destabilizing aspects of the arms race.   Disarmers such as Bernard Feld and Jerome Wiesner argued that reductions were necessary to ensure survival. However Wiesner and Feld did agree with Schelling and others that limited measures to manage the arms race could be useful. This latter position and its attendant implication that nuclear reductions would not necessarily lessen the risks of nuclear war, seemed to emerge as a lowest common denominator during the discussions in Cambridge in 1960.[32]

Third, there was no suggestion that the Russian adversaries were basically trustworthy, likeable, or "good," only that they could be rational—that is, able to perceive their interests in the avoidance of nuclear war and able to learn to appreciate the requirements this held for the development and management of nuclear weapons.[33] Although several participants in the 1960 discussions in Cambridge had special insights regarding likely Soviet behavior, relatively little attention was paid to the lessons of Soviet history and military culture compared to the weight given rationalist assumptions regarding the capability of all men to calculate self-interest.[34]

Given these premises, what were the policy prescriptions which the Cambridge Approach generated for the avoidance of nuclear war?

Objectives

Preserving the Nuclear Stigma

As suggested earlier, the Approach called for a determined effort to establish and maintain the threshold between conventional and nuclear weapons. This affirmation of the threshold could be accomplished in several ways. First, it was necessary to make sure that American capabilities for conducting a conventional war were adequate.[35] In the absence of credible non-nuclear capabilities it would be difficult to defend American interests without resorting to the nuclear arsenal. It would also be difficult for either the Soviets or the American public to believe that the United States Government recognized the hazards of their use or entertained an interest in avoiding nuclear war.

Second, it was necessary to avoid "fuzzing" the boundary between conventional and nuclear weapons as might happen when making the latter more usable. Deploying nuclear weapons with low yields or relatively "clean" (low radioactive) effects would tend to make first use more likely because governments under conventional attack might be tempted to introduce them without adequate consideration of the step's escalatory potential. Moreover, their very presence in a variety of local situations would increase the chances of their accidental involvement or of misperceptions regarding the moment or fact of their introduction. Most of the participants in the Cambridge discussions of 1960 were therefore biased against strategies of limited nuclear war, and the miniaturization of tactical nuclear weapons.[36]

Third, it was necessary to maintain the perception that first use of nuclear weapons could potentially lead to general use. Obviously, this perception was what generated the threshold concept in the first place. But as the technology spawned an ever-increasing variety of nuclear weapons, and uncertainty remained over whether intra-war limits on their use were possible, it became necessary to affirm the initial motivating condition: nuclear weapons constitute a class of weapons which are taboo because of the horrible consequence of their use in any form.

Maintenance of the firebreak required secrecy with regard to weapons production and security against the transfer of dangerous materials and technology. But it also required efforts that might be considered counterproductive on other grounds—namely, the readiness of Washington to defend allies with the U.S. arsenal if necessary (i.e., a "first use policy"), to share benefits of atomic technology with those states willing to forego weapons production, and to de-emphasize the military value of nuclear weapons. The first suggested the need to make nuclear weapons seem usable in Europe; the second suggested the need to transfer nuclear information and technology, a policy which could not be risk free; the third required denial or at least de-emphasis of the "weapons-stability nexus," a concept which lies at the heart of the Cambridge Approach to stability.

Managing Escalation

Maintaining the escalatory potential of nuclear use required that there be a continuum of force from tactical to strategic systems, that the essential characteristics of nuclear weapons remain intact (explosive and fall-out effects), that command and control be centralized and secure, and that each side believe in the other's commitment to go to the strategic level if necessary should the threshold be breached.

The belief in maintaining the escalatory *potential* of nuclear use did not preclude efforts to make command and control as smooth and efficient as possible so that intra-war bargaining could be effectively pursued if necessary.[37] Some analysts such as Schelling took the next step of advocating a "no cities" option for intrawar bargaining should deterrence fail. Though this "no cities concept" evolved as an argument for a "hard target kill" capability in some quarters of the strategic community, in its arms control context it was essentially an argument for reserving the capability for devastating cities (counter value targeting) while manipulating risks to weapons capabilities and homelands in order to terminate war. It was arms control for the period after deterrence had failed. Schelling went on to develop concepts of intrawar bargaining in his work on coercive diplomacy.[38]

Reinforcing Stability

The most important objective of the Cambridge Approach was the improvement of strategic stability to guard against accidental war, preventive war, and surprise attack. The Cambridge theorists advocated hardening and dispersal of strategic delivery systems to preserve safe weapons exchange ratios; providing robust, hardened command, communication and control capabilities; and reducing the time-urgency of strategic forces. The Cambridge arms controllers generally endorsed the development of the triad of delivery systems including the air, sea and land-based legs. Passing attention was even paid to the possibility that the development of a space based leg in the form of an orbiting bomb might be potentially stabilizing—though this did not seem widely supported in the discussions.[39]

Apart from such unilateral measures the participants in the Cambridge discussions believed that it was important to conclude agreements which would institutionalize strategic stability on both sides. This meant that both Washington and Moscow were to encourage each other to develop those nuclear forces necessary for "assured destruction." In order to be capable of assured destruction, nuclear forces had to be as secure as possible against a surprise first strike and sufficiently plentiful and powerful to do devastating damage to the other side even after having ridden out an initial attack. The Cambridge Approach called for such force characteristics *on both sides* in order to maximize the deterrent capabilities of each and, therefore, their joint security. It was assumed that in the nuclear era, the more secure one side could be made to feel, the greater the security of the other due to the reduced likelihood of preemptive attack.[40]

In theory assured destruction was primarily a force sizing and declaratory concept; it met the need to define the level of forces necessary for credibly deterring an all-out nuclear attack. In general the Cambridge arms controllers did not examine closely the issue of use: that is, what capabilities both sides should actually have or employ if nuclear war were to break out on a less than total scale. However they recognized that development of a nuclear force with predominantly counterforce capability would threaten the other side's ability to hold its adversary's population hostage. Therefore, improvements in accuracy, especially of the quickest delivery systems, and the development of population defenses, from civil evacuation plans to anti-ballistic missile systems, were discouraged.[41] Agreements codifying this relationship of assured destruction, also called "positive deterrence," would allow positive verification (i.e., the use of inspection to assure adversaries of the pacific intentions of both sides) or other procedures for the de-escalation of tension in times of crisis.[42]

The relationship of assured destruction to force development and deployment was an important one and, for the Cambridge theorists, time-urgent. They hoped that if both sides could be persuaded of the benefits of this approach to stability, a limit to the building of ballistic missiles could be quickly achieved and a rationalized approach to nuclear sharing pursued with the allies. In any event, if a relationship based on assured destruction did emerge, a natural plateau in force levels could be reached where additional weapons for either side would seem superfluous. If both sides were convinced of each other's interest in avoiding nuclear war and were also confident of their abilities to destroy each other should general nuclear war begin, there would be no incentive for additional nuclear acquisitions. If each side respected the integrity of the other's assured destruction capability and emphasized the second-strike or retaliatory role of its own (e.g., by developing relatively slow, recallable, invulnerable, and verifiable systems) the atmosphere of tension and suspicion would decline. The Cambridge analysts believed in 1960 that the target year for achieving this strategic balance was at least three years away. The most often discussed ballistic missile limit was 200.

Speculation along these lines led the theorists in Cambridge to hope that in the long-term, a force deployment policy based on positive deterrence would lead to a "neutralization" of the nuclear relationship. That is, nuclear forces would be so obviously unprofitable to use that they would eventually become irrelevant. Lack of use together with mutual agreement to halt further testing of new types of warheads, would lead to the ossification of both sides' arsenals. Once neutralization and obsolescence became the nuclear norm, perhaps significant weapons reductions could begin without jeopardizing stability.

As mentioned above, the Cambridge theorists' approach to stability did not address outstanding political differences between the Soviets and the Americans. Rather, it was assumed that they existed and that the bipolar relationship would continue to be one of essential hostility for a long time. All that was hoped was that each side would gradually become confident of the other's intent to do all that was possible to avoid nuclear war. Such intentions could be clarified through declaratory and deployment policies, through commitment to the process of negotiation, and through the preservation of secrecy regarding the details of all potentially provocative plans. This would reduce the likelihood of pre-emptive war based on the fear of surprise attack and reduce pressures on each side for additional competitive force acquisitions.

The positive political angle to the Cambridge Approach related principally to its long-term stability objectives. It was hoped that the process of reaching understandings based on common interest and the establishment of a network of agreements derived from these, would gradually increase the interests each side would have in the status quo and improve the understanding between both parties regarding the nature and limits of those interests. The more certain both sides could be of each other's perspective in this regard, the easier the arms control process would become, since the adequacy of verification would become easier to judge in political terms at the same time that the political risks of abrogations would mount. Some adherents to the Cambridge Approach even hoped that the long-term result would be a relaxation of Soviet secrecy and a realization at last of peaceful co-existence, if not accommodation. Moreover, to the extent that both sides could convince each other of their distaste for and disinterest in nuclear warfare, the greater would be the apparent disutility of nuclear capabilities. This, it was hoped, might aid the nonproliferation effort by dampening other states' incentives for acquiring a nuclear capability.

Methods

The Cambridge arms controllers suggested a variety of methods to achieve their stability objectives. They tended to de-emphasize orthodox pursuit of formal agreements in favor of more subtle and innovative means. For example, the whole Approach suggested the importance of communication to the initial identification of mutual interests and the development of each side's confidence in the other's recognition of them. Communication could be accomplished in a variety of ways, from tacit observance of precedents and limits to public declaration of policy. It might include explicit exchanges of views during negotiations or implicit declarations of intent embodied in force acquisition and deployment decisions. Although arms control at its heart was still the art of mutual restraint, the Cambridge Approach's emphasis on changing the expectations of both sides through decisions and actions as well as negotiations provided a rationale for considerable arms control input in the process of designing unilateral defense and security policies.

Of course, the design and conclusion of explicit arms control agreements remained an important method of arms control. But the priorities placed on different kinds of accords depended on assessments of their respective contributions to the stability requirements discussed above. Negotiations for radical disarmament were, therefore, less urgent than confidence-building measures or accords aimed at joint abnegation of destabilizing technologies.

Logic suggested that useful accords might also provide incentives for one side to restructure its forces by encouraging it to build more weapons of a certain type or with improved technology. Certain kinds of information exchanges or technology transfers from the United States to the Soviet Union might even be indicated in such cases.

The emphasis on bilateralism in the Cambridge Approach suggested another departure from past practice: multilateral fora would be eschewed in favor of secret two-party negotiations. International institutions would have less to do with arms control than would summits, back-channel diplomacy and secure "hotlines" for direct contact during crises. At the international level then, the Cambridge Approach suggested recognition of the need for equality of superpower representation, a de-emphasis on propaganda efforts, and affirmation of the hierarchical structure of the international system.

At the domestic level, the Cambridge Approach called for a melding of defense and arms control considerations in the formulation of security policy. This was logical given its emphasis on the arms control effects of domestic decisions regarding force acquisition and deployment. Such a well-rounded security policy would ensure that non-conflicting signals would be sent abroad and that defense decision-making would take due account of the impact of weapons programs on international stability. The result, as mentioned earlier, was that arms control literature became almost coincident with that of security studies and the role of research institutes or "think tanks," universities, and consulting firms expanded.

The Cambridge Approach provided a rationale for broadening the domestic security community; yet its eventual application by policy-makers had no domestic political angle. Nothing in the theory suggested the need to encourage the broad public's involvement in the development of arms control ideas. The focus on bilateral, secret negotiations precluded the involvement and, therefore, the public mobilization and information functions of inter-governmental and non-governmental organizations. The embrace of relatively complex deterrence theory and often unstated theoretical assumptions about inter-state bargaining, meant that even the interested layman was faced with a formidable task when trying to understand American policies and priorities. The Cambridge Approach presented no method for conducting arms control in a democracy, just as it suggested no method for reconciling arms control's bilateralist methods with alliance interests.

Summary and Conclusion

The Cambridge Approach suggested the following objectives for arms control policy:

- *Re-affirmation of the conventional/nuclear threshold* through development of conventional war capabilities, and a discriminating approach to force deployment at the tactical nuclear level—especially with respect to "special effects" weapons.
- *Reaffirmation of the firebreak* through a vigorous nonproliferation policy.
- *Pursuit of arms race stability* through the advocacy and practice of second-strike, "assured destruction" nuclear force deployments and the negotiation of arms control agreements based on these concepts.
- *Pursuit of crisis stability* through the securing of enhanced methods of communications, the assurance of safe, invulnerable strategic postures on both sides, and the development of confidence-building measures (including methods of positive verification).
- *The attainment of a long-term relaxation of tension* based on mutual recognition of the strategic interests both sides share in the avoidance of nuclear war.

The last objective carried with it the hope that strict Soviet secrecy and controls would gradually lose their rationale, making peaceful coexistence and the verification of future accords relatively easier with time. In this long-term sense, the Cambridge Approach was a world order policy of the liberal Jeffersonian political tradition, fully compatible with—indeed complementary to—the general policy of containment. That is, it sought not to change the sovereign state system, but to open it up enough for the continued pursuit of American interests overseas and the preservation of American democratic institutions at home. As will be pointed out in later chapters, the American public was impressed early on with the threat nuclear weapons in the bipolar context posed to this traditional American objective.

However, the liberal underpinnings of the policy were not associated with the purpose of international structural change; the approach was in fact highly conservative in this respect since its success would stabilize the bipolar international regime. Nor were there any implicit beliefs in the essential "goodness," ideological flexibility, or pacific intent of the adversary. Rather, there was a belief in the possibility that mutual respect, based on the gravity of shared interests, could lead to enough of a reduction of tensions that the rationale for Soviet secrecy and national barriers would be reduced or eliminated. In the meantime, the existing distribution of international power would be maintained in stable state.

Intellectual Divisions

To recall an earlier warning, this presentation of the dominant postwar arms control paradigm has been misleading insofar as the attempt to generalize for analytical purposes has conferred upon it an artificial degree of coherence.[43] The contributors to the Cambridge Approach were not engaged in the conscious pursuit of a single, collective design. The approach which they fashioned did not emerge as a phoenix from the pyre of the country's past disarmament efforts. Rather, it developed slowly as a result of exchanges of ideas inside and outside government over the course of at least a decade.

Indeed, within the boundaries of the Approach there was considerable room for disagreement. For example, the Cambridge arms controllers debated the height of the threshold. To what extent should the development of tactical nuclear systems be constrained? What was the trade-off between preservation of a high threshold and preservation of the firebreak (e.g., restraining tactical nuclear deployments and curtailing nuclear proliferation)? A related question concerned the importance of the firebreak and nonproliferation policy to strategic stability. Were horizontal and vertical stability directly linked and if so, to what extent?

A second area of debate concerned the purity with which theoretical stability formulas ought to be applied to unilateral defense policies. Given that assured destruction capabilities and second-strike characteristics were desirable features of strategic forces, did this mean that all new weapons acquisitions ought to conform to these requirements and that systems, old or new, which had contrary characteristics ought not be deployed or maintained under any circumstances?

A related area of debate concerned the issue of parity. Was parity desirable and if so, how should it be defined? What were the trade-offs between the political benefits of parity and its effects on strategic stability? How far should the United States go, for example, in encouraging the development of redundant Soviet nuclear capabilities similar to the American triad?

Finally, should effort be exerted on the long-term political goal of relaxing tensions, or should this be de-emphasized? Should potential political payoffs of the arms control approach be regarded more as positive by-products than as explicit objectives of the negotiating process? This was partly an issue of linkage: the extent to which political understandings should be an explicit part of the arms control record. It was also partly an issue concerning negotiations: whether or not direct communication should be valued in and of itself as a means of promoting peaceful coexistence.

For some supporters of the Cambridge Approach, political objectives were central and motivating. Their hope was that arms control might eventually pave the way to real changes in the international relationship of forces. For them, the Cambridge Approach was, more than anything else, the "first step to disarmament." But such views were not shared by the majority of contributors. Most perceived the arms control process as primarily technical, though based on certain political givens such as the nature and limits of states' interests in the status quo. The approach was geared to stabilizing existing force relationships; positive political results would be a happy secondary by-product of a policy whose rationale lay elsewhere.

This raises an important point: a distinction may usefully be made between contributors to and advocates of the Cambridge Approach. Many of the earliest and most important contributors to the paradigm became its harshest critics before the entire system of thought had fully evolved. To some extent this was because of the close relationship between deterrence theory and arms control. Contributors to the former also contributed to the latter to varying degrees.[44] But others who were directly engaged in developing arms control ideas *per se*, turned against the final approach in whole or in part and became potent detractors.

An example of such a contributor was Donald Brennan, a mathematician who played an important role in organizing the systematic exploration of arms control ideas in the early 1960s. Although he helped to develop the theoretical requirements of mutual stability, he ultimately rejected the Cambridge Approach to the problem. He became convinced that the Soviets would never appreciate the joint strategic interest in assured destruction and he balked at the extension of the theoretical argument for mutual invulnerability to the practical policy of urging Soviet development of redundant systems in the mid-1960s.[45]

The contribution which Brennan made to the Cambridge Approach cannot be overlooked in any intellectual history of modern arms control. Yet he cannot be considered an adherent to the Cambridge Approach in the same sense that Thomas Schelling might be. The latter's contribution lay primarily in the theoretical exploration of cooperative behavior in adversary relationships and the implications of this for strategic stability in the short- and medium-term. Although he did not agree with the emphasis some arms control advocates placed on certain elements of the Cambridge Approach, he did not take a position outside its framework or seek its dissolution.

In yet another category are those who supported the prescriptions of the Cambridge Approach but did not support or accept many of its premises. For example, certain disarmers made vigorous efforts to reconcile the policy of assured destruction with the requirements of Just War theory and associated ethical principles. Although such exercises were intended to provide a basis for supporting the established arms control approach, the authors did not fully accept the implicit assumptions of its limited design.[46]

These qualifications to the widespread acceptance of the Cambridge Approach suggest that a particularly interesting feature of modern arms control's intellectual history has been the number of people of disparate views who became involved in developing and advocating the dominant approach. In a manner reminiscent of the spread of certain ancient religions, individuals interpreted the Cambridge Approach in a variety of ways, choosing to de-emphasize or to ignore selected concepts without rejecting the whole. This flexible, feedback aspect of the Approach may account, in large measure, for its longevity as a conceptual policy framework.

Yet the flexibility of the framework also makes more complex any discussion of the history of the Approach.[47] The following chapters will explain how the central features of the Cambridge Approach evolved and discuss what technological, international, and domestic conditions were conducive to their development. The exploration of how and why these ideas crystallized into a widely accepted paradigm in the early 1960s will be of secondary importance. The focus will thus be on the contributors to the approach and not on the ideas of all its advocates or critics.

The story of the development of the Cambridge Approach begins in the immediate postwar period. It was during these years that notions about the special nature of nuclear weapons and their implications for the expansion and control of force first evolved. But it was also during these years that arms control's political utility was delimited. In the failure of the Baruch era's grand effort to shape world order through arms control, lay both the rationale for emphasis on more limited measures as well as the hardy seeds of hope that political changes in the Soviet state might be a long-term by-product of the arms control process.

Notes

1. Participants included: Jerome B. Wiesner, Director of the Research Laboratory of Electronics at the Massachusetts Institute of Technology and member of the President's Science Advisory Committee, Robert R. Bowie, Director of the Center for International Affairs, Harvard; John T. Edsall, Professor of Biology at Harvard and Chairman of the Committee o the Technical Problems of Arms Limitation of the Academy; William T.R. Fox, Director of the Institute of War and Peace Studies at Columbia University; Stephen R. Graubard, Historian at Harvard and Managing Editor of *Daedalus*; Gerald Holton; Henry A. Kissinger, Director of the Harvard Defense Studies Program; Louis B. Sohn, Professor of International Law, Harvard; and Donald Brennan, Guest Editor of the Daedalus volume.
2. Donald G. Brennan (ed.), *Arms Control, Disarmament, and National Security* (New York: George Braziller, 1961).
3. The Summer Study participants included Sidney S. Alexander, Professor of Industrial Management, Massachusetts Institute of Technology (M.I.T.); Arthur Barber, Air Force Cambridge Research Laboratories; Hans A. Bethe, Professor of Physics, Cornell University; Lincoln P. Bloomfield, Associate Professor of Economics, M.I.T.; George F. Bing, Lawrence Radiation Laboratories; Lewis C. Bohn, Systems Research Center, Lockheed Aircraft Corporation; Frank E. Bothwell, Director, Laboratories for Applied Sciences, University of Chicago; Donald G. Brennan, M.I.T.; David F. Cavers, Professor of Law, Harvard University; H. Roberts Coward, Political Science Section, M.I.T.; Paul M. Doty, Professor of Chemistry, Harvard; John T. Edsall, Professor of Biology, Harvard; Bernard T. Feld, Professor of Physics, M.I.T.; David H. Frisch, Professor of Physics, M.I.T.; Morton H. Halperin, Center for International Affairs, Harvard; Marvin I. Kalkstein, Air Force Cambridge Research Laboratories; Dalimil Kybal, Lockheed Aircraft Corp.; Seymour Melman, Professor of Engineering, Columbia University, Thomas W. Milburn, USNOTS; Max F. Milliken, Professor of Economics, M.I.T.; John Mullen, Air Force Cambridge Research

Laboratories; John B. Phelps, Department of Physics, Mershon National Security Program, Ohio State University; Ithiel D. Pool, Professor of Economics, M.I.T.; Gary L. Quinn, Atomic Energy Commission; Harry Rowen, Center for International Affairs, Harvard; Thomas C. Schelling, Center for International Affairs, Harvard; Max Singer, RAND Corporation; Arthur Smithies, Professor of Economics, Harvard; Louis B. Sohn, Professor of International Law, Harvard; Victor F. Weisskopf, Professor of Physics, M.I.T. Jerome B. Wiesner, Professor Electronic Engineering, Director, Research Laboratory of Electronics, M.I.T. There were 55 participants in the Summer Study.

4. Thomas Schelling and Morton Halperin, *Strategy and Arms Control* (New York: The Twentieth Century Fund, 1961). The volume resulting from the conference, *Collected Papers: Summer Study on Arms Control* by Gary Quinn and Karin Plaskett, included detailed minutes of the discussion but was distributed in limited numbers with the standard prohibitions on quotation and duplication. The analysis presented in this chapter draws heavily on the record of discussions in order to give the flavor of this most important gathering. However the remarks recorded in the *Collected Papers* were never cleared by the participants and therefore may not, in all cases, be completely accurate.

5. Thomas Schelling has noted that the book which he co-authored with Morton Halperin was rapidly translated into French, German, Italian and even Arabic.

6. This title perhaps confers on the approach a somewhat greater aura of coherence and geographical exclusivity than was in fact the case. The name was chosen to indicate the geographical location of the seminal meetings described in this chapter.

7. Obviously, contributors to the approach did not have to believe in all or even the majority of its features. Some contributed key ideas or concepts while remaining hostile to or ignorant of the overall framework that was to evolve.

8. For a contemporary formulation of most of these assumptions and goals, see *Arms Control and National Security: An Introduction* (Washington, D.C.: Arms Control Association, 1989), pp. 5–17.

9. Martin J. Sherwin has emphasized this point. See his chapter, "Scientists, Arms Control and National Security," in Norman A. Graebner, ed., *The National Security: Its Theory and Practice 1945–1960* (New York: Oxford University Press, 1986), pp.105–122.

10. A thorough chronological account of the introduction of U.S. nuclear weapons into Europe may be found in a series of draft papers prepared by Phillip Karber for the Nuclear History Program (NHP). Comments on the ease of integrating nuclear weapons into the conventional battlefield, at least on the U.S. side, may be found in Karber's "An Annotated Source Chronology of NATO Ground-based Nuclear Delivery Systems: Deployment in Europe 1954–1984."

11. For the importance of this point and the impact of the thermonuclear revolution on altering this fundamental premise, see Marc Trachtenberg, "Strategic Thought in America," *Political Science Quarterly*, Volume 104, Number 2 (1989): 301–309.

12. For an excellent discussion of how this happened within NATO see Robert A. Wampler, "NATO Strategic Planning and Nuclear Weapons: 1950–1957," *Nuclear History Program Occasional Paper* (April 1990, forthcoming.)

13. This thinking underpinned arguments in favor of a nuclear test ban in the early 1960s. See Donald Brennan and Morton Halperin, "Policy Considerations of a Nuclear Test Ban," and Thomas Schelling, "Reciprocal Measures for Arms Stabilization," in Donald Brennan, ed., *Arms Control, Disarmament, and National Security* (New York: George Braziller, 1961), pp. 235–266, 175–177. See also by Schelling, "The Role of Communication in Arms Control," in Evan Luard, ed., *First Steps to Disarmament* (New York: Basic Books, Inc., 1965), pp. 206–207. Schelling was, however, more inclined than many other arms control theorists, to consider the punitive, limited use of nuclear weapons in certain contingencies. Explicit mention of the threshold was made by Donald Brennan in the volume cited above: "It should be noted ... that in the absence of a comprehensive arms control program, an extremely good general-war capability might be required in the event of a failure of Type C deterrence, simply to persuade the enemy that it is unmistakably in his interest to refrain from transgressing the HE-nuclear boundary when the subsequent HE war begins to go badly for him." Donald Brennan, "Setting and Goals of Arms Control," in Brennan, *Arms Control*, p. 26.

14. See for example, Brennan and Halperin, "Policy Considerations of a Nuclear Test Ban," in Brennan, *Arms Control*, pp. 239–240.

15. Of course a key arms control theorist of the Cambridge Approach, Thomas Schelling, argued for creating options for limiting conflict or escaping from it should war break out. These limits fit within the objectives of arms control by seeking to limit destruction in case of war. But in practice they worked against the threshold concept upon which much of the strategic stability theory was based—offering the safety of multiple stopping points at the expense of reduced saliency for arguably the most important one: that boundary between conventional and nuclear use.

16. See the remarks by Bernard Feld in *Collected Papers*, p. 97. The desire to preserve the stigma against nuclear use ran up against the emerging possibility that use could be controlled and therefore destruction be limited. J. Orear pointed out the possibility that Khruhschev's threat to retaliate with nuclear weapons for the next U2 transgression (after the Gary Powers incident) was a single launch threat. The point was that the Soviets might see the potential for avoiding massive nuclear exchanges by limiting strikes and at the same time exploiting the fear of nuclear war. *Ibid.*, p. 102.

17. See for example, Herman Kahn, "The Arms Race and Some of Its Hazards," in Brennan, *Arms Control,* pp. 89–121.

18. For the best argument to the contrary see: Kenneth Waltz, "The Spread of Nuclear Weapons: More May be Better," *Adelphi Paper 171,* The International Institute for Strategic Studies, 1981.

19. See for example, Morton H. Halperin, *Limited War in the Nuclear Age* (New York: John Wiley and Sons, Inc., 1966), p. 71. Halperin writes here: " The use of nuclear weapons in a local war by either the United States or the Soviet Union might substantially speed up the process of the diffusion of nuclear weapons to Nth countries. Certainly, if one of the reasons that a number of countries have not made the decision to develop nuclear weapons is, as Kahn [Herman Kahn, *On Thermonuclear War* (Princeton: Princeton University Press, 1960)] has argued, the feeling that somehow these weapons are not used in wars, then their use in a local war would have strong effects leading to the diffusion of nuclear weapons."

20. A number of arms control analysts have criticized the bipolar orientation of earlier theorists, and have argued that American nonproliferation policy has been hampered by the resulting insensitivity to Third World security interests and aspirations. See for example, F.A. Long, "Arms Control from the Perspective of the Nineteen-Seventies"; Abram Chayes, "Nuclear Arms Control After the Cold War"; and Richard A. Falk, "Arms Control, Foreign Policy and Global Reform," in *Daedalus,* Journal of the American Academy of Arts and Sciences (Summer 1975): 1–13, 15–33, 35–52.

21. *Collected Papers,* p. 45.

22. See Arthur Barber, "Are We Talking to Ourselves?" in *Collected Papers,* pp. 17–18.

23. *Collected Papers.* Later chapters will demonstrate that this rationalist orientation was not unique to the period or the theorists of the time, but rather representative of an American orientation to nuclear controls evident from the beginning of the postwar period.

24. Although in general, arms control theorists of the Cambridge Approach opposed the use of nuclear weapons in limited conflicts, and therefore concentrated on the requirements of avoiding general nuclear war, some did consider the problem of limiting or stopping a nuclear war once begun. This involved considering punitive or counterforce targeting, the acquisition of "special effects" weapons—for example "clean" nuclear devices which could minimize collateral damage—and improvement of accuracy for certain weapons systems even when accuracy was, in the larger context of assured second strike capabilities, anathema. Thomas Schelling was one such analyst. Yet he wrote in his book co-authored with Morton Halperin, that arms control is, or should be, more concerned with reducing the incentives that may lead to war or that may cause war to be more destructive, than with reducing national capabilities for destruction in the event of war. [Thomas C. Schelling and Morton H. Halperin, *Strategy and Arms Control* (New York: The Twentieth Century Fund, 1961), p. 1–5.]

25. This refers to the dangers of making nuclear weapons appear too usable as well as to Schelling's notion of "the threat that leaves something to chance." See Thomas C. Schelling, *Arms and Influence* (New Haven: Yale University Press, 1966).

26. Arthur Barber, "Arms Control: A Search for Policy," in *Collected Papers*, p. 12.

27. See for example: Richard J. Barnet, *Who Wants Disarmament?* (Boston: The Beacon Press, 1960); James E. Dougherty, *Arms Control and Disarmament: The Critical Issues* (Washington, D.C.: The Center for Strategic Studies, Georgetown University, 1966), esp. pp. 1–22; Michael Mandelbaum, "International Stability and Nuclear Order: the First Nuclear Regime" in David C. Gompert, *et al., Nuclear Weapons and World Politics: Alternatives for the Future* (New York: Council on Foreign Relations 1980s Project, McGraw Hill Book Co., 1977), pp. 15–80. This last piece represents an attempt to distill the dominant nuclear arms control approach as understood in the 1970s.

28. The work of John B. Phelps on "psychological inspection" was of importance here. See his "Information and Arms Control," in *Collected Papers*, pp. 253–260.

29. Arthur Barber, "Arms Control: A Search for Policy," in *Collected Papers*, p. 13. Barber describes our weapons as "powerful, silent spokesmen."

30. See for example: Donald G. Brennan, "The Roles of Inspection in Arms Control," in *Collected Papers*, pp. 247–252.

31. Seminar comments by Thomas Schelling in *Collected Papers*, p. 62.

32. *Collected Papers*, pp. 44–48.

33. See comments by Ithiel Pool and Jerome Wiesner in *Collected Papers*, pp. 47–48.

34. *Ibid.* esp. pp. 47–48. Comments during this portion of the Summer Study sessions demonstrate a concern with political issues. The preference for examining force requirements in an arms control regime reflected the sense of urgency felt by analysts anticipating a new American administration, allied concerns about nuclear control-sharing, and the emergence of Communist China as a potential threat to international stability.

35. See for example, the comments of Frank E. Bothwell in *Collected Papers*, p. 114.

36. Arthur Barber was a particularly sharp critic of plans for deploying nuclear weapons in Europe. See his papers, "Arms Control: A Search for Foreign Policy," "Are We Talking to Ourselves?" and "NATO: A Reappraisal" in *Collected Papers*, pp. 1–41.

37. Though the concept of intrawar bargaining for the purpose of controlled war termination is usually identified with Schelling (see note following), others were preoccupied by the idea during the Cambridge Summer Study debates in 1960. See the remarks by Tom Milburn in *Collected Papers*, pp. 84–87.

38. Schelling made many of these points during the Cambridge Summer Study seminars in 1960, see *Collected Papers*, p. 55. For the elaboration of these views after McNamara's "no-cities" speech of June 1962 see Schelling, *Arms and Influence*, pp. 24–25 and 105–125. Schelling forcefully makes the point that the purpose of the flexibility one seeks is not to "conventionalize" nuclear war but to change the stakes of the conflict and to use the impressive weight of both sides strategic reserves to bring the battle to a swift end. It is therefore not a "tactical" war one fights but a strategic war of threat and maneuver. The implication is that limited nuclear war would end swiftly. The inconsistency between the "no cities" approach and the requirements of a stable deterrent were suggested during the 1960 Cambridge discussions by Morton Halperin, see *Collected Papers*, pp. 59–60.

39. *Collected Papers*, p. 164.

40. The "reciprocal fear of surprise attack" was considered a major problem of the nuclear age since it seemed that war could be the *rational* result of a fear of a war which neither side wanted.

41. This did not mean that research and development of nuclear capabilities should in all cases be halted or restrained. It was necessary to know what was technically possible in order to prevent a breakthrough that might lead to superiority on the other side.

42. Recognition of the importance of keeping the weapons exchange ratio greater than one was evident in the Cambridge Summer Study discussions. Remarks by Dalimil Kybal, in *Collected Papers*, pp. 65–67. These were based on a paper prepared for the Asilomar Strategy Seminar on April 27,1960. "The critical parameter in counterforce exchanges is the ratio R of the number of weapons expended by a force to the number of weapons killed...if R is less than one, a situation of high vulnerability, a decisive advantage is gained by the side making the initial attack." *Ibid.*, pp. 65–66. See also remarks on *Nuclear Exchange Ratios* by John Mullen of the Air Force Research Division, esp. p. 137. The beneficial qualities of ICBMs for the weapons exchange ratio was noted by Barber (*Ibid.*, p. 159) and apparently generally accepted by the group. Schelling did point out that the *type* of ballistic missile mattered—even alluding to the danger that would attend the development of a multiwarhead missile. "To go on, there is the question of exchange rates among missiles. Two hundred missiles says nothing about size. We could say that a missile is a missile, whether it carries 500 pound, 5000 pound, or 50,000 pounds of payload, whether it has a single warhead or multiple warheads, whether it is dispersed as an individual target, clustered with other missiles in a silo, or is shipmate to a dozen other missiles on a submarine. Just as missiles may differ from each other in their penetration and payload capability, they may differ from each other in their target significance; three missiles in a silo may be like one missile in their vulnerability. All of this suggests that one may need exchange rates among missiles. *Ibid.*, p. 207.

43. For another generalized description of the elements of the postwar approach to nuclear weapons see "International Stability and Nuclear Order: the First Nuclear Regime" by Michael Mandelbaum, in Gompert, *et al.*, *Nuclear Weapons and World Politics*, pp. 15–80.

44. For example, theorists on limited war contributed to the development of the concept of the threshold, and deterrence theorists contributed to stability analysis.

45. Personal communication, February 15, 1980.

46. An example is the notion of the weapons-stability nexus. For an example of a disarmer's sympathetic treatment of assured destruction, see Pierce S. Cordon's "Ethics and Deterrence: Moving Beyond the Just-War Tradition," in Harold P. Ford and Francis X. Winters, eds., *Ethics and Nuclear Strategy?* (Maryknoll, New York: Orbis, 1977), pp. 156–180.

47. To take the previous analogy further, an explanation of the history of Buddhism would require dipping into Hinduism, Shintoism, and certain animistic sects of Southern Asia; the distillation of the religion's essence and the selection of its most important contributors would remain contentious.

PART TWO

Arms Control as Political Instrument

In the days of the founding of this Republic...politics and science were of a piece. The hope that this might in some sense again be so was stirred to new life by the development of atomic energy. In this it has throughout been decisive that openness...was the one single essential precondition for a measure of security in the atomic age.
—J. Robert Oppenheimer
"The Open Mind," *Bulletin of the Atomic Scientists*, Vol. 5, No. 1 (January 1949): 4.

3

The Age of Atomic Innocence

The Nature of the Period

The immediate postwar period is usually described in uncomplicated terms as far as American arms control policy was concerned. During these years of nuclear monopoly, the United States Government sought an international agreement that would have banned national nuclear weapons programs after the establishment of an effective system for the international ownership, development, and safeguarding of the technology's peaceful uses. The British, Canadian, and American Governments first outlined this proposal for conditional disarmament in November 1945, then embodied it in a plan to the United Nations Committee on Disarmament the following year. Known as the Baruch Plan, this ambitious appeal for nuclear disarmament was widely perceived in the West as historic and unprecedented in its generosity. But the Soviet Union saw in its phased and conditional character an American effort to ensure Moscow's continued military inferiority in an important new technology and to penetrate and control the Soviet economy. This clash of interests resulted in stalemate for the next decade of disarmament negotiations.

Within the context of postwar American arms control thought the period from 1946 to 1953, which might be called the Baruch era, seems to stand apart, indeed to be almost irrelevant to the later arms control ideas embodied in the Cambridge Approach. Not only did official policy seem geared to disarmament, but agreement was pursued on a multilateral basis with a view to strengthening international institutions for the preservation of peace. Such notions contrast sharply with the bilateralist, statist orientation of later arms control thought.

Yet despite their anomalous image, the first years of America's nuclear age were formative ones for the development of concepts central to the country's later arms control approach.[1] This was true despite the apparent confusion in policy circles over the military meaning of atomic weapons, the relationship between arms control and military strategy, and the implications for our domestic institutions of the advent of an atomic arms race. For out of the

debates generated by these issues emerged a set of premises about
nuclear weapons and their relationship to prospects for peace which
were to become strengthened and institutionalized over the next
several decades. Among these premises were early, if limited,
appreciation of the threshold between conventional and nuclear
weapons, the bilateral context for controls and the weapons-stability
nexus.[2]

But these years also were significant for their role in establishing
a long-lasting hope: that arms control negotiations some day could
change the nature of the Soviet state, thereby contributing to long-
term stability. Although the Cambridge Approach to arms control
was to de-emphasize this goal substantially, in part because of the
failures of the Baruch era, it never denied or rejected it. Indeed, it
lent it some credibility by suggesting that the Soviets could be
educated about the benefits of a benign nuclear relationship of
American design. With such a special relationship would come
improved understanding and perhaps a measure of detente. It was
on this basis that many disarmers who sought substantial
international political and structural change, came to support the
limited measures of later years. In the Baruch era lies a key to the
appeal of the Cambridge Approach.

The arms control goal of international political change was rather
bluntly pursued during the Baruch era under the Cold War banner of
"Openness." The idea was to use America's nuclear headstart to
encourage the establishment of free flows of information, ideas and
population worldwide. It was believed that if such freedoms could
be established as international norms, it would be an important step
in the development of an international system compatible with
American institutions and ideology. As the political underpinning of
our arms control purpose, the notion of an "Open World" provided
the central concept around which disparate views could rally, thereby
providing the consensual basis for our early arms control policy. The
flaw in the consensus was that some believed the goal of openness
required early rejection of atomic secrecy and American abnegation
of its weapons capability, while others believed it required
maintenance of the American nuclear advantage in both weapons and
information in order to pry open the rapidly descending Iron Curtain.
For the first, the central threat was the new technology, for the
second it was the Soviet state.

Although positions differed on methods and the extent to which
sovereignty ought to be impinged for the purpose, the broad appeal
of the objective of an Open World provided the basis for consistent

public support for the official approach to international control. Moreover, the pursuit of global openness through arms control established an informal "contract" between the advocates of atomic arms development and the historically isolationist and fiscally conservative public. This tacit understanding assured that concomitant with increasing defense expenditures the government would pursue arms control to moderate and justify America's new global role.[3]

The primary purpose of this section of the study is to identify the origins of these early ideas about arms control and, in particular, to explore the full dimensions of "openness" as a political objective. The process will expose some of the more paradoxical aspects of the period. For example, controversies have raged over whether we seriously considered giving up the atomic bomb at a time when the Soviets had superiority at the conventional level; why we focused on atomic weapons and not on other weapons of mass destruction; why arms control thought seemed so detached from our military strategy—especially as regards its assumptions about the implications and effects of atomic technology. Perspective on these questions may be partially gleaned from a discussion of the fluid international conditions to which analysts of the time had to adjust, and from the domestic political conditions which attended America's entry into the nuclear age.

At the international level, the structure of power was changing at the same time that the United States' ability to shape outcomes was being affected by a new consciousness of power, an old national egoism, and a deep moral uncertainty in the wake of the country's use of two nuclear bombs against Japan. These conditions predisposed Washington to shape the international system, provided that an instrument or method could be found to make such an effort ethically and politically supportable. In this context, the political use of arms control—that is, as a lever to reform the Soviet Union—became eminently attractive.

At the domestic level, the nuclear policy community was both small and sharply divided—not only because of the legacy of secrecy and intermittent hostility between scientists and military during the years of the Manhattan Project, but also because of philosophical splits in the international outlook of the relevant policy groups. At the technological level, the lack of collective experience with nuclear fission meant that there was at first no thorough or widespread appreciation of the implications of this discovery for world security. Although some scientific prophets and strategists did begin to speculate about future conditions, restrictions on information and communication meant that their ideas rarely spread very far or had much impact.

This chapter will explore each of these conditioning factors with a view to setting the context for the emergence of the Baruch era's consensus on arms control. The highly volatile and fragmented nature of the period contrasts with the apparent unity in policy presented in the succeeding chapter. But in this contrast lies a key to the importance of the period, for it shows the power of the idea of openness for collective action, the force with which this idea impressed itself upon arms control's attentive public, and yet the nature and gravity of the latent fissures in America's attitude towards nuclear weapons and their management.

International Conditions

The advent of nuclear technology contributed to the crumbling of Washington's designs for postwar peace. The hope for continued allied cooperation in the establishment of a secure order fell before the circumstances of Anglo-American partnership in the and the postwar American monopoly on nuclear arms.[4] The former arrangement not only alienated the Soviets, it caused tensions between London and Washington as disagreements over its content and fulfillment proliferated. Moreover, America's dramatic introduction of its nuclear monopoly at Hiroshima, which so shifted the balance of power, seemed to compromise, if not preclude, the low profile and the beneficent and liberalizing role in the international system for which Americans had hoped. Thus, America's fabulous new power was met with both possessiveness and much hand-wringing. Indeed, as Hanson Baldwin has put it, America seemed "branded with the mark of the beast"—a circumstance which chroniclers of the country's vainglorious and messianic past found both ironical and portentous.

In contrast to American power there was European prostration. The desperate need for cheap power sources for European recovery, the growing hostility toward the Soviet Union, and a general awareness that the American atomic monopoly could not survive, lent a special urgency to the search for a means of exploring the peaceful potential of the atom while controlling its destructive effects. Arms control was perceived as more than a means of avoiding holocaust. It was also seen as a means of liberating a new industry and reestablishing a lost moral authority in the international system.

However, there were limits to America's self-flagellation and search for atonement for having become the "beast" with the bomb. The hubris which came with victory in war and science contributed to a growing international egoism and a continuing tendency to underestimate the technical and military capabilities of others—especially the Russians. Even many of those scientists who believed that the United States had no monopoly on basic nuclear science nonetheless believed that the totalitarian state system would constrain the advance of Soviet science and thus Soviet military capability in general.[5]

After the explosion of the Soviet Union's first atomic device in 1949, some commentators admitted their surprise at the earlier than expected achievement. Yet, the reluctance to credit the Soviets with skills commensurate to Americans' was evident. Bernard Brodie wrote:

> What does the relative earliness of the Soviet success indicate about the level of Soviet technology? Clearly it is not as bad as most of us thought. But what can we say beyond that? The Russians knew what we did not know in 1942—that atomic bombs could be made and were decidedly worth making. They were further informed by the Smyth report (an American publication) ... A great deal has been made of the phenomenal complexity of the bomb mechanism itself...but the Russians may have found it possible to dispense with what would be a typical American standard of efficiency and reliability. Or they may have learned more from us than we intended. When viewed in the light of these considerations ...the Russian accomplishment does not look so spectacular. They appear to have done in the four years...something we did in the two-and one-half years following the close of 1942, but whether they produced a production plant comparable to the one we had by July 1945 is still another question.[6]

Hans J. Morgenthau, a political scientist at Chicago, was one of the minority to criticize Brodie's kind of perspective: "Nations have a natural propensity to underrate their enemy or to overrate themselves. These distortions are the weeds in the garden of patriotism and national pride."[7] Yet even Morgenthau failed fully to appreciate our singular self-confidence, for Americans underestimated their friends as well. For example, it was with much reluctance and incredulity that Congressional overseers came to understand the significant role the British and Canadians had played in the wartime atomic project. Indeed, the view persisted into the 1950s that these Western allies were beneficiaries of American largesse, an opinion which in turn created problems for those Administration officials responsible for the implementation of wartime arrangements for raw materials distribution, information sharing and joint nuclear decision-making agreed to by President Roosevelt and Winston Churchill at Quebec in 1944.[8]

The sense of American superiority was evident in other non-scientific fields as well. The Russians were perceived by American diplomats as being somewhat crude and unsophisticated. The relatively simple disarmament plan offered as a counter to the innovative Baruch proposal of 1946 reaffirmed this prejudice, while the obstinacy and apparently irrational dogmatism with which the Gromyko Plan was later championed, only strengthened it.[9] As for the British, many Americans criticized London's inability to get the nation's economic house in order despite American aid, and the country's turn toward domestic socialism.

This national chauvinism, based on intellectual and scientific prowess, contributed to the fear among many Americans that espionage was the chief means by which others would come to match the country's nuclear achievement. The technical assumption upon which this view was based was that other states could not soon acquire the engineering know-how for building a nuclear bomb even if they possessed the theory behind nuclear chain reactions.

It was with respect to this technical assessment and threat perception that the most significant domestic differences were to be expressed. The debate involved differing philosophies of social progress, including the role of modern technology, as well as opposing premises regarding the origins of conflict in the international system.

Domestic Conditions

There were essentially three domestic groups with consistent influence on American arms control thought after the war: the official policy-makers in government, the military, and the scientists. In values and international outlook, the last two of these remained essentially hostile, while the first was more fluid both in membership and bias. Whereas military and scientific thought suffered from lack of cross-fertilization, Congressional and Executive thinking was fully exposed to, and indeed caught between, these opposing forms of expertise.

Politicians and Bureaucrats

The official community within which arms control compromises would be wrought for policy purposes was small and easily influenced by the contrasting views of the scientists and military, depending on the issue and, *inter alia,* the state of international politics. With the National Security Act of 1947 and the creation of the National Security Council, the post war emphasis on developing a holistic approach to national security policy became institutionalized.[10] This self-conscious need to develop an integrated politico-military approach to a variety of international challenges and threats was to shape the evolution of arms control planning as well. Indeed, during these early post war years arms control was more an instrument of political maneuver than an adjunct of defense planning as it was to be envisaged in the 1960s.

Because the "secret" of America's atomic achievement was both cherished and believed easily lost, only a limited number of people were fully informed about atomic technology and the nuclear arsenal. Therefore, the most influential thinkers on arms control policy were closely associated with or were members of the government. Operating in an "official" intellectual climate, these few were inevitably participants in the framing of America's broader international goals such as multilateralism, free trade, and collective defense. Just as these ideals were expressed in bipartisan American support of the United Nations Organization, the design of international monetary institutions and the handling of lend-lease arrangements, so they would be reflected in American arms control planning.

Yet in the realm of nuclear politics and controls, strains in the bipartisan alignment on foreign policy during the early years of the Cold War were particularly evident. The question of the disposition of America's dramatic nuclear advantage activated the vested interests of segments of the military and the unilateralist proclivities of influential conservative senators. The temptation to rest American defense on a limited arsenal of nuclear weapons strategically delivered was intensely appealing to those alarmed by the possibility that the Communist challenge might otherwise bleed the West into economic weakness and submission. Opposed to these views were those who believed that a return to domestic normalcy and reclamation of our moral authority abroad were at least as important as the Soviet military threat, and required vigilant maintenance of civilian control of our domestic institutions and bold new initiatives in the realm of nuclear arms control. Given the limited size of the informed policy community, the conflicting pressures on those charged with the earliest development of ideas regarding nuclear arms control were understandably intense.

This fragmentation of the official arms control community had its roots in the alienation of America's scientific and military communities. The prestige and influence of both had been dramatically heightened by the role of the first in creating the atomic bomb and the ingenuity of the second in organizing the effort and keeping it secret. But the Manhattan District Project had also fostered great suspicions and hostility between these groups as the tendency for scientists to discuss and question clashed with the military's bias towards secrecy and regimentation.

The Scientists' Movement and Scientific Rationalism

At the close of the war the scientists who had been involved in the Manhattan Project were quick to organize themselves for the political purpose of wresting control of the atom from military hands. They were anxious for civilian control of the atom because they feared that the military's bias toward secrecy and hierarchical controls would lead ultimately to government control of science—a trend that had been developing since the turn of the century.[11] Not only did this suggest the kind of political interference from which many of these emigre scientists had fled, it also was believed to imperil both the chances for international control and the very scientific progress which the military desired for the American defense effort. With a rapidly developing political agility that astounded many, the scientists won their first victory with the passage of the McMahon Bill for civilian control of the national nuclear program.[12]

The scientists' considerable public stature was evident in their popularity as speakers and in their inclusion in official circles. Shedding the ethical positivism that had left many isolated from their respective national polities in the past, post-war scientists in the U.S. organized themselves, wrote numerous policy-oriented articles, took government positions and made presentations across the country on governmental affairs.[13] They owed their elevated public position largely to their fascinating role as the experts who conceived and developed the "winning weapon" and to the prestige conferred upon them by the post war nuclear establishment.

Yet there was a deeper attraction to the arguments of the scientists than simple admiration for their war-time accomplishments. Excessive reliance on secrecy and military formulas for atomic security threatened to damage our domestic institutions; yet the scientific spirit and method seemed to embody the kind of individualism, enterprise, and rational approach to problem solving upon which the American way of life was believed to be founded. As the Cold War developed during the late forties and early 1950s and Soviet ideology grew increasingly threatening, the exaltation of a reasoned, scientific approach to problem-solving based on public understanding of the "facts" at issue, became ever more pronounced in the United States. The scientists' arguments recalled an aspect of the American myth that politicians and commentators had identified since the founding of the Republic: technological superiority through fair play. An increasing number of lay thinkers, many of whom held official positions, found an intellectual compatibility with the scientific community on this basis and allied with them on certain arms control questions. Although the special place accorded scientific expertise was temporarily lost during the McCarthy hearings and the Oppenheimer trial in the early 1950s, it reemerged in the late Eisenhower Administration, as indicated by the role played by the Presidential Science Advisory Committee.[14]

At one level, these intellectual trends were apparent in the way the first government-sponsored arms control effort, the Acheson-Lilienthal Plan, was developed and publicly received. In the critical analyses of this report, which quickly followed its publication, almost as much was made of the method by which it had been devised as of its contents. Commentators from both ends of the political spectrum applauded the measured, reasoned, and collegial style with which the drafting committee had deliberated. In reflecting on his committee's work, Lilienthal wrote:

> What I am trying to do is to emphasize the fundamental importance of *facts*. It is an absence of knowledge of the facts that has led to some of the unfortunate occurrences in the field of policy thus far, and they must be corrected as well as they can be. This is a supreme test of my faith that it is not in the discussion of dogma or abstract propositions that social progress lies, but in ascertaining the facts and evolving policies and action from them.[15]

Although by eschewing passion and dogma, Lilienthal attempted to distance himself from the idealism of World Government advocates, he shared with them a faith in the fundamental educability, goodness, and rationality of world public opinion. He was convinced that when taught the facts, people could be trusted to make "right" and thus good choices. He lauded the methods of science as a model for rational men to follow in all their fields of endeavour.

> It is my opinion that the only hope to control atomic energy and prevent its use for destruction lies in applying the scientific spirit and the scientific method to this problem. The essence of the scientific method and spirit to me—a layman—is that it does not start with the answer, but with the facts, and draws its insight and its overtones from the facts.[16]

Lilienthal's position was shared by Bernard Baruch, the first postwar American arms control negotiator, who referred to himself as "Mr. Facts" and by a majority of scientists who believed that politics and sociology in particular, had lagged behind science in both discipline and progress.[17] Perhaps the most frequently heard analysis of modern man's dilemma was that social institutions and thought had failed to keep pace with scientific progress and the challenge which it posed.

Theoreticians and advocates of international law and organization were quick to offer a reasoned approach to filling the gap. They took "scientific rationalism" to another level by suggesting very reasoned, legalistic solutions to the nuclear age in the form of new international institutions or forms of world government. Among the most active of this theoretical (as opposed to policy-oriented) school, were James T. Shotwell of the Carnegie Endowment for International Peace,[18] and Robert Hutchins, President of the University of Chicago.[19] President Hutchins established in the early fall of 1945, an Office of Inquiry into the Social Aspects of Atomic Energy which included leaders in the fields of economics, sociology' politics and international law. This office existed in partial alliance with those resident natural scientists who were interested in atomic policy during peacetime.[20]

Under the rationalist banner, natural and social scientists applied their expertise to the arms control problem and gained fame for doing so. Although at the time there were few journals devoted to arms control or national security policy, ideas generated by the scientific community were promoted in public fora (where almost anyone with credentials was in demand) and in trade journals. *The Bulletin of the Atomic Scientists* (referred to hereafter as the *Bulletin*) founded in 1945 by the Atomic Scientists of Chicago, borrowed heavily from these diverse sources to form perhaps the best record of unofficial arms control thought for the period. In addition, the editorial contributions of its founders provide an excellent liberal-rationalist commentary on the evolution of American arms control policy.

Aside from the motivation provided by the rationalist paradigm, the involvement of academics and scientists in the interdisciplinary subject of arms control had much to do with the successful relationship which science and government had established through the operation of the Office for Scientific Research and Development during the war. New links between the government and universities were established as public financed and planned research began to supplant the traditionally private, individualistic endeavor. Many scientists, and the academic departments which they represented, held professional and financial interests in the evolution of public programs in science and technology at the national and international levels at the same time that they feared the implications of state-dominated research. The evolution of this love-hate relationship can be traced through the debates over establishment of the Atomic Energy Commission, the legitimacy of requiring security clearances for AEC fellows engaged in non-classified research, and the organization of the National Science Foundation.[21]

It was widely believed among scientists that the structure of the domestic nuclear establishment and the relationship of science to government would have a profound effect on the prospects for international control by setting an example for other countries. Similarly, progress on international control would lighten the suffocating burden which official controls for secrecy's sake were having on scientific progress.

It should be noted that scientific opinion was not monolithic during these years. Among atomic scientists there were divisions between the younger generation and the older leadership arising out of the latter's role as a wartime conduit for scientific opinion on atomic policy—a role which the younger scientists believed was ineffectively performed. Moreover, several of the leading elder scientists were implicated with the military in their early advocacy of military involvement in the AEC.[22] Political differences also arose between those who felt the state system could be radically changed through the mobilization of public opinion and those of a more "realist" bent who believed that sovereignty was too well entrenched for that.[23]

Nevertheless, the scientific community did have a core set of beliefs which won allies within academia and unified its members in the face of challenges from opposing groups. These precepts included faith in the scientific method as an approach to social issues, and the necessity of a free "marketplace of ideas" for social progress and international peace. The orientation of the scientists was internationalist and their ideal world order, for which arms control was instrumental, was one in which the role of states was as constrained as science and individual enterprise was exalted.[24] Somewhat ironically, it was the philosophical embrace of rationalism and free expression that provided scientists with both their unity and their greatest challenge in the realm of arms control thought.

The Military's Influence and the Realists' Challenge

The early antipathy between scientists and the military did not ease with the unfolding of the 1940s. As the Cold War intensified there were increasing concerns about the potential for leaks—especially from the growing number of scientists in the nuclear establishment for whom secrecy ran against the grain. This led to intensive personal investigations backed by the military and its congressional allies, the process and publication of which many scientists considered to be harassment. The scientific community also suffered considerable loss of prestige and public trust as accusations about spies within its ranks continued into the 1950s.

As a result of the intensification of the Cold War and the declining influence of the scientists, the relative influence of the military grew in the field of atomic policy. Though the military's direct input into arms control thinking was minimal at this time, its perception of the central threat as one emanating more from the Soviet state than from atomic technology and its control, affected the development of official arms control thinking dramatically and tended to overshadow the more theoretical and speculative reflections of those concentrating on arms control *per se*. By the time a decision had been made on the wisdom of developing a hydrogen bomb, balance of force considerations took precedence over bold new initiatives to halt the arms race. In particular, the Air Force's interest in the development of its nuclear capability was supported by those congressmen who feared the Soviet economic threat most of all. Saving American domestic institutions through deterrence had begun to seem more credible than doing so through nuclear disarmament.

At the theoretical level, there developed a yet more significant challenge to the scientists' approach than the temporary dominance of a particular policy school. The rationalist spirit of the scientific movement for arms control was being increasingly challenged by the rise of the realist school of thought within academia. The "realists" took rationalism to task for its positivist orientation and its faith in the global relevance of "scientism." Hans J. Morgenthau, a leader of the realist school since the publication of *Scientific Man Versus Power Politics* in 1946, believed that America's internationalist bias, as reflected in much of its arms control thought, was symptomatic of man's excessive faith "in the power of science to solve all problems and, more particularly, all political problems which confront man in the modern age."[25] Morgenthau believed that scientism's universalistic, liberal bias had come to dominate Western political thought since the 18th century, and had led to its decline. Indicative of this trend had been the rise of legalistic, ahistorically optimistic solutions to world order problems as epitomized by Wilson's League of Nations and evolving notions of "scientific disarmament."[26]

In a set of articles published in the *Bulletin* at the end of the decade, Morgenthau stressed the need for resolution of the outstanding political differences between the Soviet Union and the United States as the only effective step to a negotiated peace. Morgenthau believed that "...disarmament can succeed only as a by-product of a political settlement, not as a substitute for it. Both historic experience and political analysis bear out these propositions."[27] In advocating a "spheres of influence approach" as the political handmaiden of effective arms control, he parted with the mainstream thought of his time and anticipated the operating premises—if not the ultimate objectives—of the arms control school which would dominate in the 1960s.[28]

Morgenthau was joined in his critique of rationalism by the eminent theologian Reinhold Niebuhr, whose realism was based on an Augustinian Christianity interpreted through a German-Lutheran framework.

> Niebuhr warned that reason and particularly faith in science, could never be trusted, for both reason and science too often refused to use religious and historical insights required to solve secular problems.[29]

Yet Niebuhr also inveighed against those of the American "civil religion" whose Christian positivism had gone to their heads, deluding them into believing in Anglo-Saxon grandeur and the perfectibility of man.[30] He believed that the resulting messianic drive to shape the international system according to America's idealist-democratic image was based on "... a profound instinct for the superiority of the Anglo-Saxon race; a sectarian, utopian spirit of concern; a complacence with the grace that God, through science, industry and progress, daily sheds upon America."[31]

Thus, Niebuhr found that the postwar movement for universal and legalistic solutions to international control of the atom added "a touch of pathos to the tragedy of our age":

> Our problem is that technics have established a rudimentary world community but have not integrated it organically, morally or politically. They have created a community of mutual dependence, but not one of mutual trust and respect.[32]

Although Niebuhr lauded efforts to strengthen the world community where possible, he also believed that "the notion that world government is a fairly simple possibility is the final and most absurd form of the 'social contract' conception of government which has confused modern political thought since Hobbes."[33] Niebuhr noted that proponents of world government argued that atomic weapons had created the necessary common interest for global integration. Since the Soviets had never had a chance to accept or reject a true constitutional order such proponents believed a sincere effort to devise one not weighted against the Soviets might lead to their ultimate participation. Niebuhr was intensely critical of such optimism:

> This answer contains in a nutshell the rationalist illusion implicit in world government theories. It assumes that constitutions can insure the mutual trust upon which community rests.[34]

By contrast, Niebuhr and Morgenthau believed that the cohesion provided by common fear of destruction was still weaker than the centrifugal forces inhering in the state system. For Niebuhr, as for Morgenthau, the best hope for peace lay not in the scientists' appeal to international reason and for international cooperation, but in the careful maintenance of the balance of power.

> Realism means particularly one thing, that you establish the common good not purely by unselfishness but by the restraint of selfishness. That's realism.[35]

Niebuhr's audience extended beyond the confines of academia to the broader public through his extensive publications and political activism.[36] He led the opposition to the postwar Progressives' call for an open door to trade and political understanding with the Soviets, including willingness to guarantee Soviet security needs in Eastern Europe. Niebuhr preferred to emphasize the necessity of containing the Communists. In early 1947, Niebuhr chaired the founding meeting of the Americans for Democratic Action, a group of liberals who disassociated themselves from Henry Wallace's Progressives by supporting the Democratic Party as explicit anti-Communists.[37]

Neither Niebuhr nor Morgenthau became extensively engaged in the arms control debates of the 1940s, but the realist framework which they helped to elaborate was usefully employed by some of their colleagues. Jacob Viner, a professor of economics at the University of Chicago, lauded the scientists' activism in the realm of nuclear policy while at the same time criticizing proposals for world government as constituting an overly simplistic approach.[38] He noted that

> many ... (scientists) think that all that stands in the way of adoption of this remedy is the stupidity of politicians and ordinary citizens, or their failure to understand how terrible the atomic bomb is or how impossible it is for any country to retain a monopoly of it.[39]

But Viner thought that the problem was more complex than the "rationalists" allowed: the global distribution of power which had left the Soviet Union and the United States preeminent, meant world government was impossible.

> We are told that when some danger menaces the ostrich he buries his head in the sand. Here we are advised to meet the menace of the atomic bomb by hiding our heads in the clouds. Neither approach appeals to me as wise procedure.[40]

Others joined Viner in attacking the designs, if not the motives, of rationalism's most radical school of thought. In *The Absolute Weapon,* the earliest collection of realist analyses of the implications of nuclear weapons, William T.R. Fox's particularly thorough critique of world government solutions to the atomic dilemma established him and his Yale colleagues as the intellectual opponents of this developing arms control community.[41]

The philosophical and political fragmentation over arms control approaches was exacerbated by the third condition affecting arms control thought in the immediate postwar period: limited and imperfectly distributed technological information.   Information on atomic resources and possible developments in the field was at first speculative and essentially monopolized by the military and scientific communities; then the requirements of secrecy and arsenal improvement distorted both its assessment and its dispersal.   The results were technological pessimism and political apathy.

The State of Atomic Knowledge

At the end of the war the feasibility of improving efficiency, increasing various effects, and miniaturizing the bomb were all uncertain.   Whether atomic weapons would ever be plentiful depended to some extent on whether thorium, uranium 238, or hydrogen could be used in addition to the relatively rare uranium 235 isotope. Moreover, the requirements of secrecy and the lack of full communication and cooperation between the military and scientific communities meant that the theoretical possibilities that were gradually appreciated by nuclear physicists were not always absorbed by the military or the political leadership in a timely fashion.   Knowledge of the parameters of nuclear power production were even more limited due to official secrecy and the preoccupation of the AEC with its weapons testing program during its first few years.   This relative atomic innocence had significant effects on the events which shaped, and the premises which governed, the thinking of the period.   The first and most obvious effect was delayed appreciation among non-scientists of the unique and revolutionary quality of the new technology.

Technological Conservatism

From a contemporary vantage point it is hard to imagine how the atomic revolution could have been missed or overlooked by anyone; in fact many were slow to see the broad implication of this new technology. Towards the end of the war when policy-makers had both the organization for systematic planning and much of the information about the technological future that they needed, their preoccupation with present military requirements and the scientific establishment's uncertain mastery of the atom tended to drive out speculative thoughts about the implications of atomic technology for conventional strategies of war or for the projection and control of force in peacetime.[42]

Secretary of War Stimson's account of the decision-making process that led to the use of the bomb against Japan suggests that while the weapon was considered horrible, it was also considered by many to be an extension of conventional military capabilities. It was not perceived as representative of a class of weapons inherently deserving of special opprobrium or indeed capable of being segregated from other highly destructive types.

> ... It was our common objective, throughout the war, to be the first to produce an atomic weapon and use it. The possible atomic weapon was considered to be a new and tremendously powerful explosive, as legitimate as any other of the deadly explosive weapons of modern war. The entire purpose was the production of a military weapon ...[43]

Stimson believed his critics erred in presuming that United States policy "... was or should have been, controlled or at least influenced by a desire to avoid the use of the atomic bomb." Stimson viewed all methods of total war—including the fire raids—as barbaric; "in recommending the use of the atomic bomb he was implicitly confessing that there could be no significant limits to the horror of modern war."[44]

The lack of reflection on the potential threshold between nuclear and conventional forms of force continued in some circles even after the results of Hiroshima and Nagasaki were widely publicized. This might well have been because atomic weapons, unlike more exotic biological and chemical types, fit more easily into the military's conventional paradigm since they involved relatively familiar explosive effects.[45] Stimson's recollection, quoted above, seems to confirm this at least as regards the decision on first use.

Bernard Brodie, in analyzing the Army and Navy's strategic plans in 1947, noted that the services seemed to ignore, or at least undervalue, those revolutionary implications of the new weapons which he had identified in *The Absolute Weapon* a year before.[46] At most, atomic weapons were viewed by the War Department as a method for blunting enemy capabilities while the United States mobilized for a conventional war of the World War II type.[47] The

Bikini tests conducted during the summer of 1946, seemed to confirm this belief for the Navy, which concluded, according to Brodie, that "... the amount of protection already built into modern class naval vessels ... provide a very high degree of immunity to (atomic) bomb blast." The only additional defensive measure required by the atomic environment would be somewhat greater distances between vessels underway.[48]

Clearly missing from the military's plans were recommendations for practical overall strategic adjustments to America's imminent vulnerability, the implications of the new salience—indeed potential decisiveness—of the Air Force in any future war, and the effects of possible scientific or technological developments in the field of atomic warfare. This was perhaps most evident in the Army's concentration on mobilization scenarios, but "the principal goals of all the services ... had been set before the end of World War II. Whatever relevance they had to the needs of the Cold War were fortuitous."[49] There was little attention paid to the concept of deterrence by forces-in-being; deterrence was the peculiar function of the bomb and strategic air power, not the armed services in general.

Such a lack of early innovative thinking about atomic weapons was due in part to the military's awareness of the scarcity of fissionable and fissile material, but it also reflected their preoccupation with the successes of the last war, the imminent reorganization of the services, and their previous exposure and adjustment to Guilio Douhet's thesis about the decisiveness of strategic air attack for which the atomic bomb seemed to provide but an exclamation point.[50]

Moreover, the developing recognition of the need for politically useful forces to meet the requirements of containment meant that much energy was exerted by certain military and State Department officials, to ensure the development of American ground forces—preferably of a highly mobile type. This effort implicitly recognized the special quality of nuclear weapons, but made no headway toward the development of a strategic design.[51] As Huntington put it:

> The implications of neither limited war, nor mobilization, nor nuclear airpower were fully spelled out. An inadequate balance existed but no overall strategic plan.[52]

Thus, the stasis in military planning reflected doctrinal bias, interservice rivalry, and the natural conservatism of a recently victorious power. But it also reflected the lack of a cooperative framework for information sharing between scientists and the military despite early efforts to create one.[53] It was not until the explosion of the first atomic bomb by the Soviets in 1949, that the military and its associated strategists began to adjust to the implications of the new technology.

Although Brodie's critique of the military's strategic analyses seems remarkably prescient in the light of subsequent events, it should be noted that he, as well as many of his colleagues in academia, were basing their more radical views regarding the strategic implications of atomic weaponry on highly conservative technological assumptions of a different sort.[54] For example, Brodie and Viner believed that atomic weapons could not be significantly reduced in size. This, combined with their scarcity due to expense, meant that minor targets were believed unlikely to be atomic ones. William T.R. Fox, while admitting the technological instability of the era, held that the sacrifice of an early American monopoly in nuclear capability could be supported by a political realist since the use of atomic weapons could never be a response proportionate to conventional provocation due to the inalterably excessive effects of this technology.[55] It was not until the 1950s when it became public knowledge that fissile material was more abundant than previously thought and that scientific advances could lead to significant miniaturization, that Fox, as well as others, came to appreciate the tactical possibilities of nuclear devices.[56] Paradoxically, this early technological innocence actually simulated some of the conditions brought about by later technological developments such as the hydrogen bomb. Thus, the theorists at Yale became among the first to elaborate the notions of the atomic threshold and strategic stability and to suggest their implications for limited war and the secure deployment of nuclear forces.

As has been frequently noted, the work of these early strategic analysts had only limited impact in policy circles and on public opinion. The intellectual community which Brodie, Fox, Viner and others constituted, was small during the 1940s. This was in part due to the American nuclear monopoly and the government's control on information, both of which made strategic studies seem highly speculative, less than urgent, and therefore not widely marketable. As Colin Gray writes: "A self-conscious community of extra-official strategists began to emerge only at the end of this decade."[57] And though a "thin if promising trickle" of strategic studies began to be produced by RAND, a post war Air Force creation for advice on the technical, political and operational aspects of strategic warfare, its effectiveness was constrained by the limited number and relative inexperience of its staff, its limited budget, and its lack of incentive in the form of a climate of urgency.[58]

Thus, at the end of World War II, an external community of strategic thinkers did not yet exist as an information bridge between the scientific and military communities or as a consulting network for arms control and force planning. These roles were not to be performed by the civilian strategists until the 1950s. One of the most important implications of this was that the state of knowledge about atomic technology was slow to develop and to diffuse through the policy-making community. Moreover, the secrecy requirements attending our atomic monopoly meant that the public was not able to provide political pressure either for more information on nuclear technology or for new initiatives in the arms control area.[59] Military and arms control expertise remained highly compartmentalized.

These limitations on the nuclear dialogue meant that the development of technological knowledge, a function of the AEC, became defined by the debate between military and scientific interests with little input from the public through its representatives. The deliberations of the Joint Committee on Atomic Energy (JCAE) were largely secret, which in turn made its members highly vulnerable to the arguments of the experts in the context of a general appreciation for the public's desire to keep public spending down.[60] Such circumstances meant that the case for research into peaceful uses of atomic technology or radiological effects of present and potential nuclear devices was rarely heard.[61] The quite rational emphasis on weapons development became an almost exclusive preoccupation of the government. As a result, some scientists even became wary of "progress" in their own work, demonstrating interest in defining and controlling government involvement with it. Thus, the second effect of our atomic innocence was a new technological apprehension within the scientific community.

The greatest appreciation of what lay ahead technologically was held by the members of the scientific community. Their understanding of the principles behind the nuclear chain reaction and the theoretical possibilities for fusion devices made them initially radical in their predictions. However, differing views on the wisdom of furthering technological development and on the Government's capability to manage it caused friction within the scientific community and exacerbated the free information flows between public, experts and officials, which scientists themselves had long championed.

The first systematic, theoretical consideration of thermonuclear possibilities had occurred in the fall of 1942 among a group of scientists organized in Berkeley by the Director of Los Alamos, J. Robert Oppenheimer. The group was sufficiently impressed by the thermonuclear possibility to give special notice to the S-1 Executive Committee.[62] Within a short time most scientists involved in the project at Berkeley and Chicago knew of the startling possibility.[63] Intensive work on developing a "super"—as the device was cryptically called—had to await development of a fission trigger. However, a small group of physicists continued to examine the feasibility of this next stage of atomic capability. Although they eventually determined that the fusion bomb would not be feasible in time for use during the war, several important physicists had become convinced that its development was inevitable.[64]

Among the first to warn the public about what atomic technology had in store was Dr. Edward Teller, a member of Oppenheimer's Berkeley group. In an article published in the January 1947 edition of the *Bulletin*, Teller noted that it was possible the United States could survive a war in which 1 to 10,000 of the current generation of atomic weapons were used, provided proper dispersal and hardening of forces and industry had been accomplished.[65] But he went on to point out that conventional and atomic "tonnage" could never be truly comparable due to the latter's "flash" and radiological effects. Moreover, he urged his readers to think about the future in which bigger nuclear bombs would become available, bombs potentially one thousand times greater than the Hiroshima weapon. This "natural" development within the atomic field would make concerns about radioactivity and thus mankind's very survival more salient.[66]

Teller's interest in the implications of the "super" was widely shared, but others were either more skeptical about the inevitability of its development or more concerned about its implications and wary of the world's ability to manage it than he later became. Indeed, one of the main causes of dissension within the scientific community was differing attitudes concerning the feasibility and propriety of constraining technological development.

Typifying one school of thought was Teller, whose attitude towards the "super" was shaped by firmly-held beliefs concerning politics and social progress. He believed that scientific and technological change were both inevitable and good. As long as the world remained divided into sovereign states—a condition which he took to be inevitable given Soviet secrecy and the need to contain

Stalin's communist ambitions—countries would compete for technological advantage. In Teller's view, this competitive advance was both inevitable and necessary in order for the stability of the system to endure. Attempts by governments to intervene in the process either by establishing controls or by internalizing the scientific process would put a "competitive premium on infringement" of any international agreement; for any state which managed to violate the accord—especially considering the long lead times involved in modern technological advance—would gain such a coup that the balance of international power would swing to its advantage.

Thus, Teller's requirements for adequate verification of agreements were extremely strict and intrusive. He believed that until the state system could be radically altered, either by diminution of sovereignty or democratization of its peoples, the risks of agreement would always be greater than the risks of technological competition. Fundamental to Teller's view were two notions: a) that technological change is integral to progress and that no particular technology is inherently more vile or otherwise distinguishable from any other and, b) that democracies are inherently incapable of enforcing strict secrecy and are therefore more likely to fulfill international agreements than are totalitarian regimes.

Leaving the second premise to discussion in the following section, it is left to point out that Teller's colleagues did not all agree with his assessment of technology's modern dynamic or role. Eugene Rabinowitch, a fellow scientist and editor of the *Bulletin,* wrote an article in October 1947 in which he drew a distinction between scientific progress and technological development. He believed that the latter was not only potentially bad, but that it could only be safely controlled by the exercise of individual morality. Thus, the *Bulletin* by its own admission, refused to publish any articles speculating on the possibility of a hydrogen bomb until a leak came from other sources.[67] Rabinowitch was not alone: as early as March 1946, a prominent physiologist urged all scientists to develop a moral code similar to medicine's hippocratic oath. He went on to argue that scientists ought to boycott any project in which they had no control over the disposition of the product.[68] Taking a similar position, Norbert Weiner, a mathematician who worked on missile technology during the war, refused to release significant results of his work to a researcher of the staff of an aircraft corporation for fear they would contribute to the arms race. In his view, to disseminate information "in the present state of our civilization is to make it practically certain that that weapon will be used." As far as controlled missiles were concerned, "their possession can do nothing but endanger us by encouraging the tragic insolence of the military mind."[69]

These scientists all believed that the fruits of research could and should be subject to personal censorship for the public good when deemed necessary. They were not so much elitist in their sense of mission as they were highly suspicious of national intervention in the conduct and use of their work. In their view, science was being discredited by a corrupt state system which turned theoretical advances into technological monsters. Since they believed all modern technologies available for war represented a continuum of force, the advent of atomic weapons meant war itself had to be abolished. Thus, technological and individualist prejudices fed the "one world" visions of many, reinforcing the notion of world government as the solution to atomic terror long after others, such as Teller, had given up on the idea.

Between the technological prejudices of Teller and Rabinowitch lay the views of such scientists as Oppenheimer and Hans Bethe. They believed that while scientific and technological advance was inevitable, mankind could manage the development and use of technology through national and international controls. Atomic technology ought neither to enhance nor to diminish the role of the state in the pursuit of peace; rather, it should lend new urgency to the development of national and international arrangements for technology's control.

The differences between Oppenheimer and Rabinowitch were subtle yet significant. Oppenheimer agreed that the advent of atomic weapons meant that a war was likely to be a total one, but he was equally certain that states must therefore create a barrier between conventional and nuclear forms of force. In his view, national politics could serve to limit, direct, manage and control the course of technological development. This faith in the ability of politics to create useful distinctions for policy purposes was evident in Oppenheimer's position on national technical controls. Whereas the more radical scientists feared that modern technology's essential coherence meant that national controls on one field of research would inevitably stifle all, with grave effect for American science and culture, Oppenheimer believed atomic technology could be distinguished from all others if the will to do so was widely shared and quickly acted upon.[70] For him technology could be either good or bad, it was the task and purpose of politics—not the individual scientist—to neutralize it when necessary.[71]

Regardless of such differences over the government's capability to manage nuclear developments, scientists generally shared a trepidation about what the new technology had in store. This provided much of the motivation behind their political activism. Yet despite the fact that they brought their ideas to the American people more vigorously than any other interest group, the general public registered little continuing sympathy with their case. While this was partly due to factors mentioned earlier such as government secrecy, the declining prestige of the scientists after the war, and growing hostility toward the Soviet Union, it also was another reflection of general atomic innocence.

Public Complacency

The American people were not experienced with a technology which could either develop faster than their understanding of it, or invade their daily lives. After the initial shock of Hiroshima and Nagasaki, awe of technology was soon supplemented by a renewed confidence in American skilled expertise.

Early in 1946, the Committee on the Social Aspects of Atomic Energy of the Social Science Research Council suggested an assessment of public views regarding the effects of nuclear developments on international politics. Financed by contributions from Cornell University, the Rockefeller Foundation, and the Carnegie Corporation, a large study was launched under the Council's auspices. The results showed that while 98% of the American people knew about the atomic bomb by August 1946, most were not greatly preoccupied by it. The general public did believe atomic bombs constituted a unique class of destructive weapons, but they also expressed confidence that the United States would find a technological fix for, or defense against, nuclear warfare before any other state could get ahead in the technology.[72] Indeed many scientists acknowledged that their early popular support largely reflected mass fear of losing civil liberties in a militarized society rather than sympathy with the scientists' worst nuclear fears.[73]

It was not that the American people were unconcerned about atomic weapons. The American people were aroused by the widely-published views of scientists such as Teller, who warned of the potential need to disperse population and industry in a nuclear environment, and Louis Ridenour, who wrote a playlet describing a future nuclear catastrophe.[74] The graphic articles on the effects of Hiroshima and Nagasaki bombs evoked horror and guilt. But the most salient political fact was the general willingness of Americans to let the government cope with the formulation of an answer to the new technology. This lack of the kind of broad grassroots activism on disarmament which affected later arms control efforts arose from four factors.

First, the radiological implications of nuclear testing and use had not yet become widely appreciated.[75] The public was largely unaware of the capability for nuclear weapons to affect their lives or those of future generations in peacetime as well as in war.

Second, the public was eager for a return to normalcy after the war, both in the operations of domestic institutions and in the conduct of their daily lives.

Third, faith in government was high after World War II and its spectacular finish. There was a readiness to believe that the expertise which brought the victory and nuclear breakthrough could also generate answers to the technological and political challenge these posed. Indeed, the very group which pressed hardest for public recognition of the atomic danger, the scientists, promoted the rationalist view that there "must" be a solution to the problem of control and that this solution would be found if proper regard for the facts was paid.

Finally, and related to the last point, the government did produce a program, with the apparent cooperation of military and scientific experts, that captured bipartisan support and the public's imagination. Soviet rejection of the plan masked the fact that the proposal rested on superficial consensus in the U.S., and that the bond which united most of the disparate views already discussed, was the elusive objective of an open world.

Only a few political commentators noticed the potential explosiveness of the situation and the tacit compact between government and public to which the scientists' movement had contributed. In 1947, Edward Shils wrote the following:

> Perhaps only when the situation has gone beyond the point of reclamation by compromise, will the mass of those threatened by annihilation awaken into the state of reason-destroying fright and anxiety. The political expression of such a state of mind will scarcely contribute to the maintenance of the tact and the clear perception of alternatives on which wise political judgement rests.[76]

Conclusion

The foregoing description of conditions which affected arms control thought highlights several policy problems which confronted the United States at the end of World War II. First, how could the United States regain its moral leadership and ensure a moderate role in a democratic world order when the weapon with which it became the preeminent victor was widely perceived as both deterrent and destabilizer? At the domestic level, how could the United States protect its institutions from the socialization, secrecy and regimentation which control of nuclear weapons technology implied? Finally, how could nuclear weapons best be controlled when the nature of the technology and its requirements were so poorly understood?

The limited number of those persons adequately informed, plus the lack of cooperation between those who could best answer these questions, meant that U.S. arms control thought was bound to be closely allied to the development of arms control policy, and to reflect the lowest common denominator as far as objectives were concerned. After an initial surge of creativity, arms control thought became reactive and essentially conservative; planning was almost non-existent. Indeed, the original U.S. policy position designed in 1946 was able to survive largely in spite of changing international conditions and the Soviet acquisition of Atomic weapons.

The consensus which so delicately supported U.S. arms control policy during this period was thin, yet it survived because it was based on an ideal on which Americans of diverse backgrounds could agree: an open world. This concept embraced the freedoms and respect for reason around which the scientists rallied, the ideology which conservatives believed set us apart from Communism, and the philosophical rationale for a military policy of containment.

In the following section we will trace the development of this "openness" theme for arms control and its variations through the immediate postwar years. Although differences in the premises of various arms control thinkers will be noted, the broad attractiveness of the concept's central tenets should be emphasized. Although the Cambridge Approach would downgrade the importance of openness as an arms control goal, the political agenda for arms control, of which the openness concept was a part, was never completely lost. Following a brief concluding section on the implications of this ideal for the development of arms control thought in the 1950s, we shall turn to a final analysis of the roots of the American nuclear arms control paradigm.

Notes

1. Some of these linkages are explored by Martin J. Sherwin in "Scientists, Arms Control and National Security," in Norman A. Graebner (ed.), *The National Security: Its Theory and Practice 1945–1960* (Oxford: Oxford University Press Inc., 1986), pp. 105–123.

2. For example Martin Sherwin has noted that the "winning weapon, combined with the apocalyptic vision of it in German hands, assured that its importance would not be underestimated by policy makers." *Ibid.*, p. 108. Many of those who advocated use against Japan, such as Arthur Compton, director of the Manhattan Projects University of Chicago lab, felt the weapon could only be effectively stigmatized if its first use was appalling. *Ibid.*, p. 114.

3. Evidence of official belief in this "contract" or rhetorical bond appears throughout the post war years. It informed the rationale for "Operation Candor" and "Open Skies" during the Eisenhower Administration and was referred to explicitly in the report of the Executive Committee on Regulation of Armaments, which was presented to the NSC on 26 May 1953. See Charles A. Appleby, *Eisenhower and Arms Control, 1953–1961*, a dissertation submitted to the Johns Hopkins University, Baltimore, Maryland (1987), pp. 22–25; on NSC 68, pp. 49–50.

4. The relative importance of the bomb to the origins of the Cold War is still hotly debated, and will not be addressed in this study.

5. Responsible estimates on the number of years it would take for the Soviets to duplicate our atomic achievement ranged from 5–25.

6. Bernard Brodie, "What is the Outlook Now?" *Bulletin of the Atomic Scientists*, Vol. 5, No. 10 (October 1949): 268.

7. Hans Morgenthau, "The Conquest of the U.S. by Germany," *Bulletin of the Atomic Scientists*, Vol. 6, No. 1 (January 1950): 21.

8. For a discussion of the Quebec Accords, see Richard G. Hewlett and Oscar E. Anderson, Jr., *The New World 1939/1946, Vol. 1: A History of the United States Atomic Energy Commission* (University Park: Pennsylvania State University Press, 1962), pp. 278–280. Also Gregg Herken, *The Winning Weapon* (New York: Alfred A. Knopf, 1980), pp. 61–64.

9. Such views were even shared by many scientists who were more willing than others to grant the Soviets greater expertise in the scientific area.

10. For more on this see, Richard D. Challener, "The National Security Policy from Truman to Eisenhower: Did the 'Hidden Hand' Leadership Make Any Difference," in Norman A. Graebner, *The National Security:*, pp. 42–43.

11. On these developments see Alice Kimball Smith, *A Peril and a Hope: The Scientists' Movement in America, 1945–1947* (Chicago: University of Chicago Press, 1965), and Robert Gilpin, *American Scientists and Nuclear Weapons Policy* (Princeton: Princeton University Press, 1962).

12. The passage of this bill signalled the legislative failure of the May-Johnson Bill which had been drafted by the War Department. Among other contentious provisions of the government sponsored legislation, it allowed for military participation on the Atomic Energy Commission (AEC). The McMahon Bill as finally passed called for a civilian commission, a military liaison board to advise on military applications and requirements and a General Advisory Committee of scientists for technical counsel. Despite the legislative victory, the tension between military and civilian influence within the AEC continued to trouble the organization. Hewlett and Anderson, *The New World*, pp. 482–530; David Lilienthal, *The Journals of David E. Lilienthal: The Atomic Energy Years 1945–1950*, Vol. II (New York: Harper & Row, 1954), *passim*.

13. See Robert Gilpin, *American Scientists and Nuclear Weapons Policy*, pp. 3–38. Also Richard Rhodes, *The Making of the Atomic Bomb* (New York: Simon and Schuster Inc., 1986).

14. "Confessions of a Weaponeer," transcript of an interview with George Kistiakowsky, broadcast on PBS, 3 March 1987 (Boston: WGBH Transcripts, 1987), pp. 1–23.

15. Lilienthal, *Journals*, p. 15.

16. David E. Lilienthal, "How Can Atomic Energy Best be Controlled?" *Bulletin of the Atomic Scientists*, Vol. 2, No. 7/8 (October 1946): 14.

17. In commenting on the purge of genetics in the Soviet Union, the editors of the *Bulletin of the Atomic Scientists* wrote: "We believe—and this belief is the basis of all activities of the 'atomic scientists'—that this conflict (between technological progress and the persistence of outworn patterns of social and political behavior) cannot be resolved without a more widespread knowledge of the facts and methods of science, and increased application of this knowledge in the formulation of national and international policies." [Vol. 5, No. 5 (May 1949): 130.] For a similar view from a more "establishment" scientist of the 1940s, see Robert J. Oppenheimer, "Physics in the Contemporary World," *Bulletin of the Atomic Scientists*, Vol. 4, No. 3 (March 1948): 86.

18. Shotwell believed in supplementing the United Nations Charter with a Tripartite Advisory Body in arms control and a treaty providing a binding covenant against war itself. See "The Atomic Bomb and International Organization," *Bulletin of the Atomic Scientists*, Vol. 1, No. 7 (March 1946): 8–9.

19. See Robert Hutchins, "Unrealistic Realism," *Vital Speeches*, Vol. 11 (15 July 1945): 601–603.

20. See John A. Simpson, "The Scientists as Public Educators: a Two-year Summary," *Bulletin of the Atomic Scientists*, Vol. 3, No. 9 (September 1947): 245.

21. The Atomic Energy Commission will be referred to hereafter as the AEC.

22. This refers to the May-Johnson Bill which was supported for example, by President Conant of Harvard, a physicist, and Vannevar Bush.

23. See Chapter 4, pp. 83–94 for a discussion of these differences.

24. See Robert Gilpin, *American Scientists and Nuclear Weapons Policy* (Princeton: Princeton University Press, 1962), pp. 28–34.

25. Hans J. Morgenthau, *Scientific Man Versus Power Politics* (Chicago: The University of Chicago Press, 1946), p. vi.

26. *Ibid.* According to Morgenthau, rationalism brings the philosopher to four erroneous conclusions: (1) that the rationally right equals the ethically good; (2) that the rationally right choice is the successful one; (3) that the rationally right choice can be learned through education; (4) that the laws of reason, as applied to the social sphere; are universal in their application."

27. Hans J. Morgenthau, "The H Bomb and After," *Bulletin of Atomic Scientists*, Vol. 6, No. 3 (March 1950): 76–79.

28. Hans J. Morgenthau, "On Negotiating with the Russians," *Bulletin of the Atomic Scientists*, Vol. 6, No. 5 (May 1950): 146–147.

29. Walter LaFeber, *America, Russia, and the Cold War, 1945–1971* (New York: John Wiley and Sons, Inc., 1972), p. 40.

30. Jennifer Sims, "Reinhold Niebuhr, the Christian Realist," Unpublished manuscript (May 1978), p. 3.

31. Michael Novak, "Needing Niebuhr Again," *Commentary*, Vol. 54, No. 3 (September 1972): 52–62.

32. Reinhold Niebuhr, "The Illusion of World Government," *Bulletin of the Atomic Scientists*, Vol. 5, No. 10 (October 1949): 289.

33. *Ibid.*

34. *Ibid.*

35. Novak, "Needing Niebuhr Again," p. 52.

36. *Christianity and Power Politics* (1940); *The Children of Light and the Children of Darkness* (1944); and a journal, *Christianity and Crisis* begun during the war.

37. For more on the Niebuhr-Wallace debate, see Walter LaFeber, *America, Russia and the Cold War 1945–1971* (New York: John Wiley and Sons, 1971), pp. 37–41.

38. Jacob Viner, "The Implications of the Atomic Bomb for International Relations," *Proceedings of the American Philosophical Society*, Vol. 90, No. 1 (January 1946): 53–58.

39. *Ibid.*, p. 55.

40. *Ibid.*

41. Bernard Brodie, ed., *The Absolute Weapon* (New Haven: Institute of International Studies, 1946).

42. Studies of the effect of the nuclear technology on our national security were conducted before the first use of the atomic bomb but their audience and impact were severely limited by the press of wartime

priorities.   See the discussion of the Tolman Committee in Hewlett and
Anderson, *The New World*, pp. 324–325.

43. Henry A. Stimson, "The Decision to Use the Atomic Bomb,"
Harpers Magazine 194 (February 1947): 97–107.

44. Henry A. Stimson and McGeorge Bundy, in *On Active Service
During Peace and War* (New York: Harper and Brothers, 1947), p. 632.

45. Insight contributed by Pierce Cordon, a physicist with ACDA,
during a personal interview, 15 September 1981.

46. Bernard Brodie, "War in the Atomic Age" in Bernard Brodie, *The
Absolute Weapon*, pp. 21–70.

47. Colin Gray, *Strategic Studies and Public Policy: The American
Experience,* unpublished manuscript (Hudson Institute, 1980), pp. 179;
Samuel Huntington, *The Common Defense, Strategic Programs in National
Politics* (New York: Columbia University Press, 1961), pp. 25–47.

48. Bernard Brodie, "Navy Dept. Thinking on the Atomic Bomb,"
Bulletin of the Atomic Scientists, Vol. 3, No. 7 (July 1947): 198.

49. Huntington, *The Common Defense*, p. 45.

50. For a discussion of this debate and the implications of the atomic
bomb for the use of force in the postwar world, see Chapters 1–3 in Robert
E. Osgood's and Robert W. Tucker's *Force Order and Justice* (Baltimore:
Johns Hopkins University Press, 1967).   For an explanation of Douhet's
importance one can do no better than John Shy, "In the 1920s Guilio
Douhet and other early theorists of 'air power' did for the airplane what
Mahan in the 1890s had done for the warship; they developed a doctrine
for its optimal strategic employment that closely resembled the Jominian
version of Napoleonic warfare"; "Jomini" in Peter Paret, ed., *Makers of
Modern Strategy from Machiavelli to the Nuclear Age* (Princeton: Princeton
University Press, 1986).

51. Among those who were active in this effort were General Greunther,
Secretary of State Marshall and George Kennan.   Their efforts were
constrained by budgetary limits, domestic political considerations' and the
military bias toward Preparations for total war. Huntington, *The Common
Defense*, pp. 39–40.

52. Huntington, *The Common Defense*, p. 47.

53. During the war, Vannevar Bush and James Conant had thought at
some length about this issue.   Early efforts by Bush to establish a Research
Board for National Security with both scientific and military participation,
were denied funding.   Later efforts became input for the formulation of
domestic control legislation by the War Department.   As will be shown,
fears of excessive military influence on atomic policy more generally meant
that coordinated planning and national security research was never realized
during this period.   See Hewlett and Anderson, *The New World 1939/1946*.

54. Brodie was later to recognize the assumptions behind his early
thinking about nuclear weapons.   Looking back at this period from the
vantage point of the early 1950s, he commented that the simple atomic
weapon was "not so absolute a weapon that we can disregard the limits of

its destructive power." Quoted in Marc Trachtenberg, "Strategic Thought in America, 1952–1966," *Political Science Quarterly*, Vol. 104, No. 2 (1989): 303.

55. William T.R. Fox, "Atomic Energy and International Relations," in William F. Ogburn, ed., *Technology and International Relations* (Chicago: Chicago University Press, 1949), pp. 102–125, esp. p. 109.

56. Personal interview with William T.R. Fox on 27 August 1981.

57. Gray, *Strategic Studies and Public Policy*, p. 166.

58. *Ibid*.

59. David Lilienthal, first chairman of the AEC was to be an active and vocal critic of this circumstance by the end of the decade. See D.E. Lilienthal, "Where Do We Go From Here?" *Bulletin of the Atomic Scientists*, Vol. 5, No. 10 (October 1949): 294.

60. The JCAE, created by the McMahon Bill, was responsible for overseeing the work of the AEC.

61. Towards the end of his tenure as Director of the AEC, David Lilienthal focused on this problem and started a public campaign to promote peaceful technology.

62. The group included John H. Van Vleck, Robert Serber, Edward Teller, Emil J. Konopinski, Stanley P. Frankel, Hans A. Bethe, Eldred C. Nelson and Felix Bloch. S-1 was the early designation for the secret atomic project.

63. There was an effort to keep the prospect of a hydrogen bomb from spreading, but it was futile. See Hewlett and Anderson, *The New World: Technology and International Relations*, p. 104.

64. *Ibid.*, p. 240. Tolman reported to General Groves, Director of the atomic project, that the "super cannot be completely forgotten if we take seriously our responsibilities for the permanent defense of the USA."

65. Edward Teller, "How Dangerous Are Atomic Weapons?" *Bulletin of the Atomic Scientists*, Vol. 3, No. 2 (February 1947): 35–36.

66. *Ibid.*, p. 36.

67. Eugene Rabinowitch, "Secrets Will Out," *Bulletin of the Atomic Scientists*, Vol. 6. No. 3 (March 1950): 67–68.

68. A.V. Hill, "The Moral Responsibility of Scientists," *Bulletin of the Atomic Scientists*, Vol. 1, No. 7 (March 1946): 3, 15.

69. Norbert Weiner, "A Scientist Rebels," *Atlantic Monthly,* December 1946 and *Bulletin of the Atomic Scientists*, Vol. 3, No. 1 (January 1947): 31.

70. For the radical view, see Eugene Rabinowitch, "Military or Civilian Control of Atomic Energy?" *Bulletin of the Atomic Scientists*, Vol. 1, No. 7 (March 1946): 1–16.

71. Robert Oppenheimer, "Physics in the Contemporary World," *Bulletin of the Atomic Scientists*, Vol. 4, No. 3 (March 1948): 65–68, and "The International Control of Atomic Energy," *Bulletin of the Atomic Scientists*, Vol. 1, No. 12 (June 1946): 1–4.

72. Sylvia Eberhart, "How the American People Feel About the Atomic Bomb," *Bulletin of the Atomic Scientists*, Vol. 3, No. 6 (June 1947): 146–147.

73. Eugene Rabinowitch, "A Victory and an Impending Crisis," *Bulletin of the Atomic Scientists*, Vol. 2, No. 2/3 (August 1946): 1.

74. Edward Teller, J. Marshak, and L.R. Klein, "Dispersal of Cities and Industries," *Bulletin of the Atomic Scientists*, Vol. 1, No. 9 (April 1946): 13–15, 20.   [See also Tracy B. Augur, "The Dispersal of Cities as a Defense Measure," *Bulletin of the Atomic Scientists*, Vol. 4, No. 5 (May 1948): 131–134.] Louis N. Ridenour, "Pilot Lights of the Apocalypse"; one act play, *Fortune*, Vol. 33 (January 1946): 116–117.

75. The first official report on atomic weapons effects was issued by the AEC in 1949.   See *Bulletin of the Atomic Scientists*, Vol. 5, No. 3 (March 1949): 68.   However, the debate on radiological and other effects had been going on for some time, especially in the wake of the Bikini Tests.

76. Edward Shils, "American Policy and the Soviet Ruling Group," *Bulletin of the Atomic Scientists*, Vol. 3, No. 9 (September 1947): 238.

4

The Open World: Arms Control as an Instrument for Achieving Long-Term Political Stability

The Consensus on Openness

In the immediate postwar period American arms control thought was inchoate and lacking in cohesiveness. There were at least five reasons for this. First, since relatively few people were informed about or engaged in nuclear policy, there was a lack of institutional "memory" and thus consistent thinking about nuclear arms control. Second, the nature of wartime relations and philosophical barriers between scientists and government officials (especially in the military) lead to considerable hostility between these groups. The result was a lack of early cooperation in the formulation of arms control ideas. Third, and in part because of the second point, an official view of the implications of nuclear technology for domestic and international conditions was slow to develop. Fourth, military strategy was the province of the professional military and few civilians were concerned with the nexus between defense and arms control policy.

Finally, Americans were ambivalent on nuclear issues. On the one hand, many were awed and troubled by the effects of nuclear use against Hiroshima and Nagasaki. On the other hand, there was both considerable pride in the American nuclear achievement and relief that the war could be brought to a close so swiftly. Both of these attitudes served to raise the prestige of the scientists and to lend weight to their positions on arms control. Such attitudes also led to the expectation that America's wise men would provide answers to the problems of finding an adequate defense against nuclear bombs and/or discover the key to their adequate control. There was an early sense of urgency fired by the scientists' public crusade for controls, and a gradually developing, though contradictory, complacency resulting from confidence in American technical leadership.

Despite the conflicting tendencies in arms control thought, any student of the period must be impressed with the apparent consistency of arms control policy after the war, and with the broad consensus which ultimately developed in support of the first official American disarmament effort—the Baruch Plan. How was it that incoherence became consistency and divergence gave way to consensus? What finally bound disparate views on technology, international politics and policy priorities to a single policy approach—an approach that was to remain relatively unchanged throughout the forties?

The answer to these questions is the concern of this chapter. It will be shown that consensus became rooted in arms control's larger purpose: the political objective of an Open World. The chaos of the period offered the opportunity for reorganization of the international environment while America's nuclear advantage lent it the power to assert its own design through arms control initiatives. While few could agree on short-term policy issues regarding nuclear strategy, secrecy or domestic controls, all could endorse the long-term opportunity for stability which political accommodation with the Soviets—on American terms—would ensure.

What was required was Soviet willingness to participate in an inter-state system characterized by the reduction of political, economic, and cultural barriers.[1] In such an effort, some hoped for more and others for less, but all could agree that the Soviets had to meet part way. And though some favored use of our nuclear advantage as leverage while others preferred an initial peace offering, all readily agreed that nuclear weapons had to be presented to the modern world as a unique and unprecedented danger since herein lay the strength of the American negotiating position. Because this arms control position had little to do with questions of short-term stability or military strategy, it was notable but apparently irrelevant that American military strategy was being developed on rather different grounds.

The basis for the consensus having been stated, it remains to point out that in another respect the conventional wisdom about this period is inaccurate or at least misleading: the consensus was both slow to develop and somewhat superficial. Before the development of the Baruch Plan in early 1946, there was no agreed approach to nuclear controls within policy circles. That a consensus crystallized at all must be credited to the timely rise of moderates on the issue; it was they who drafted the compromise known as the Acheson-Lilienthal Report, which later became the Baruch Plan. Once the consensus was established, the negotiating position of the Soviets and the wider development of the Cold War ensured that it would, for the most part, endure.

This chapter will begin by discussing the views on openness held by the official and scientific communities, stressing the differences in their implications for arms control priorities. Included here will be a discussion of the rather haphazard way in which the earliest American initiatives on the subject came about. This will be followed by a discussion of the emergence of the intellectual compromise offered by the Acheson-Lilienthal Plan of 1946. If the analysis seems to focus excessively on the development of policy, it should be understood that the monopoly on information which the government could claim, practically ensured that official policymakers would be in the forefront of the intellectual developments of the period.

Finally, the following discussion of the development of the openness objective has a two-fold purpose. Besides revealing the complexity of the concept and the related superficiality of the consensus on arms control policy, it will provide the intellectual background for understanding the later American approach to negotiated stability. In a melding of the scientific and official views of the 1940s, many arms controllers of the late 1950s and 1960s were to believe that American example in the disposition of its forces and international discussion of models for stability might buy time or even form the basis for a long-term political "relaxation of tensions." This mix of faiths provided the cement which bound disarmers to arms controllers in the consensus on limited measures of the 1960s and early 1970s.

The Scientists' Movement for an Open World

The common denominator of all "openness" concepts was the belief in the free marketplace of ideas and the right of all peoples to self-determination. The "Open World" was an ideal world order in which freedom of information, ideas and movement would be maximized. The belief in the ideal of one world and America's power to bring it about by example and reason separated the scientists' concept of openness from the one accepted in official circles.[2] Serious abnegation of sovereignty in the pursuit of international integration or world government was never an objective of government policy during this period. The official view was more of a piece with traditional American pursuit of an international system open to, and supportive of, American political principles; scope for unilateralism and acceptance of the sovereign state system were implicit. While a nod was given to the scientists' views in deference to their logic and obvious domestic appeal, in fact the scientists' political isolation and early preoccupation with domestic control policy, meant that their substantive impact on the course of official arms control thought was limited.[3]

The scientists' postwar approach can best be understood through an appreciation of its relation to the philosophy of rationalism. Perhaps more than any other domestic group, the scientific community believed in the applicability of the scientific method to all human affairs—including international politics. It will be recalled that this method embraced a connection between progress and freedom of communication which made the postwar scientists' movement fit neatly within the broader American intellectual tradition of openness.[4] The domestic application of rationalist principles led to the scientific community's strong endorsement of democratic systems and, in particular, the freedoms protected by the American Bill of Rights.

Where most scientists parted with American tradition was in their denial of the historic corollary to an open, if sovereign, state system—the preservation of scope for unilateralism in the conduct of the nation's foreign policy. Scientists distrusted the state. After all, was it not national barriers which prevented men from reasoning together, and was it not the state that, in its marshalling of force against the liberal tide of the 19th Century, fostered fascism?[5] Though such suspicions were shared by most scientists, only a few went on to deprecate the role of national governments in devising the best solution for the conflict-ridden postwar world.

While such differences will be explored in greater detail later in this section, for now it suffices to point out that they rested on varying beliefs regarding the primary threat to peace and the malleability of international politics. With respect to the first, many scientists believed that the threat to domestic institutions posed by the spread of Soviet communism was most important. If the world came to be dominated by this revolutionary ideology, the basic freedoms on which all social progress was based would be lost. Therefore, the first task was to shore up defenses for the democratic way of life. The existence of the Iron Curtain meant that any negotiated outcome short of world government, including arms control and disarmament agreements, would be unwise since the Soviets would have an incentive to cheat. In the view of these scientists it was best to let the natural advantages of western democratic systems ensure our technological lead through free competition. The premises of these scientists were rationalist, but their policy prescriptions were in harmony with the realists.

As the Cold War developed, an increasing number of scientists moved toward a nationalist point of view. Yet others believed that ideological differences between states were of secondary importance to the threat of nuclear war. They held that the only way to peace lay in dissolving national barriers and the only way to protect democratic institutions, which were in any case imperiled by atomic weapons, was through arms control and disarmament. National measures to defend against communism would lead to militarism and excessive domestic controls, thereby stifling essential freedoms as well as the very technological progress upon which the more nationalistic scientists counted.

But these technologically oriented scientists differed among themselves with respect to the second factor mentioned above: the malleability of politics. Whereas some organized and supported initiatives for world government, others felt that this was too big a step for states to take in practice. The latter generally supported a functionalist approach to integrating an atomic world.

None of the above distinctions, while helpful in distinguishing individual views at particular times, warrant rigidly classifying particular scientists. Many of those who started out as fierce "one-worlders" became fierce advocates of national defense with the growth of East-West tension. Some who favored a functionalist approach to world integration, but had little faith in the practicality of world government, joined the advocates of containment after the Baruch Plan's proposal for limited measures of cooperation foundered on Russian intransigence.

Yet, what was most important for the long-term development of the American approach to nuclear arms control was not the particular differences of the moment, but the one message all scientists delivered to a receptive American public immediately after the war: an open world and a stable order could be achieved if men would reason together on the basis of the facts. Perhaps the most prominent and influential espouser of this message was the foreign scientist Niels Bohr.

The Influence of Niels Bohr

The Danish physicist Niels Bohr, creator of the quantum theory of atomic structure, was the first scientist to make an official appeal to the United States Government for unfettered information flows as the international solution to the atomic era. In memoranda to the President and private visits with him during 1944 and early 1945, Bohr sought to convince him of the urgency of a Western initiative in this direction. Though he was ultimately to fail in his purpose, he contributed to, and reflected, a developing orientation among scientific participants in the Manhattan Project.

Bohr's argument for openness was essentially rationalist and based on the following four premises: first, conflict is not integral to international politics; second, individuals can change the conflictual pattern of traditional international relations through concerted action based on reason; third, the necessary but insufficient condition for such concert is the threat to all nations posed by atomic technology; and fourth, the necessary facts and international understanding upon which such action must be based may be ensured with uninhibited information flows among all nations and maximized opportunities for education and cross-cultural contact. Bohr repeatedly asserted that peace had to be based on a spirit of world community, but he did not specifically advocate world federation or government. In his view, the abandonment of secrecy would lead to a healthy competition among nations confined to asserting themselves solely through contributions to the common culture.[6]

As previously noted, the idea that individuals could change the international system through force of will, and choose its new form via the exercise of reason, was a fashionable belief. Bohr advocated the use of the already extant and internationalistic scientific community as the vehicle for early initiatives in this regard. Yet at the same time he did not depreciate the role of governments, for he felt that an atmosphere of trust and goodwill had to be reinforced by the leadership of the states concerned. Moreover, those states with the greatest store of nuclear knowledge had a special responsibility to open their doors to curious outsiders, for only in this way could dangerous suspicions be dispelled.

Bohr's belief that nuclear technology was modern man's fire—both intensely destructive and potentially civilizing—inspired his sense that the nuclear age presented man with a magnificent opportunity. Yet such positivism had a catch: it was based on the technologically conservative assumption that things nuclear would always be analytically discreet and that the balance of the technology's debits and credits would remain intact. The nuclear threshold was, for Bohr, a fact about which individuals had to be educated, not a condition towards which policy had to strive. Once educated, the world's public would know only one solution to the nuclear dilemma—an open world. It did not apparently occur to him that increased knowledge might obscure the peaceful utility or revolutionary aspects of the technology.

Bohr's policy recommendations during the war were directed to Washington and London since these allies had the advantage in both nuclear knowledge and technology. At first he stressed early consultations between the Big Three "about the best ways jointly to obtain future security," and urged such discussions before tensions arising from the development of the bomb and the political frictions attending victory dissolved the glue of common purpose which bound the partners of war. He recommended complete information-sharing regarding military and industrial efforts among the three, together with the institution of controls on dangerous activities.

When this first effort to win Churchill and Roosevelt to his cause failed, Bohr used the occasion of the San Francisco conference on the establishment of a United Nations Organization to make a second appeal. This time he stressed the need for the future international security organization to incorporate a body for technical and expert advice on the development of international controls. He wrote:

> Detailed proposals for the establishment of an effective control would have to be worked out with the assistance of scientists and technologists appointed by the governments concerned, and a standing expert committee, related to an international security organization might be charged with keeping account of new scientific developments and with recommending appropriate adjustments of the control measures.
>
> On recommendations from the technical committee the organization would be able to judge the conditions under which industrial exploitation of atomic energy sources could be permitted with adequate safeguards to prevent any assembly of active material in an explosive state...[7]

Although Bohr's recommendations to the Western Allies were not implemented, his ideas were absorbed by his scientific colleagues and seemed to have some effect on the development of their views.[8] The extent of Bohr's influence is difficult to delimit since ideas similar to his were "in the air" at Manhattan District Laboratories. He did make several extended visits to Los Alamos where he not only aired and shared his ideas, but also "acted as a father confessor to the younger men."[9] Indeed, even scientists who were to hold as diverse views as Robert Oppenheimer and Edward Teller later acknowledged their intellectual debt to Bohr in the realm of arms control as well as in atomic theory and design.[10]

Despite Bohr's authoritative position within the scientific community and the appeal of his philosophy, the American scientific movement, in practice, developed as a separate effort. Bohr's wartime campaign was highly personal and based on extra-institutional contacts at the highest levels of the American and British Governments. The scientists' wartime campaign was collective and necessarily institution-bound. In general, project scientists did not have the freedom to pursue their ideas outside the channels rigorously monitored by the military. Still, the concept of openness was the central feature of both. That Bohr's emphasis was international, and the other scientists' more domestic, reflects their somewhat divergent preoccupations while it also differentiated their contributions.

The Origins of the Scientists' Movement

The scientists' movement essentially began at Chicago in early 1944 when the Metallurgical Laboratory (MET Lab) faced imminent cutbacks in funding.[11] A significant number of the staff became concerned that scientific momentum in the nuclear field would be lost if the national labs were allowed to dissolve once their wartime purpose had been achieved. As they turned their thoughts to the implications for nuclear studies and industry, such current issues were augmented by the concern that excessive domestic controls enforced by continuing military involvement and a lack of forethought regarding the international implications of first use would combine to make the necessary international controls on atomic technology impossible. This dual concern for unimpeded nuclear research and international control lay at the heart of the scientists' special contribution to the openness concept and characterized it throughout the early postwar period. In their view, whether and how the United States pursued nuclear development at home would seriously affect prospects for international control. Preservation of the American way of life, as exemplified by the scientific spirit and method, depended upon the country's approach to nuclear education, research, and control of information. The United States had to provide an example to the world. Similarly, they believed that the way the United States pursued international arms control would seriously affect the health of the nation's democratic institutions. Although the scientists' movement failed to achieve its programmatic goals during the early years it did not fail in branding this powerful idea on the conscience of the American public.[12]

An early and important example of the thrust of this thinking at Chicago may be found in the Jeffries Report, which was inspired by concern over the future of American nuclear research and submitted to Arthur Compton, Director of the MET Lab, on 18 November 1944.[13] Section VI of this report discussed the international and social implications of nuclear technology. After pointing out the revolutionary effects atomic weapons would have on the conduct of war, the authors posed a choice: we could either stop all technological progress and wait for social institutions to catch up (here mention of a central, global authority was made) or we could proceed to inform all the people of the facts so as to ensure the moral prerequisites to abandonment of old habits of thinking and international behavior. The authors sided unequivocally with the latter alternative. Like Bohr, the group felt that once nations understood the facts they would recognize that international control was the only way to ensure survival and would thus recognize their common interest in accepting limits on sovereignty.

Towards this end they recommended that complete information on most phases of the subject be made available as soon as national security would allow—that is, after the war. Quoting Rear Admiral J.A. Furer, they wrote:

> True security lies in speed of accomplishment. It is the only way we can keep ahead of the enemy in this complex technical war of measure and counter-measure.[14]

Moreover, it was clear that the authors considered domestic conditions to be of critical importance:

> The nations which establish conditions favorable to extensive research and industrial development in nucleonics may be expected to show a greater advance in the science and art than nations which, intentionally or otherwise, have policies or laws which discourage research and development in this field.[15]

Thus, the Jeffries Committee came to the conclusion that maximum public and private development of "nucleonics" had to be encouraged and that we should aspire to international control of all dangerous activities. The best means to accomplish these goals was to encourage cooperation between a private nuclear industry, government, and university research labs in the context of a mass public education campaign on the horrors of nuclear war. The authors stressed that cooperation with friendly nations—particularly regarding the effort at mass education—should begin promptly and seriously. They wanted maximum scientific and technological progress at home while maximum information flows could begin to establish the international cooperation which would ensure military security.

The tension between the apparent need for early controls and the desires for an atmosphere conducive to research in "nucleonics" was implicit in the Jeffries Report. It became both more obvious and more complex in the work of Chicago's Committee on Social and Political

Implications. This committee headed by James Franck, produced
recommendations on international control in June 1944 which were
subsequently sent to Washington.

The Franck Report, as this report came to be called, was designed
to stimulate government thinking about international control and foster
greater awareness among officials about the future implications of
current decisions.[16] In this attempt at specific policy advice, Chicago
scientists dipped further into the political kettle than they had with the
Jeffries Report and did so because they felt international politics would
condition domestic developments regarding this new field. They tied
the notion of openness to concrete recommendations for international
action. Unlike Bohr, they did not specifically call for immediate
consultations with the Soviets. Instead they focused on the question of
first nuclear use against Japan, which had become a major issue for the
scientists. This was a pressing policy decision in which degree of
information sharing—and thus "openness" and security—was a critical
element. Denigrating a minority view that the bomb's feasibility ought
to be hidden through continued secrecy, the Franck Committee extended
the logic of the scientist's rationalist approach to openness by arguing
that first use could only be made legitimate if it served to educate the
world to the horror of nuclear weapons while preserving the moral
integrity and leadership of the United States.

The Franck Committee stressed that a nuclear arms race had to be
prevented until such time as world government became feasible. For
only such an arms agreement could provide an acceptable defense
against total nuclear annihilation.[17] A prerequisite for such an accord
was a fund of international trust so that nations would be able to
abandon certain elements of sovereignty and institute international
controls. In view of this, the authors opposed surprise use of nuclear
weapons against the Japanese since they believed international
cooperation would be irreparably damaged by such an act of unilateral,
indiscriminate, and unrestrained force. Instead, it was urged that
wartime secrecy be abandoned with the harmless demonstration of our
nuclear potential; for even if chances for accord were slim, keeping the
feasibility of atomic arms secret while developing our nuclear
capabilities as quickly as possible had the drawback of being both
deceitful and extremely difficult. Not only would intensive nuclear
development be constrained by the public's skepticism and ignorance,
but the prospects for future arms accords would be damaged by the
record.

The Franck Committee's advocacy of openness at the international
level incorporated elements of Bohr's conception: first, international

goodwill could be created by the example Western Allies set; second, knowledge of the facts of nuclear technology in the context of this spirit of goodwill would lead states to abandon certain sovereign rights for the purpose of establishing international control.[18] But, in failing to take Bohr's next step, in which he suggested that a spirit of world community would quickly revolutionize international politics, the authors' more limited design ran into logical snags. The question of how to address the apparent trade-off between establishing international trust and hedging against duplicity was left unresolved in the report. Instead, the Committee nodded at the issue and then ducked.

> One thing is clear: any international agreement on prevention of nuclear armaments must be backed by actual and efficient controls. No paper agreement can be sufficient since neither this or any other nation can stake its whole existence on trust in other nations' signatures. Every attempt to impede the international control agencies would have to be considered equivalent to denunciation of the agreement. It hardly needs stressing that we as scientists believe that any system of control envisaged should leave as much freedom for the peacetime development of nucleonics as is consistent with the safety of the world.[19]

Nevertheless, the scientists' domestic and international objectives did not really conflict during the war. Most felt that the primary domestic objective should be to educate the public as soon as possible to the revolutionary features of the bomb while purchasing both international goodwill and cooperation through timely sharing of nuclear information. Towards this second end, the majority of scientists favored some kind of military or symbolic demonstration of the device after fair warning or appropriate announcement.

Though rarely if ever made explicit, the inclination to use information as an international peace offering was based on the theory that once scientific inquiry was facilitated by domestic openness, any duplicity by totalitarian states would be negated by the more rapid scientific advance of the free. Thus, a liberated scientific community would generate its own hedge against the secrecy of others. Those taking this position could thus argue simultaneously for the necessary sacrifice of sovereignty integral to the concept of openness and for the national interest in technological advantage which the military sought to protect.[20]

The one approach to openness which rankled most scientists was the attempt to use American scientific advantage as an instrument for cracking Soviet secrecy, for this implied severe state controls on

information and a coercive—not exemplary—approach to international
suasion. Yet it was this second conception of openness which the
government was to embrace.

Official Openness: Information as Power
in Arms Control Policy

Unlike the scientific community, the official Washington policy-
making community initially lacked cohesion and continuity of thought
on arms control policy. This is not at all surprising given the scarcity
of information, the non-institutionalized methods of dealing with the
issue after the Manhattan Project's demise, and the diverse interests of
those individuals who were both informed and involved. Nevertheless,
by mid-1946 an arms control approach had developed which included
clear and relatively consistent notions about methods and objectives.

In essence, this official arms control approach consisted of an effort
to use the American nuclear advantage as a bargaining chip with which
to pry open the Soviet Communist Bloc and thus expose the regime to
the pressure and influence of world opinion. Though essentially
bilateralist, the approach was dressed in moralist, multilateralist cloth
as official arms controllers sought to reconcile security interests with
moral example. Due in part to a lack of an integrating framework,
official thought became caught in the netherworld between foreign and
defense policy and, at last, became irrelevant to both. Yet it managed
eventually to capture a consensus among the American people which
sustained American arms control policy throughout the 1940s.

The Influence of Vannevar Bush and James Conant

The origins of the official approach to arms control lay in the latter
part of the war when American postwar planning began to receive
greater attention. On the one hand, the proximate success of the bomb
had inspired Manhattan Project Administrators to press for high-level
recognition of the problems which the nuclear discovery would soon
pose for certain postwar and international objectives. On the other
hand, the developing tension between Soviet and American interests
caused movers of the United States' broader foreign and defense
policies to caution against excessive optimism regarding Soviet
cooperation in the maintenance of an acceptable postwar peace.
Whereas the former resulted in a multilateralist thrust to official
methods, the latter kept American arms control purpose fully wedded
to bilateral considerations.

Official interpretation of scientists' concerns rested chiefly with Vannevar Bush, Director of the Office of Scientific Research and Development (OSRD), and James Conant, Chairman of the National Defense Committee and unofficial deputy to Bush on atomic energy matters. In the summer of 1944, these scientists considered the postwar problems nuclear weapons would raise and in September drafted a memo to Secretary of War Stimson on the matter. In it they "pointed out the totally new and alarming situation which would result if no United States policy was developed before the war ended and the knowledge of the existence of the bomb was made public." They went on to advocate "free interchange of scientific information with other nations, including the Soviet Union, under arrangements by which the staff of an international office would have unimpeded access to scientific laboratories, industrial plants, and military establishments throughout the world."[21] In short, they warned that security did not lie in an attempt to hold secret the country's present nuclear knowledge.[22]

In its international aspects, particularly its reference to early exchange of information with the Soviet Union, this first memo from Bush and Conant resembled the general recommendations which Bohr had made. Yet the views of the authors were not fully formed; little systematic thought had been given to how much or what kind of information would be suitable for sharing, or how such exchanges might be effected given the asymmetrical nature of interallied relations on the subject. Evidence suggests that at the time of this early memo, Bush was concerned that Roosevelt's interest in continuing close ties with Britain after the war would lead to a falling-out with the Soviet Union and a destabilizing arms race.[23] Indeed, Roosevelt and Churchill had just agreed to far-reaching postwar cooperation on raw material supplies and nuclear use policy in what later became known as the Quebec Accords.

In this context the appeal Bush and Conant were making for a non-secretive, multilateral approach to postwar planning was more an attempt to balance a developing Anglo-American alliance in official policy than it was an appeal for the kind of magnanimous gesture which Bohr had advocated. In fact, in subsequent memoranda on the subject, Bush and Conant called for a form of information classification:. following the bomb's demonstration, all information except manufacturing and military details of the bombs, should be made available to the general public.[24] This caveat became the critical point of official departure from the scientists' approach to openness; for though the need for an information clearing-house under an association of nations was recognized, the idea that some secrecy was both possible and in the American interest, had found voice within an authoritative and informed part of the government.

This early belief that there was knowledge that could and should be withheld from adversaries lay at the heart of the official postwar concept of openness. For if we had something a potential adversary might want, we had a bargaining chip—a basis for political *quid pro quos*. It was not a much further step to conclude that the better the country could control this information, the better the bargaining would go. The logic of such an argument fit comfortably within the realist—as opposed to rationalist—paradigm for it admitted the concept of nuclear advantage if not the weapons stability nexus *per se*.[25] Moreover, it implicitly endorsed a degree of national secrecy. In the official approach to openness, information-sharing was not to be an international peace offering on the altar of world government, it was to be an instrument for world order according to the American design.

The Early Influence of Stimson and Byrnes

Such a purpose was made explicit in the writings of Secretary of War Henry Stimson. Bush and Conant directed many of their wartime memos on postwar planning to him, and his advice to Roosevelt and Truman clearly reflected their influence. But he was also highly sensitive to changing relations with the Soviets and tended to view nuclear policy in a more explicitly bilateral context than did the scientific administrators. In December 1944, Stimson pointed out to Roosevelt that General John R. Deane's warning from Moscow concerning the futility of concessions and the importance of *quid pro quos* had a bearing on the nuclear question. He urged that we withhold information until we could get something for it.[26]

This message was repeated in a memo to Truman on 25 April 1945. After noting the tremendous destructive force of the bomb and its potentially revolutionary strategic consequences, Stimson observed:

> If the problem of the proper use of this weapon can be solved, we would have the opportunity to bring the world into a pattern in which the peace of the world and our civilization can be saved.[27]

It was the Soviet Union's internal system as well as its international objectives that concerned Stimson. Given the admitted need for controls and inspection in a nuclear world, it was difficult to conceive of the role a police state would play in any cooperative effort. In a memo written about Russia at the time of the Potsdam Conference, Stimson wrote:

> I therefore believe that before we share our new discovery with Russia, we should consider carefully whether we can do so safely under any system of control until Russia puts into effective action the proposed (liberalizing) constitution which I have mentioned. If this is a necessary condition, we must go slowly in any disclosures on agreeing to any Russian participation whatsoever and constantly explore how our headstart in X and the Russian desire to participate can be used to bring us nearer to the removal of the basic difficulties which I have emphasized.[28]

Thus, nuclear weapons and potential negotiations for their control were perceived as a means by which Russia's international behavior and domestic institutions might be changed to coincide more with our own. But this would be done not by example and concessions as the scientists wanted, but through traditional diplomacy buttressed by a degree of secrecy. The most pressing threat, according to this analysis, was the ideology and interests of the Soviet State, not the weapon which it might one day wield or the effects a nuclear environment might have on American institutions.

Stimson changed his mind on information sharing, though not bilateralism, after Hiroshima.[29] This left Secretary of State Byrnes as perhaps the most influential and active advocate of such views after the war. Byrnes had little trouble reconciling his views with Bush's emphasis on multilateralism; neither the purposes nor the proposed means of these policymakers conflicted. This was evident in their mutual satisfaction over the development of Washington's arms control approach in late 1945. The first international conference on the subject held in November of that year between the heads of the United States, Canada, and Britain, left both men pleased.[30] The Secretary of State was satisfied that the Western allies agreed to make negotiations conditional on Soviet behavior, while Bush could be happy that the prospect of information-exchange with Moscow marked a step away from the exclusivity of the wartime nuclear alliance between London and Washington. Besides this mutually acceptable "phased" approach to information-sharing, the multilateralist coin forged by the agreement to pursue arms control negotiations within the United Nations Organization had American hegemony and thus bilateral implications on its reverse side.[31] That the Moscow leadership succeeded in changing the relevant forum from the General Assembly to the Security Council (where the American majority was less and each state had a veto) had the long-term effect of stalemating the negotiations; it did not expose the flip side of the American coin and thus damage the developing American consensus on arms control.[32]

It should be noted that one assumption behind the highly political thrust to official arms control thought—especially within the State Department—insured that international objectives would dominate nuclear control policies. It was assumed that the United States had control of nuclear technology and was therefore in a position to bargain effectively. In contrast, most scientists viewed nuclear technology as inherently unstable and the United States to be less in control of, than captured by, the inevitable logic of its unfolding. This difference meant early domestic disunity on the priorities of openness.

Certainly it was with some surprise that government administrators found that the first and most vigorous efforts by dissenting scientists pertained to domestic legislation. The scientists' belief that international peace and openness in the nuclear world would depend to a great extent on the nature of domestic controls was at first strange and then threatening to these administrators. They found themselves caught between the security requirements of nuclear possession and the anti-militarist thrust of the scientists' approach.

This battle, regarding the importance of domestic example for arms control, was joined in Congress as legislation for an atomic energy commission began to take shape. The compromise embraced by the McMahon Bill, though only a superficial resolution of the dilemma, freed the scientific community to participate more actively in the evolution of an approach to international nuclear arms control approach.

The Development of an American Consensus

The foregoing discussion of the concept of openness as conceived by the scientific and diplomatic communities does not fully explain how this ideal unified domestic opinion on arms control. Domestic consensus arose in the context of the intensifying Cold War in 1946 and because of the cooperative development and special formulation of the Acheson-Lilienthal Plan earlier that year. Whereas the former impressed many scientists and their allies with the growing nature of the Soviet threat, the latter embodied within an ambitious arms control plan, many of the realists' prerequisites for international bargaining as well as a functionalist step towards international integration. Thus, both conceptions of openness and how it ought to be pursued found official expression.

The Stimson Memo and the Influence of Acheson

The Acheson-Lilienthal Plan was drawn up in anticipation of the convention of the United Nations Commission on Arms Control and Disarmament mandated by the Truman-Atlee-King Declaration of November and the Moscow Conference of early December 1945. Though there was considerable urgency to the project, there were few preceding directives to form a basis for it. The members of the Committee charged with the task of devising the American approach therefore had considerable discretionary power. It was this unique collection of men that devised an approach both politically acceptable to all sides and scientifically informed. It was their plan, and the process by which it was created, that won the liberal-rationalist scientific community to the official approach to openness.

The head of the drafting committee was Deputy Secretary of State Dean Acheson who, at the time of the assignment in January 1946, had been largely excluded from the designing of the official arms control approach. Indeed, he had been an early critic of the kind of phased, multilateral approach which the November summit, orchestrated by Byrnes and Bush, had embraced. Instead, he had supported Stimson's last memo on the subject which had been aired at the highest policy levels in September 1945.[33]

Basically the Stimson-Acheson position was a bilateralist, extra-institutional approach to openness that implicitly recognized the link between domestic and international controls. To explain the premises of their approach and contrast it with the one which Stimson previously held and Byrnes was carrying on, one can do no better than to quote directly from the book co-authored by Stimson and his assistant, McGeorge Bundy:

> Granting all that could be said about the wickedness of Russia, was it not perhaps true that the atom itself, not the Russians, was the central problem? Could civilization survive with atomic energy uncontrolled? And was it practical to hope that the atomic "secret"—so fragile and short-lived—could be used to win concessions from the Russian leaders as to their cherished, if frightful, police state? A long talk with Ambassador Harriman persuaded Stimson that such a hope was unfounded; the Russians, said Harriman, would regard any American effort to bargain for freedom in Russia as a plainly hostile move. Might it not then be better to reverse the process, to meet Russian suspicion with American candor, to discuss the bomb directly with them and try to reach agreement on control? Might not trust beget trust; as Russian

confidence   was   earned,   might   not   the   repressive—and
aggressive—tendencies of Stalinism be abated?[34]

The result of Stimson's agonized reflections was a memo to the
President. In it he recommended direct discussions with the Russians
on nuclear matters in the interest of developing mutual trust,
encouraging positive internal changes within the Soviet State, and
thereby avoiding war. He specifically advised against using the United
Nations as a forum for discussion of controls, or raising the issue in
the context of threats or near threats associated with peace negotiations.
As the heart of the memo, he wrote:

> ... relations (of mutual confidence) may be perhaps irretrievably
> embittered by the way in which we approach the solution of the bomb
> with Russia. For if we fail to approach them now and merely continue
> to negotiate with them, having this weapon rather ostentatiously on our
> hip, their suspicions and their distrust of our purposes and motives will
> increase.[35]

And in what the author considered to be the most important point of
all he wrote:

> I emphasize perhaps beyond all other considerations the importance of
> taking this action with Russia as a proposal of the United States—
> backed by Great Britain. But action of any international group of
> nations, including many small nations who have not demonstrated their
> potential power or responsibility in this war, would not, in my opinion
> be taken seriously by the Soviets.[36]

Acheson, who had read and agreed with Stimson's position, raised
the issue of timing such international action with the formulation of
domestic legislation. In his view, the substance of international and
domestic proposals had to be harmonized. On 25 September, Acheson
sent a memo to the President on this subject. Here he took the
position that a policy of scientific secrecy would be futile and
dangerous. Instead, he advocated a direct approach to the Soviets, after
discussion with the British:

> to attempt to develop a program of mutual exchange of scientific
> information and collaboration in the development of atomic power to
> proceed gradually and upon condition that weapons development should
> be renounced with adequate opportunity for inspection.[37]

In due course, other nations might join in the arrangements. But it was essential that a fully-informed Congress develop domestic legislation concurrently with, and in appreciation of, the international discussions.

Acheson's position on international control was highlighted by his views on the course of negotiations in the fall of 1945. Commenting on the results of the November summit, he called the phased institution of controls through United Nations mechanisms "the opposite pole" from Stimson's position—and his own.[38] However, this was not quite the case. Stimson and Acheson had carved out a position on control which incorporated elements of both the developing "official" (Byrnes-Bush) approach and the scientists' concept of openness.

On the one hand, Stimson emphasized that the central threat to the world order was the atomic bomb—a weapon which he now considered categorically different from all other known weapons, including gas. American monopoly of the weapon and collusion with the British in its management could, in his view, become the central source of Soviet-American hostility. This acceptance of the threshold and the scientists' threat perception led to a prescription which the scientific community could endorse: share confidential information with the Soviets as a form of peace offering. On the other hand, Stimson embraced the views of the realists in Washington by arguing that the American arms control approach had to be bilateral and outside of the multilateral institutional framework of the United Nations. There was no reference to the aim of developing a spirit of world community at the sub-state level through the removal of boundaries on travel and information. Instead, the methods were to be intergovernmental and secret.[39]

Acheson's elaboration of Stimson's middle ground on openness moved the latter's ideas yet closer to those which he was later to criticize. Whereas Stimson sought to stress the necessity of bilateralism, Acheson balanced this requirement with reference to the "gradual" and "conditional" release of information in view of progress on inspection and the prohibition of nuclear weapons development.[40] It was not a much further step to refer, as November's three-power agreement did, to the free interchange of information after the establishment of "effective, reciprocal, and enforceable safeguards acceptable to all nations," or to advocate that work proceed "by separate stages, the successful completion of each one of which will develop the necessary confidence of the world before the next one is undertaken."[41]

The lack of specificity in the Stimson-Acheson proposals regarding the nature and scope of the information-sharing which they were recommending ultimately derailed their efforts to gain acceptance of their position within the government. Leaks from policy meetings raised Congressional fears that the government was planning to give away "the secret"—though few were sure just what that was. Byrnes and Bush, neither of whom had raised any objections to the thrust of Acheson's memo of 25 September, were thus left relatively free to set the official approach in the cement of the November declaration.[42]

Acheson's absence from the arms control scene over the next four months was abruptly terminated with his appointment as the chairman of the committee charged with developing the American arms control plan to be presented at the first meeting of the United Nations Arms Control and Disarmament Commission. With this re-introduction to the field, Acheson was given another opportunity to present his views, albeit within a new set of constraints: the involvement of the United Nations in any international control scheme was preordained.

The Acheson-Lilienthal Report

Interestingly enough, Acheson was to share his new responsibilities with Bush, Conant, General Leslie Groves, former head of the Manhattan Project, and John J. McCloy, former assistant Secretary of War under Colonel Stimson. Except for Acheson, all had supported the official approach to nuclear arms control as it had developed since September 1945; indeed, all had favored the original May-Johnson approach to domestic controls against which the scientific community had organized.[43]

This group was supported in turn by a Board of Consultants who, in fact, generated the draft which was to become sanctioned as the official report. Its members included: David E. Lilienthal, Chairman of the Tennessee Valley Authority (T.V.A.); Chester I. Bernard, President of New Jersey Bell Telephone Company; Dr. J. Robert Oppenheimer, former Director of the Los Alamos Atomic Laboratory; Dr. Charles A. Thomas, Vice President of Monsanto Chemical Company; and Henry A. Winne, Vice President of General Electric Company. The manner in which this group of consultants arrived at their conclusions, as well as the substance of their report, brought formerly disparate views on control into harmony.

First, and as previously discussed, the members of the advisory board sought to approach the subject with as few pre-conceived notions as possible both with regard to the "facts" on which policy had to be based and the objectives which the American proposal was to meet. In large measure, this conscious effort to apply scientific methods to their study was the work of the Board's chairman, David Lilienthal.[44] The publicity which accompanied the later publication of the report made much of the unique and collegial way in which the report was produced—winning many to its position. But the nature of the Board's conclusions was in fact heavily influenced by the one person on it who had had a significant role in the development of the arms control debate both during and after the war, and who had first-hand scientific expertise on the subject—Dr. Robert Oppenheimer. He held very strong, though moderate, views on how best to use nuclear arms control to achieve an open and peaceful world order. Since it was both the Board's use of scientific methods and the report's conclusions which led to broad domestic support for the Plan, the views of Lilienthal and Oppenheimer are important for an understanding of the development of the domestic arms control consensus. Indeed, their resulting celebrity status among informed individuals accentuated their prominent roles during the following years as shapers of American attitudes on nuclear arms control.

David Lilienthal's approach to arms control was heavily influenced by his adherence to rationalist premises.[45] He believed that proper attention to the facts by logical and unprejudiced thinkers would lead to an answer or set of answers to the nuclear question. This orientation was affirmed for him by his experience as head of the T.V.A. The collegial style of management which had proven so effective in his experience seemed to underscore his essential belief in the importance of facts and reliable information to the solution of any dilemma. He therefore joined the scientists in their effort to debunk the notion that America's nuclear secrets could be usefully withheld from other states, and he was critical of the Army's interest—as epitomized by General Groves—in using information as leverage.[46]

Though in his views on openness he seemed to side with the scientists, Lilienthal was, like Stimson and Acheson, a realist about the state system. He had little patience with those who advocated world government as the only answer to the nuclear threat. Instead, he endorsed the kind of functionalist approach to public resource issues that the T.V.A. represented. The Lilienthal Report's emphasis on cooperative international development of nuclear technology—as opposed to "controls"—was largely a reflection of this shared orientation among Board members. The objective was not to subvert the state system, but to supplement it; just as the New Deal's Valley Authority had supplemented interstate relations domestically.[47]

Dr. Robert Oppenheimer was Lilienthal's most informed ally in the formulation of a "cooperative" approach to nuclear security. To

Lilienthal's emphasis on a fresh, functionalist approach to the issue, Oppenheimer brought clear views on the best means to integrate these with the grander objective of an open world. The greatest influence on him in this regard was Niels Bohr, though Oppenheimer was perhaps more realistic than the Dane about what could be accomplished with the Russians. In his role as advisor to Stimson's wartime Interim Committee on nuclear policy Oppenheimer had repeatedly urged contact with the Soviets and the exchange of scientific information as an important prior step to first use. But he had joined the official community in favoring military use since his preoccupation with the bomb's fitful development left him skeptical that any other kind of demonstration could be spectacular enough.[48] After the war, Oppenheimer became active in furthering official recognition of the destabilizing developments which atomic technology had in store. In terms of his emphasis on the importance of bilateral information-sharing, his preoccupation with the international dimension of the issue, and his appreciation of the threshold between atomic and other weapons, he felt most comfortable with the Stimson-Acheson approach to openness.

The result of the Board's deliberations—during which Lilienthal served as Chairman and Oppenheimer as informal teacher to laymen—was a report that differed in several important ways from the thrust of past policy:

- Emphasis switched from controls and inspection to "cooperative development" of nuclear technology under the management of an international agency possessing a monopoly on research and development.
- The approach was to be an integral one; that is, not so phased that the American nuclear advantage would be held in reserve until proof of Soviet compliance was obtained.

Both of these proposals were bound to meet with wide approval among most scientists. But to this, the Board added such "realist" provisions as the concept of "strategic balance." Plants were to be "equitably distributed so that if the plan should break down; innocent nations could defend themselves" by access to compensating weapons technology.[49] The premise here was that a conflict-ridden international system in which deterrence and balance-of-power principles inhere, would continue to exist even after a nuclear accord was reached.

In this sense, and in the recognition that peaceful and destructive nuclear technologies were practically indistinguishable, the Lilienthal team proposed more of an arms control than a conventional disarmament agreement.[50] Moreover, the ideas regarding international management and the minimization of inspection was reached out of respect for nationalism and sovereign sensitivities. Controls were to impinge as little as possible on the internal affairs of participating states. Many scientists were to have difficulty grasping this motive and therefore accepting the principle of minimal inspection.

The proposal produced by the Board of Consultants had to go through two substantive reworkings before it was to gain official status as the American Plan. First, the Board had to present its ideas to Acheson's Committee; second, it had to be transformed from a framework to a true policy position. Concerning the former, Lilienthal believed that there was scant hope of approval.[51] However, with the leadership of Acheson, the atmosphere turned out to be one of general support, albeit with certain individual reservations.

The most serious of these were raised by Conant and Bush who wanted more on what would happen if the scheme were to break down either in the process of being established or thereafter. According to Lilienthal, they seemed to be committed to "the step-by-step" plan, and while "conceding the necessity" of an integral approach, still wanted a chapter on safeguards.[52] After considerable discussion, the final version of the Acheson-Lilienthal Report accepted the notion of implementation through successive stages. Furthermore, the Committee effectively argued that the prohibition of bomb production should only be instituted after the international machinery of development and control was set up.

Despite these significant changes in the spirit—if not content—of the Report, the members of the Board of Consultants continued to be pleased with the results. This was because the grander purposes and principles of the plan remained intact. Among these, the affirmation of certain openness principles were salient.

The Report implicitly supported the necessity of free pursuit of information since, as Oppenheimer was later to remark, " ... no proposals predicated on forbidding enquiry and learning could, in the end, survive."[53] Private enquiry itself was not to be banned, only experimentation with significant quantities of fissionable material. The premises upon which this recommendation was based bear repeating. As Oppenheimer later explained: "knowledge about explosives is, in a situation such as we are here contemplating, more dangerous if not disseminated than it is if disseminated." He went on to explain that "... it is not enough to declare something is open. It requires instruction;

it requires work to get an understanding of these things abroad. I know this from experience."[54]

To this liberal goal of free information and internationalized research, including the implicit notion that instruction was necessary, was added the belief that openness in this area could lead to a change in the Soviet Union. According to Oppenheimer, the framers of the postwar approach "saw an opportunity to cause a decisive change in the whole trend of Soviet policy, without which the prospect of an assured peace were indeed rather gloomy, and which might well be, if accomplished, the turning point in the pattern of international relations."[55] Though Oppenheimer was later to regret that awe of the technology became as absorbing as it did relative to the bilateral context, he nevertheless felt that:

> The question of the future of atomic energy thus appeared in one main constructive context: what can be done with this development to make it an instrument for the preservation of peace and for bringing about those altered relations between the sovereign nations on the basis of which there is some reason to hope that peace can be preserved?[56]

Indeed, awe of the technology was in part what gave hope that nuclear controls might be a means of "reaching" the Soviets: the technology was terrible in its destructive effects; its benefits required an international approach for effective development and exploitation; effective control of the technology required intensive, ongoing collaboration with other peoples and supra-national patterns of communication; and the development of atomic principles had been an international effort, originally untouched by national controls.[57]

It was uncertain at the time whether the hope, that nuclear arms control could provide the means for long-term political accommodation, was already futile. It was possible that Soviet hostility was too developed, and cooperation among the Western Allies too prejudicial at that point, to leave any possibility of a useful outcome in this regard. Oppenheimer later expressed the view that the " ... relegation of problems of atomic energy to discussions within the United Nations, where matters of the highest policy could only be touched upon with difficulty and clumsily, would appear to have prejudiced the chances of any genuine meeting of minds."[58]

Indeed, the development of the consensual approach to arms control as embodied in the Acheson-Lilienthal Report could well have bought domestic unity at the price of international unacceptability. The special Anglo-American nuclear relationship had already been underscored as a result of the early influence and diplomacy of Bush and Byrnes; this record was not mitigated by the reemergence of more explicit bilateralists on the issue such as Acheson and Oppenheimer. Insofar as they could not change the multilateral framework in which their ideas would be articulated, their major role would be in bringing the skeptics of official designs to the support of an official approach. In this, they succeeded admirably.

The Acheson-Lilienthal Plan attracted realists and rationalists, world federalists and unilateralists, since all could find a reflection of their views in the proposal. William T.R. Fox described the basis for reconciliation between the world government advocates and their critics in an article in the *Bulletin of the Atomic Scientists.*[59] He pointed out that the Report offered the prospect of a new international authority with intrinsic, yet precedential, integrative effects for the international system. Nevertheless, the proposed Atomic Development Authority (A.D.A.) would have functional limitations and would, by the nature of its structure and operations, minimize the need for police-style inspection. Moreover, the agreement was designed to maintain the underlying strategic balance while offering the possibility of eliminating a weapon so powerful that many realists could not imagine its use ever serving the political purposes of the United States. Here was the middle road to openness, neither world government—the old banner of idealists and closet imperialists—nor unilateralism and secrecy alone.

If anyone was inclined to be skeptical of the Plan it was the realist who believed that: (a) the openness objective was futile even in the long run; (b) the atomic bomb was not categorically different from conventional weapons, (i.e., that it could be a useful instrument for the projection of force); and/or (c) the American nuclear monopoly was crucial to counterbalance the Soviet advantage on land. But such views were rare in 1946. They were not to be widely accepted until the 1950s when Soviet intransigence had transformed the openness principle from objective to propaganda tool, and the tactical potential of atomic bombs had become highlighted by testing, development and comparison with thermonuclear possibilities. As Hans Morgenthau was to point out in 1950, the complacency which characterized the official response to news of a Soviet atomic test in 1949 could only be reconciled with containment policy if one believed that maintenance of the American nuclear weapons monopoly was not critical to the balance of power.[60] The framers of the official arms control approach of 1946 not only assumed that maintenance of the American nuclear monopoly was impossible, they implicitly acknowledged that the powers of nuclear and conventional weapons were incomparable—thus making discussion of their "balance" fallacious. Few were those who disagreed in early 1946, though by 1949 opinions had changed.[61]

Of more concern at the time were those who questioned whether the A.D.A.'s power, particularly with regard to inspection, would be adequate. These tended to be scientists distrustful of the state system and fearful that anything short of world government would be dangerous. In this regard, the few additions which Bernard Baruch was to make to the Plan further strengthened the domestic consensus.

The Baruch Plan: Reaffirmation of Arms Control as Leverage

The second hurdle the Acheson-Lilienthal Report had to cross was its transformation into a policy proposal. To the dismay of most of Lilienthal's Board, this was to be left in the hands of Bernard Baruch, long-time advisor to presidents, darling of Congress, and personal choice of Secretary Byrnes. Again, the thin nature of the arms control bureaucracy threatened to inject inconsistency into policy, since Baruch was of no mind simply to articulate a previously developed plan.[62] However, the early leaks, combined with later publication and widespread distribution of the Plan, had led to such broad public support that significant changes were made politically difficult. In the end, Baruch added only two substantive elements to the original plan. First, he recommended "condign punishment" for violators, and second, he insisted upon the abolition of the veto over the operations and decisions of the new international authority.

However, there were also changes made in the emphasis and tone of the Report. The Baruch team stressed the role of inspection instead of diminishing it as the Lilienthal team had done in the interest of establishing an atmosphere of "cooperative development." This followed from Baruch's preference for A.D.A. "dominion" over raw materials and mining as opposed to international ownership.[63] The Baruch Plan also emphasized the notion of implementation by successive stages, depending on Soviet good behavior and beginning perhaps with a general assessment of the worldwide distribution of uranium and thorium. Such a first step was in part conceived as a test of Soviet willingness to provide access to its territory and generally cooperate with the international community.[64] By contrast, the Lilienthal team had referred to phases only under protest and had explicitly rejected the initial step of a raw materials survey as likely to provoke Soviet hostility and suspicions.

The toughness which Baruch's team lent the American position, especially the emphasis on a phased approach during which American secrets would be safeguarded, was welcomed by such influential Senators as Vandenberg and Connally and ensured their support. The unfolding of international events had not only strengthened bipartisan feeling in the Senate that American knowledge about nuclear energy should be used for leverage on Soviet behavior, it had also lent legitimacy to the notion that the country's nuclear arsenal provided security which had to be preserved—indeed guaranteed—during any transition to atomic disarmament.

Many scientists were similarly pleased with the new emphasis on inspection since in the absence of world government, states would still be prone to old habits and rivalry. Others joined the politicians in seeing in the abolition of the national veto on atomic matters both a lever on, and a litmus test for, Soviet willingness to participate in a free and open international order. This purpose for arms control proved particularly important as the political atmosphere of 1946 turned colder.

By 1947 the Baruch approach had become a useful counterpart to containment; it emphasized to the broad public that the purpose of America's new international role, as well as its nuclear arsenal, was to protect the country and the international system from a state whose ideology was antithetical to the basic freedoms for which the United States stood. At the same the formulation of the Baruch Plan, including the early record of its origin and the rhetorical flourish with which it was presented to the United Nations, seemed to shift Americans' perception of the moral burden of nuclear agreement from the perpetrator of Hiroshima to the rejectionists of an open world . After all, the Soviet Union had simply proposed, in response to the Baruch Plan, an international convention requiring the destruction of nuclear weapons and a prohibition of their manufacture or use. Later it was to propose national management of nuclear energy together with limited inspection. However, the terms of the latter were never elaborated and, in any case, an initial atomic disarmament convention was to come first.

In an ironic way, our arms control effort thus seemed to legitimize the existence of our nuclear arsenal and the maintenance of secrecy. When the Soviets had failed to reply with an equally methodical and potentially far-reaching plan by the end of 1946, many who had favored concessions in the interest of rapid disarmament or world government had become fully allied with the Baruch position. In such an atmosphere, the idea of a phased approach—even the suggestion of coercive diplomacy—had lost its negative aura of "power politics." The politically insignificant splash made by Henry Wallace's challenge to Baruch's position on this matter only serves to highlight the minor status the scientists' original position on concessions then held and the relatively greater significance they ascribed to the official position on the necessity of openness first.

The Fate of the Consensus

The formulation of an official American arms control position helped to establish a consensus on the conditions and purposes of nuclear weapons restraint. On the one hand, the Baruch Plan was applauded by most scientists and their allies because of its rational formulation, its integrative and cooperative approach to a potentially divisive international issue, and its emphasis on continued research and development—albeit under international auspices. Moreover, the manner in which Baruch presented the plan to the United Nations further impressed those who hoped that nuclear controls would provide a first step or model for general disarmament.

On the other hand, those more suspicious of rationalistic premises, including traditionalists such as Byrnes, were pleased by the Baruch Plan's implicit recognition of the leverage on Soviet behavior which a phased reduction in the American nuclear advantage would provide. And the emphasis on both the inspection and veto issues exposed Soviet intransigence on matters deemed critical by world federalists and realists alike.

The unifying theme was the notion that peace and global stability could only be ensured if all nations subscribed in some measure to the goal of international openness. In the fluid international environment of the immediate postwar period such an arms control goal was not considered futile. Ironically, arms control thus became the political justification for, and counterpart to, the American strategy of containment. A fiscally conservative and traditionally isolationist public could be inspired to pay for a military arsenal which included nuclear weapons as long as it was sufficiently impressed with the Soviet ideological and military threat and the American effort to do something about it by morally persuasive, non-military means. The negotiations of the Baruch era contributed to this impression most eloquently and dramatically. Of course, with such a political underpinning for arms control, the fact that nuclear weapons were treated differently in this context than they were at the Pentagon struck few as hypocritical or even very unusual.[65]

As the Cold War intensified, the consensus on arms control strengthened.[66] In fact, by the end of the decade, the Soviet negotiating record and general foreign policy did more for American cohesion on arms policy than did the specifics of the American plan. Moderates such as Acheson, Oppenheimer, and Lilienthal voiced their growing concern about the Soviet threat and the prospects for negotiation. Lilienthal himself presided over the early development of the American nuclear stockpile in his role as the first Chairman of the Atomic Energy Commission. His example is illuminating insofar as the domestic secrecy which he abhorred in principle became an accepted and tolerable responsibility of his office in the early years of the Cold War.[67]

Most analysts believed that the Soviets' greatest objection to the American Plan was the proposed reduction in sovereignty implied by nuclear cooperation and international inspection—not the veto issue itself.[68] Harold Urey, a scientist active in the movement for world government, observed that the Soviet Union's domestic instabilities and political insecurity were exposed by the United Nations' negotiations. He predicted that the subjects of Russian dictatorship would become dissatisfied if they learned of "the greatly advanced economic and social position of the peoples of Western countries." Therefore, the Soviets could not "admit free inspection of the Soviet Union" and the Baruch Plan would never be realized.

> Such inspectors would probably learn that the Soviet Union is very weak from a military standpoint, and hence the possibility of Russia's continuing its immense bluff in the international poker game would be destroyed. Moreover, inspectors would probably learn that there are large numbers of political prisoners in Russia ... living in prison camps.[69]

Within the short space of a year and a half the American approach to arms control had provided first a hope for political reorganization of the international system and then a moral stand for military face-off in the frozen politics of the Cold War. By 1949, the Western-dominated United Nations Atomic Energy Commission (UNAEC) reported an intractable stalemate: "The Government of the USSR puts sovereignty first ... if this fundamental difference could be overcome, other differences could be seen in true perspective, and reasonable ground might be found in their adjustment."[70]

Nevertheless, the domestic American arms control consensus was, at two levels, quite fragile. First, the goal of an open world could only remain the paramount purpose of arms control as long as several conditions obtained: (a) the United States had enough of an advantage in nuclear knowledge and technology to insure its ability to bargain effectively for political concessions; (b) nuclear technology remained less intrinsically threatening than Soviet Communism in the short run; (c) the majority behind the consensus favored international political change over the stability of the status quo as a policy goal. Second, the glue which bound liberal rationalists to the official "Baruch" approach depended on the widespread assessment that domestic openness had to be subsidiary to the goal of cracking open the Iron Curtain. Soviet secrecy—not nuclear arms themselves—had to pose the greatest immediate threat to the American way of life.

By the turn of the decade these essential conditions for political arms control were disappearing, and the consensus was becoming unstuck. First, the Soviet Union exploded an atomic device in 1949. This was not only a devastating blow to the American sense of superiority, but it also suggested a Soviet capability to achieve parity in effective nuclear force projection. Realists such as Morgenthau pointed out that the balance which nuclear forces lent the Soviet-American military relationship was now tilting in favor of Moscow in view of the continued supremacy of the Red Army in Europe. Such observations began to undermine Washington's negotiating posture—how could the United States continue to entertain the notion that the Russians would "open up" in exchange for controls on a technology which they had recently acquired and which held the prospect of ensuring their own strategic advantage? In short, the Soviets' atomic test suggested that a re-examination of nuclear arms policy as a whole was in order.

Second, nuclear technology was becoming more threatening and less predictable in its rate of change. The Soviet atomic test was followed by an American decision to develop the much more powerful hydrogen bomb. Not only was the public soon exposed to astonishing new projections of nuclear force and effects, but officials in Washington began to speculate that nuclear arms would become relatively cheap and plentiful due to improved design and manufacturing economies. Citizens and their representatives began to demand more information on the government's nuclear policy, including stockpile figures.

The initial concerns of thermonuclear skeptics were soon played out as weapons tests in the Pacific brought catastrophic results with respect to fall-out, and advances in bomb miniaturization and conventional delivery capabilities on both sides threatened new instabilities arising out of fears of surprise attack. When the Soviets beat us in the task of developing the first deliverable hydrogen device, American vulnerability to unprecedented destruction began to compete with the broader fear of the Soviet ideological and political challenge as a motivating factor for arms control. In fact, after the death of Stalin, there was some hope that a new and constructive relationship with the Soviets would soon be developed. When the Soviet Union agreed to much of our disarmament position at the United Nations in May of 1955, the American public was ripe for dissent should the United States be less than forthcoming.

It was not that the Soviet challenge was no longer appreciated. Rather, it was becoming apparent that the Soviet system might survive for many years, that it might be influenced in the long run, but that political hostility was likely for the foreseeable future. Just as the early 1950s witnessed the adjustment of American military policy to requirements of containment, so arms control thought began to adjust to the same condition, including the notion that political accommodation, reconciliation, or change must be a long-term effect, not a short-term requirement, of coexistence.

Despite these incipient trends which suggested that the arms control consensus of the 1940s might be coming apart, official policy clung to the old political format throughout the early 1950s.[71] Changes in the international system and technological conditions were slow to develop and slow to be recognized. When they were, it was first among informed individuals in government. Secrecy provisions prevented general public appreciation of those new factors—especially technological—which were beginning to make disarmament much more difficult in practical terms, and military stability much more fragile. In significant measure, the restrictions on domestic openness, which buttressed arms control efforts to bargain for global openness, insured the survival of the latter policy long after its utility for arms control had expired.

Towards the end of the Truman Administration, one effort was made to change the course of official arms control policy to conform to changing political and technological factors. In April 1952 Dean Acheson, then Secretary of State, established a Panel of Consultants on Disarmament including Oppenheimer; Bush; John S. Dickey, President of Dartmouth College; Allen W. Dulles, Deputy Director of the Central Intelligence Agency; and Joseph Johnson, President of the Carnegie Endowment for International Peace.[72] The members of the consulting group decided on a broad review of nuclear arms policy since it was recognized that the past separation of weapons strategy and control was becoming obsolete. Noting the growing irrelevance of United Nations disarmament discussions given the political and technological factors mentioned above, the Panel argued for an integrative approach to nuclear arms policy based not on secrecy but on an informed public opinion.

The Panel's report cited the Iron Curtain and intensified superpower rivalry as the principal reasons for the Baruch Plan's failure. As the Panel stated it: "the differences between the free world and the Soviet Union are so deep-seated that no genuine, large-scale political settlement seems likely within the present generation."[73] Given this, and the outbreak of the war in Korea, an arms control policy which failed to recognize the need for military strength in the West would be doomed to irrelevance.

The Panel went on to argue that an isolated, propagandistic arms control policy based on a continuation of the old approach would be disastrous, since the dangers of surprise attack and nuclear devastation were growing. Therefore, nuclear weapons policy had to incorporate the important arms control objective of reducing the probability of war. By recognizing and accepting the deterrent function of nuclear weapons, the authors separated themselves from the disarmers; and by identifying military stability as the central objective of a realistic nuclear policy they brought arms control proximate to strategy.

In this sweeping and potentially revolutionary analysis, the Panel's members made the first detailed argument for the end of the excessively political arms control policy of the Baruch era. While arguing that an open world would be eminently desirable, they also argued that it was now equally unrealistic and therefore dangerous. The nation could no longer afford the luxury of devoting all efforts at control to its pursuit. Instead, the Panel urged: (a) greater domestic openness and candor about the nuclear situation; (b) strengthened alliances and a simultaneous reduction in the unilateralism with which nuclear policy is formulated; and (c) an effort to communicate with the Soviet leadership so that the threat posed by atomic weapons might be appreciated by both sides in the same terms. Although it was hoped that Moscow would become acquainted with the extent to which its secrecy contributed to long-term instabilities, it was considered of at least equal importance to gain better understanding of Soviet perceptions of the nuclear issue. The Panel thus recommended that arms control be extracted from its multilateral context as well as from its past identification with negotiations related to treaties capping or reducing arms. By placing the goal of the avoidance of war first, arms control was broadening in meaning and impact. In recognition of this, the Panel argued for a bureaucratic reorganization in which "a close coordination of the basic authority and responsibility for all major problems of atomic armament" might be carried out.[74]

This document marked the first thorough intellectual challenge to the Baruch era's political approach to arms control. By bringing issues of surprise attack and military stability to the fore, political objectives such as openness and ideological or even doctrinal convergence were relegated to second order status. In another sense, Acheson's panel modernized the approach for which Secretary Stimson had appealed in 1945: bilateral discussions for the purpose of limited exchange of information on the nuclear threat. In both cases, positive political outcomes were desired as a by-product—but not a condition—of progress towards controls. Whereas the technical and political conditions for such an arms control orientation were not present in 1945, they were emerging in 1953.

However, policy lagged behind intellectual change in this area. The Oppenheimer Panel's recommendations for an integrated nuclear policy, and candor with the American people about technological changes, were criticized within the succeeding administration as being overly pessimistic. "Operation Candor" soon was transformed into Eisenhower's "Atoms for Peace" proposal in which the atom's benefits for mankind were advertised and magnanimously offered on a global scale. In the meantime, nuclear arsenal development and multilateral arms control diplomacy continued relatively disassociated and unchanged.[75] Since domestic nuclear secrecy continued to make it difficult for unofficial observers to arrive at judgments similar to the Oppenheimer Panel's, the propagandistic United Nations approach offered a secure route to preservation of the domestic arms policy contract.[76]

Though the political objectives of arms control thus remained essentially unchanged during the early 1950s, the official format had to be altered to reflect the Soviet Union's new nuclear status and the resulting loss of American leverage. Most obvious was the decision to link nuclear reductions to more general disarmament—a move which recognized the Soviet's advantage on land and complicated the nuclear disarmament effort considerably. At the same time, emphasis was switched from schemes for "cooperative development" to general disarmament accompanied by inspection.

The push for openness after 1950 became almost exclusively an effort to obtain aerial inspection rights from the Soviet Union. This increasingly practical orientation towards openness reflected at least some official appreciation of the political and technological changes mentioned above; aerial surveys were emphasized because it was believed that this would provide the best counterbalance to the intelligence advantage enjoyed by the Soviet Union while at the same time continuing the juxtaposition of American accessibility and Soviet secrecy.[77]

In April 1952, after the establishment of a new Disarmament Commission covering nuclear and conventional weapons, the United States delegate set forth the "Six Essential Principles for a Disarmament Program," the second principle of which was the requirement that all states cooperate to establish an open and substantially disarmed world. The sixth principle added that agreements must include a progressive and effective system of disclosure and verification to "achieve the open world in which alone there can be effective disarmament."[78]   The United States working paper on verification procedures of armed forces suggested that inspection and verification procedures include, *inter alia*, aerial surveys and inspection of waterways and railways.

Not surprisingly, pessimism infused the official arms control effort of the early 1950s. Those who continued to believe that arms control negotiations could contribute directly to a change in Stalin's regime were becoming fewer in number while the ranks of the skeptical, cynical and pessimistic were increasing. This was in part a result of the conviction growing in the government and in the Pentagon especially, that new arms control initiatives would undermine the effort to gain public support for nuclear and conventional weapons build-up necessary in the aftermath of Korea. As Chuck Appleby has written in his thorough study of the period: "Neither Eisenhower nor any of his close advisors appear to have entertained seriously any notion of interfering with the major build-up of forces then underway." [79] The result was a diminished role for arms control in policy circles and rhetorical and unimaginative repetition of stale political conditions and objectives. The expiration of the notion that arms control might best be used as political prod and litmus test was bound to be a long one. In official circles where the idea had been most useful, it hung on longest.

Indeed, conventional wisdom has it that the Open Skies proposal of 1955, offered by the United States in response to a dramatic Soviet demarche in May of that year was most significant as America's first postwar control (as opposed to disarmament) effort and that its limited nature marked a significant break from the past. In fact, Open Skies is at least as significant as the swan song of the official American political approach to arms control. It was in large part an effort to test the Soviet Union's willingness to relax its secrecy and thereby demonstrate its political intentions in the post-Stalinist era, and to regain the propaganda edge if the Soviet Union were unwilling to allow aerial surveillance.

In a review of W.W. Rostow's book on arms control during the
Eisenhower Administration, Gregg Herken makes the following
observations about this initiative:

> The "Open Skies" proposal grew out of a recommendation from a top-
> secret government panel convened at Quantico to identify Russian
> vulnerabilities that might be exploited during the upcoming summit at
> Geneva.   The "Quantico Vulnerabilities Panel" (headed by Nelson
> Rockefeller) quickly perceived that one such vulnerability was the
> Soviets' mania about preserving a closed society ... what finally sold
> the Open Skies idea in the administration was the plain fact that the
> United States stood to benefit from the offer whether or not the Russians
> accepted it.[80]

When Admiral Arthur W. Radford, Chairman of the Joint Chief of
Staffs, finally understood the point of the proposal he interjected: "I
see what you fellows are doing—you are trying to open up the Soviet
Union."[81]

This emphasis on the political goals of the Open Skies proposal is
not meant to suggest that no one saw potential advantages for stability
in such a proposal. But at best, strategic arguments cut both ways: the
exchange of blueprints and the allowance of overflights could have
exacerbated fears of pre-emptive attack.[82]   Nevertheless by combining
openness objectives with a stability rationale, the proposal maximized
chances for broad domestic and international support.   Though the
Soviets pulled off a coup by calling our bluff with their earlier
concessions on disarmament, Open Skies was a perfect parry; advisors
from Dulles to Harold Stassen could find merit in the proposal.[83]

The Impact of the Baruch Era
on Later Arms Control Thought

From the perspective of the present, the approach to arms control
in the immediate postwar years seems anomalous. In contrast to the
technical orientation of later years, arms controllers were preoccupied
with the political challenge of the Cold War and the implications this
held for weapons negotiations. Divorcing nuclear weapons restraint
from broader questions of strategy, they sought to use the American
technical advantage as an instrument to penetrate Soviet secrecy and
reform the international system.

Moreover, unlike later years, the arms control community was both
small and government-centered. The morally unexceptionable objective

of international openness and control helped to bind most
others—including disarmers, world federalists, unilateralists and
traditionalists—to the official positions on nuclear control and, in the
absence of such controls, on secrecy, nuclear development, and military
rearmament.   Arms control thought was more influenced by the
premises and objectives of official architects of foreign policy than by
the theoretical musings of scholars and strategists.

For an explanation of the uniqueness of the period, one must keep
in mind the political and technical conditions described in Chapter III.
During these years of international turbulence and uncertainty, official
policy was aimed at bringing about the kind of world order for which
the nation had fought. Military strength was perceived as a prerequisite
for favorable political change and these changes were in turn a
prerequisite for true weapons restraint. It is hardly surprising that the
realm of nuclear diplomacy, where the United States had both leverage
and moral drive, became a central vehicle for advertising and seeking
political objectives.   As the seeking was frustrated, the advertising
became emphasized, proving as beneficial for domestic cohesion in the
face of growing secrecy and military expenditures as it was useful for
international propaganda purposes. As the United States consolidated
the Western alliance system and became increasingly oriented towards
preserving the status quo, arms control lost its salience as a vehicle for
international change and became a medium for reinforcing ideological
and political division between East and West.

Yet even this propagandist political role depended on technological
conditions which themselves were undergoing rapid change. Whereas
the early postwar years were characterized by a certain ambivalence
regarding nuclear weapons in many quarters, the Soviet nuclear test and
the dawn of the thermonuclear age together with rapid advances in
delivery capabilities began to increase the perceived threat posed by the
weapons themselves.   A broader and better appreciation of the
destructive potential of the atom, the rate of innovation in nuclear
technology, and the technical competence of the adversary, tended to
bring issues of nuclear stability to the fore. In short, the luxury of
pursuing the low returns of atmospherics in arms control policy had
become unaffordable. Thus it was not until international political
change became less critical for American interests than prevention of
nuclear war itself that arms control's political purpose was to lose its
primacy.

The special nature of this period for postwar American arms control
thought should not, however, obscure the impact which these years had
on later developments in the field. Indeed, an appreciation of the

political history of the American approach aids in understanding the often understated political premises of the arms controllers of later years by providing a context for their more technical orientation. Adjusted to the international status quo and jaded by the poor results of politically designed arms control policy, strategists and theorists of the late 1950s and 1960s reorganized the priorities of past policies to conform to the new imperative of avoiding nuclear war. Realists and hardened strategic thinkers encouraged the shift, noting the worthlessness—even danger—of our past offers to forfeit nuclear advantage for international agreement and intangible political objectives.

As a result, arms control became more detached from the political fortunes of the Cold War to become wedded to strategy more generally. In this context, questions of stability were most pressing. The attempt to resolve them not only characterized arms control thought for the next several decades, it also biased strategic considerations towards reducing the risks of war as opposed to prevailing in any international test of wills. International politics was not so much ignored as assumed to be a constant.

The shift from political to more technically oriented arms control thought was analogous to the reaction of strategists to massive retaliation. The development of limited war theory in the 1950s reflected a perceived need to adjust strategy to changing technological and political factors; it did not necessarily reflect a belief that total war had suddenly become irrelevant. So it was with arms control thought: the premise underlying the technical approach with which American negotiators went to the Surprise Attack Conference of 1958 was that political change had become at best a secondary objective of arms control. Rather than taking on the broad purpose of Washington's foreign policy, arms control had to be placed in the proper context of strategy.

Having said this, it is important to point out that political motives did not suddenly or completely disappear from arms control's more modern design. Many of the ideas about its potential political role persisted in somewhat altered form. Among these were:

- the notion that bilateral tension could be reduced by the explanation of stability concepts and corresponding force deployments to the Soviet Union—an effort which in turn might lead to a degree of "doctrinal convergence" in military terms;
- the notion that ongoing arms control negotiations can be valuable in and of themselves since they might provide a useful bridge to

political influence and understanding on a broader plane and across issue areas (e.g., "linkage" and detente).

Both of these ideas had been expressed in the 1940s; the first in the Acheson-Lilienthal Committee's deliberations and the second in the musings of Stimson, Acheson, and apparently Conant and Averell Harriman as well.

By the late 1950s these ideas had become secondary in importance, yet they offered a long-term political rationale for a highly technical approach to stability. Assuming each side preferred national survival to ideological victory over the other, it seemed plausible that American advocacy of an "objective" stability formula might convince the Soviet Union of our long-term intentions with respect to nuclear war. Although bilateral conflict would not be eradicated, it might be lessened and perhaps redirected to more conventional competition. Some went so far as to suggest, or to hope, that nuclear arms could thus be neutralized, allowed to obsolesce, and eventually be abolished. Indeed, this was the motivation for many disarmers' acceptance of the countervalue stability formulas of the 1960s.

Finally, the Baruch era had lasting effect on the domestic context for arms control thought. Arms control had, from the beginning, served to justify the development of the American nuclear arsenal, extended deterrence, and nuclear secrecy by advertising American restraint and morality and Soviet uncooperativeness. Arms control policy satisfied the need to protect Western democratic institutions from the nuclear threat by defining an ethical answer to the new military age at the same time that it demonstrated by its lack of results, the perhaps greater threat posed by the hostile political and social system of the adversary.

The link within the public conscience between the pursuit of arms restraint and continued nuclear expenditures ensured that arms control thought would have an audience and an impact that might have otherwise been missing. For Americans held the hope that the American nuclear posture might know bounds, and that containment and unprecedented domestic secrecy might therefore be tolerable.

From the official angle, this meant that an effective effort at arms restraint was a necessary corollary to proposals for new expenditures on strategic forces. The domestic contract upon which official defense policy was based gave "bargaining chip" a two-fold meaning: just as military systems could be used to encourage concessions from the other side at the bargaining table, so arms control proposals might be used to rationalize for the American public, new expenditures on arms. If

Moscow would not demonstrate its pacific intent at the bargaining table, then Washington had to strengthen its deterrent through improved capabilities. To this extent arms control has underscored strategic relations and—some would argue—exacerbated the arms race.[84]

Notes

1. The desire for an Open World has strong roots in American intellectual tradition. It involves the notion that the health of the country's domestic institutions and economy depends on maximizing the opportunities for American initiative, isolationism and free enterprise in the international arena. This orientation has traditionally found expression in a preference for unilateralist foreign policies. America's historical preoccupation with territorial and economic expansion has fit hand-in-glove with the desire to be left alone, free from the political rivalries and balance of power machinations of the continental powers. Moreover, since the last was believed to be the result of royal intrigues and the source of war, Americans tied the maintenance of peace and stability—so conducive to America's unilateralist expansion—to the spread of democratic freedoms internationally. Thus, the ethically "good" international system was believed to be both stable and liberal. The ironies which resulted from the implicit liberal and conservative biases which inhered in this dual premise have been described extensively elsewhere and cannot be fully explored here. Yet it is important to note that while openness became a special objective of the post World War II arms control policy of the United States, it was not a surprising development given fluid international conditions, Stalin's tyrannical mastery of Soviet power and Washington's preoccupation with a liberalized international system more generally. In the *Bulletin of the Atomic Scientists* Hanson Baldwin was to write: "If we are to put up intellectual bars around the country, intended to keep all foreign scientists out and all our scientists in, we will create as much a barrier to international understanding as if we build up tariff and cultural barriers." [Vol. 1, No. 9 (April 1946): 6.] That the idea of openness also took on a new form in this context, had much to do with the fact that the scientific community, many leading members of which were recent emigres, became its most vociferous champion.
2. The term "scientists" is used throughout this chapter to refer, not to all scientists, but only to those who organized in civil opposition to the government and became engaged in the nuclear arms control debate. There were many scientists who chose not to become involved in politics and a few who disagreed with the dissenters' views; however, these latter were a distinct minority.
3. The scientists' domestic priorities had to do both with their immediate concerns over research conditions and funding, and with their perception that the nuclear threat was as much to America's democratic institutions via

military aggrandizement and secrecy as it was to America's national defense. However, this is not to suggest that the scientists were unimportant to the development of the American consensus regarding arms control objectives. Although the scientists' direct impact on the development of official policy was slight, their eventual support of the Acheson-Lilienthal Plan meant that a large segment of domestic public opinion would rally behind the American initiative as well. The scientists' influence was great, and their grassroots organization exceptional.

4. See Chapter 3, n. 16. The Connection referred to was made explicit in the Jeffries Report. See Alice Kimball Smith, *A Peril and a Hope* (Chicago: Chicago University Press, 1965), pp. 539–559. A brief review of scientific rationalism's central tenets may be in order. The main feature of the scientific method is its focus on the rigorous and orderly development of facts and the exploration of their inter-relationships with regard to a particular problem. The ideal situation for such work is an environment where communication is unobstructed by political, technical, or ideological barriers and where education permits the greatest intellectual participation possible. The more knowledge gained, the closer one comes to a "solution," which, by definition, is good. Thus the growth of education leads to enhanced communication, which in turn allows more rapid progress toward scientific discovery or, in the case of society, the cure of social ills.

5. E.U. Condon wrote persistently on the theme of state encroachment on science and its detrimental effects. See "Science and International Cooperation," *Bulletin of the Atomic Scientists*, Vol. 1, No. 11 (May 1946): 8–11 and "An Appeal to Reason," *Bulletin of the Atomic Scientists*, Vol. 1, No. 7 (March 1946): 6–7.

6. Niels Bohr, "For an Open World," *Bulletin of the Atomic Scientists*, Vol. 6, No. 7 (July 1950): 213–217, 219.

7. *Ibid.*, p. 215.

8. See the discussion of the Acheson-Lilienthal Report in this chapter. A copy of the Acheson-Lilienthal Report may be found in the *Bulletin of the Atomic Scientists*, Vol. 1, No. 8 (1946): 2–9.

9. Hewlett and Anderson, *The New World*, p. 310.

10. Oppenheimer's understanding and appreciation of Bohr's point of view is recorded in Lilienthal, *Journals*, pp. 455–456. Teller's intellectual debt to Bohr is noted in Arthur Herzog, *The War Peace Establishment* (New York: Harper & Row, 1963), p. 18.

11. Young academic scientists mobilized in the summer of 1943 over the effects of the influx of scientists from private industry at Chicago. Although some later held that the dispute involved concern about the nuclear future, the true significance of the 1943 rebellion seems to have been in its effects on relations between the young scientists and the military, which opposed organized dissent during the war.

12. Senator Glen H. Taylor reflected such views in his appeal for world government, introduced as a resolution in October 1945. In an untitled commentary in the *Bulletin of the Atomic Scientists*, he wrote: "... modern

technology is responsible for binding the fortunes of cultures and political organizations which are vastly different from our own, and which also have yet to make their adjustments to the requirements of the modern world." [Vol. 3, No. 9 (September 1947): 289].

13. Members of the committee were Zay Jeffries (chairman), R.S. Mulliken (secretary), Enrico Fermi, James Franck, T.R. Hogness, R.S. Stone, and C.A. Thomas.

14. Quoted from Smith, *A Peril and a Hope*, pp. 558–559.

15. *Ibid.*, p. 559.

16. For a copy of the Franck Report, see Robert Jungk, *Brighter Than a Thousand Suns* (New York: Harcourt Brace and World Inc., 1956), pp. 348–360.

17. The idea of dispersing population and industry was considered potentially effective but highly disruptive if not infeasible.

18. Franck knew Bohr as a friend and colleague, but he minimized the latter's direct influence upon his thinking except as relates to the exercise of individual responsibility in these matters. See Smith, *A Peril and a Hope*, p. 31.

19. Quoted from Franck Report as reprinted in Jungk, *Brighter Than a Thousand Suns*, pp. 358–359.

20. The views of Edward Teller constitute an excellent example of this position. See Edward Teller, The *Legacy of Hiroshima* (Garden City, New Jersey: Doubleday, 1962) and with Albert L. Latter, *Our Nuclear Future: Facts, Dangers and Opportunities* (New York: Criterion Books, 1958).

21. James Conant, *My Several Lives* (New York: Harper & Row, 1970), p. 300.

22. Hewlett and Anderson, *The New World*, p. 327.

23. *Ibid.*, pp. 326–328.

24. *Ibid.*, p. 328.

25. See Chapter 2, p. 24 for a discussion of this term.

26. Hewlett and Anderson, *The New World*, pp. 334–335.

27. Stimson and Bundy, *On Active Service*, p. 636.

28. *Ibid.*, pp. 640–641.

29. *Ibid.*, pp. 641–649. For a discussion of this change of heart see this chapter, p. 98.

30. The results of the November Conference were also endorsed by the Senate leadership which favored both American guardianship over nuclear secrets and multilateral (United Nations) channels for such diplomacy.

31. Conant was apparently ignorant of this implication of using the United Nations. As late as December 1945 he was advocating special bilateral or trilateral contacts on nuclear information and scientific development along the lines of Stimson's earlier proposal. He was to write in his memoirs later: "I did not realize that the decision to place the problem of the control of atomic energy before the United Nations had already precluded the development of any arrangement involving only two or three nations." (*My Several Lives*, p. 487.)

32. The Soviet Union joined the United States and England in recommending the establishment of a Commission under Security Council auspices (but including a representative from Canada) to make proposals for the "control of atomic energy to the extent necessary to ensure its use only for peaceful purposes" and "to the exchange of information for peaceful ends." This agreement was set forth in the Moscow Declaration of 27 December 1945, concluded at the end of the Moscow Foreign Ministers Conference, attended by Byrnes and Conant *inter alia.* See Evan Luard, *First Steps to Disarmament,* p. 14.

33. Dean Acheson, *Present at the Creation: My Years in the State Department* (New York: Norton, 1969). On Stimson memo see pp. 123–125, 131–132. On the early development of policy see pp. 149–168.

34. Stimson and Bundy, *On Active Service,* p. 641.

35. *Ibid.,* p. 644. It is interesting to note that Molotov, at the first social occasion of the Conference, asked Conant, who was serving as Byrnes' scientific advisor on the nuclear question, whether he had "a bomb in his pocket." This was an interesting choice of words given the context, the fact that this was the first official meeting with an American scientist from the nuclear project, and the words used by Stimson in his September memo. See Conant, *My Several Lives,* pp. 475–477.

36. *Ibid.,* p. 645.

37. Dean Acheson, *Present at the Creation* (London: Hamish Hamilton, 1969), p. 125.

38. *Ibid.,* p. 132.

39. Acheson in defending Stimson's position, also asserted that the Secretary never intended to imply that the United States should share everything it knew about the new technology. But a careful definition of intent, especially given the sensitivity of the issue, was appropriate—and never made. See Acheson, *Present at the Creation,* p. 123.

40. *Ibid.,* pp. 124–125.

41. Acheson, *Present at the Creation,* pp. 131–132.

42. Acheson was later to describe the period between October 1945 and January 1946 as one of disarray and chaos in the area of control policy. He felt this was due to a lack of organized thinking and the usurpation of decision-making in this area by General Groves. This interpretation of his views was recorded by David Lilienthal in his *Journals,* p. 10. Vannevar Bush, in his own memoirs, suggests the same thing with specific reference to the November Conference which was apparently carried out in a very *ad hoc* and non-professional fashion [Vannevar Bush, *Pieces of the Action* (New York: William Morrow & Co., Inc., 1970), pp. 296–297.]

43. As mentioned earlier, James Conant followed Bush's lead on questions of international control and there fore endorsed the official line. However, his susceptibility to Stimson's line of reasoning was evident in his own December memorandum on bilateral information exchange with the Soviets (see note 31, this chapter.)

44. See Chapter 3, pp. 57–58.

45. See Chapter 3, pp. 57-59, and Chapter 3, n. 19.

46. Lilienthal had expressed such views at the Chicago Conference of September 1945 where he was exposed to, and affected by, a broad spectrum of scientific and academic opinion on the subject of nuclear policy, secrecy and openness. See also Lilienthal, *Journals*, p. 10–12.

47. *Ibid.*, p. 40. Ganno Dunn protested that the Acheson-Lilienthal Report was simply a public power scheme.

48. Hewlett and Anderson, *The New World*, p. 358.

49. William T.R. Fox, "The Struggle for Atomic Control," *Public Affairs Pamphlet* (New York: Public Affairs Committee, 1947), p. 12.

50. The plan did suggest that nuclear fuel could be "denatured" by the international agency, thus permitting at some future date, national operations using materials licensed by the international authority.

51. Lilienthal, *Journals*, p. 27.

52. *Ibid.*, pp. 27–28.

53. Robert J. Oppenheimer, "Functions of the International Control Agency in Research and Development," *Bulletin of the Atomic Scientists*, Vol. 3, No. 7 (July 1947): 197.

54. *Ibid.*, p. 176.

55. Robert J. Oppenheimer, "International Control of Atomic Energy," *Bulletin of the Atomic Scientists*, Vol. 4, No. 2 (February 1948): 41.

56. *Ibid.*

57. *Ibid.*, pp. 39–43, *passim.*

58. *Ibid.*, p. 42.

59. William T.R. Fox, "Debate on World Government or Discussion of Atomic Energy Control," *Bulletin of the Atomic Scientists*, Vol. 2, No. 5/6 (September 1946): 22–23.

60. See Hans Morgenthau, "The Conquest of the United States by Germany," *Bulletin of the Atomic Scientists*, Vol. 6, No. 1 (January 1950): 21–26.

61. Of course there were those in the military who were basing war plans on very different premises. Not only was their technical information less speculative and therefore less complete concerning thermonuclear potential, but they were also largely outside arms control's intellectual community.

62. Baruch wanted to go further than the Acheson-Lilienthal proposal suggested, but Truman (and others) rejected his ideas for a general disarmament scheme. Acheson seemed to think Baruch wanted to gain the spotlight with a rhetorical speech. [Lilienthal, *Journals*, pp. 31–33.]

63. This started out as the primary difference between the Acheson and Baruch teams. The latter felt that private enterprise was being compromised by the internationalization of mining and even the management of some primary plants. There was some indication that Baruch's advisors were concerned about the status of the RAND gold mines of South Africa. [Lilienthal, *Journals*, p. 51.]

64. Lilienthal, *Journals*, p. 49. This idea was contributed by Fred Searls, advisor to Baruch and mining engineer of some repute. He convinced the Baruch team that the United Nations should send 50 two-man teams all over the world to survey raw materials for nuclear production. According to Lilienthal, "Searls said that in this way we would find out what is going on in Russia. And if the Russians refused to accept this proposal, then we would know that they would not go along on any international scheme, and ... he didn't finish the statement but his eyes indicated what he thought should be recommended and it was anything but pleasant ...", *Ibid.*

65. Baruch sought the comments of certain military leaders, including Eisenhower and Groves, before delivering his prepared speech at the United Nations. However this was a late request and a reply was not received in time to effect either the substance or style of the Baruch Plan.

66. Among the dissenters were Niels Bohr who, in a memorandum to the United States Government in 1947, argued that the United States ought to make additional concessions to improve the political atmosphere and thereby break the arms control stalemate, and a minority of scientists whom Gilpin has grouped in the "control school" (Gilpin, *American Scientists*, p. 65). The latter group included scientists such as Philip Morrison, Harlow Shapely, and Linus Pauling. They believed that *uncontrolled atomic energy* (not ideology, security, or other vital interests) was the essence of the political divisions between the Soviet Union and the United States and that the Soviet Union should push new methods of control if the Baruch Plan negotiations continued to founder. And as mentioned earlier Henry Wallace also dissented from the American position, but the transient nature of the splash his critique made in the media only highlighted the unpopularity of his implicit belief in spheres of influence as opposed to openness.

67. David Lilienthal's journal makes extremely interesting reading and provides important insights on this period from a liberal perspective. The author's support of the Baruch Plan's approach seemed to strengthen with time, as did his own anxieties over the role of secrecy in a democratic society. Yet his preoccupation with the Soviet threat and the need to ensure American security through continued nuclear development insured that his anxieties would not divert him from his central task.

68. The editors of the *Bulletin of the Atomic Scientists* expressed the view that Moscow might well be stalling even in view of its more detailed proposal of June 1947. The proposal seemed late in coming and less than forthcoming on the issue of inspection [Vol. 3, No. 7 (July 1947): 201–202.] Byrnes believed by December 1946 that the Soviets were not living up to their promises of the year before in Moscow, and that they were muddying the arms control waters with extraneous issues in order to avoid coming clean on inspection [*All in One Lifetime* (New York: Harper, 1958), p. 386.]

69. Harold Urey, "An Alternative Course for the Control of Atomic Energy," *Bulletin of the Atomic Scientists*, Vol. 3, No. 6 (June 1947): 139.

70. Quoted in Bernard G. Bechhoefer, *Post War Negotiations for Arms Control* (Washington, D.C.: The Brookings Institution, 1960), p. 98.

71. See the discussion on pp. 113–114 on disarmament negotiations at the United Nations.

72. McGeorge Bundy, "Early Thoughts on Controlling the Nuclear Race. A Report to the Secretary of State, January 1953," *International Security*, Vol. 7. No. 2 (Fall 1982): 3–27.

73. *Ibid.*, p. 7.

74. *Ibid.*, note 24.

75. For a detailed account of the Atoms for Peace Plan and Eisenhower's arms control policies more generally, see the thorough study by Charles A. Appleby Jr., "Eisenhower and Arms Control, 1953–1961," Ph.D. dissertation submitted to the Johns Hopkins University, 1987. On Atoms for Peace see Henry Sokolski, "Atoms for Peace, A Non-Proliferation Primer?" in *Arms Control*, Vol. 2 (Sept. 1980): 199–232.

76. This is not to suggest that there were no divisions in the Administration on the subject. There were a few who thought in integrated terms about the relationship between arms control and military objectives. For example Robert Bowie, head of the Policy Planning Staff in the State Department, made numerous and articulate appeals for rationalizing these two instruments of security policy. He in turn believed, and continues to believe that Eisenhower held similar views. (Personal communication January 1990).

77. Luard, *First Steps*, p. 28.

78. Bechhoefer, *Post War Negotiations*, p. 179–180.

79. Chuck Appleby, *Eisenhower and Arms Control*, pp. 51–52.

80. Gregg Herken, "The Poker Game of Arms Control," *Washington Post, Book World* (23 January 1983): 1–2, 9.

81. *Ibid.*, p. 2.

82. It was questionable whether such information and intermittent surveillance would enhance stability or damage it. Each side would gain better targeting information but little assurance or additional time to prepare for a surprise blow. See Jerome H. Kahan, *Security in the Nuclear Age* (Washington, D.C.: Brookings Institution, 1975), pp. 56–60.

83. Although initially opposed to the plan and Rockefeller's role in developing it, Dulles finally backed it in the belief that the Russians would turn it down. Nevertheless, he remained concerned about Eisenhower's enthusiasm over the plan. When the Soviets finally rejected Open Skies as an American attempt at espionage, Dulles was actually relieved and "Eisenhower was reluctantly forced to conclude that Khrushchev's own purpose was evident—at all costs to keep the USSR a closed society." See Herken, *The Poker Game*, p. 9.

84. It has been speculated that our arms control policy of the 1970s did not so much inhibit development of our nuclear arsenal as it enhanced it insofar as the SALT debate publicized considerations of strategic balance. Without this debate, proposed new expenditures of MX and cruise missiles might not have proven politically acceptable. [Interview 15 May 1979 with James Timbie, a physicist and arms control expert with the United States Arms Control and Disarmament Agency.]

PART THREE

Arms Control as
Security Instrument

After deterrence is stabilized, it will be easier to make the world security system even more rational and efficient by reductions in deterrent forces. But this task is impossible until they are first rationally organized in a politically and technically stable system.
—Richard S. Leghorn
"The Approach to a Rational World Security System," *Bulletin of the Atomic Scientists*, Vol. 13, No. 5 (May 1957): 198.

5

From the Age of Innocence to the Balance of Terror: Nuclear Arms Control Thought Comes of Age

Introduction

In several important respects the period from 1945–1950 was an anomalous one for postwar arms control thought. In contrast with later years, there were only a few civilian strategists concerned with arms control. The most influential ideas on the subject were generated by a quite limited group—those associated with the government and therefore privy to information on nuclear technology. In addition, arms control was pursued in a multilateral context, independent from defense policy and with a salient political objective: to shape the international system into one which would be receptive to American institutions and values. Any nation unwilling to conform became an "aggressor" by definition. If American arms control policy failed in its direct and primary purpose of preventing an arms race, it became highly successful in its indirect and secondary one; for it served to define the enemy and highlight the threat for the defense community and the general public.

During the 1950s, the purposes of arms control were to change dramatically. New arms control ideas generated by a broadened and better informed intellectual community shifted the focus of arms control away from political and propaganda purposes to the more immediate concern of securing strategic, bipolar stability. Before examining the conditions which set the stage for this shift, it is useful to identify and to review those prophetic thinkers of the immediate postwar period who, by anticipating the future, set themselves apart from the general intellectual trend of the immediate postwar period to become the intellectual forbearers of the Cambridge Approach to arms control.

Prophets of the 1940s

One of the significant differences between the 1940s and the 1950s in the field of arms control thought was that, by the latter decade, nuclear weapons were no longer novel. Ideas and policies had already been shaped around them and, while the technology itself was evolving, the nature of the nuclear problem was becoming less arcane.

Thus, one of the new factors in the intellectual environment for arms control thought was the history of ideas about nuclear control. While the dominant strain of thinking in this respect has been covered in the previous chapter, other more prophetic analysts had laid some groundwork for the Cambridge Approach to arms control. In this chapter the intellectual environment for arms control thought during the 1950s will be described—including the ideas "in the air" but not yet widely held at the turn of the decade.

Early Notions of Bipolarity

Although the international system was unquestionably bipolar by the close of World War II, arms control thought did not generally reflect this. Perhaps the most important reason was that the bipartisan constituency for America's new international role had become enamored of international organizations as bulwarks of international order. Indeed, the consensus which supported the political purpose of openness did so in part because the instrument for its pursuit was the United Nations Organization. But it was also true that many who thought in bipolar terms nevertheless spoke the language of multilateralism for political purposes; the Western bloc was at an unquestionable advantage within the United Nations Organization as a whole.

Yet during these early years there were those who were not only aware of the bipolar context for arms control thought but were willing to argue for more attention to it at an early date. Robert Oppenheimer was one of the minority advising the government during the summer of 1945 who favored a direct approach to the Soviets on the atomic energy issue.[1] Even after the United Nations format was chosen, he, as well as others drafting the Acheson-Lilienthal Report, hoped that its adoption would lead to critical social and political changes in the Soviet Union.[2] Stimson and Acheson favored a direct approach to the Soviet Union on the subject immediately after the war and argued explicitly against the multilateral route as likely to foster suspicions and delays.[3]   Others, such as James Conant, recognized the importance of the Soviet Union to any arms control scheme but did not fully appreciate the extent to which bilateral and multilateral routes would be mutually exclusive until after the latter was officially chosen.[4]   Jacob Viner, whose ideas on nuclear strategy were prescient in a number of other respects, argued that the two great powers should discipline their rivalry within the United Nations context and thereby engage a Concert of Powers to maintain the peace but within the conciliatory and legitimating structure offered by the United Nations.[5]

By 1948 Oppenheimer was to lament that other preoccupations had caused early arms control thinkers to overlook what, in his view, should have served as "the well-spring" of our policy: the bipolar context. He wrote:

> We have allowed our own internal preoccupation to make us content to put forward our views in the United Nations without pursuing early enough, on a high enough plane, or with a fixed enough resolution, the objective of making the heads of the Soviet State in part at least, party to our effort.[6]

Whereas Oppenheimer had hoped that atomic energy could provide the incentive for Soviet leaders to change the secretive and authoritative trends in their policies, two years of fruitless negotiations in a multilateral context left him ultimately pessimistic. In his view, atomic control had become a security instrument more dependent on, than conducive to, political evolution in the Soviet State.

> My own view is that only a profound change in the whole orientation of Soviet policy, and a corresponding reorientation of our own, even in matters far from atomic energy, would give substance to the initial high hopes.[7]

By 1947 the bipolar international context was obvious to most observers but the wisdom of abandoning the multilateral approach to arms control still was not. Those on the left argued either for a new American arms control proposal within the United Nations context, or a grand effort at World Government excluding Communist regimes if necessary. Others argued for maintaining the Baruch Plan approach and the negotiating forum offered by the United Nations Organization. After all, the majority of its members had backed the

American Plan, making the institution an ideal setting for an East-West stalemate from an American diplomatic point of view.

Although recognition of bipolar circumstances was implicit in positions such as these, it was generally absent from prescription. With atomic monopoly and an international political majority supporting American policy, why stew over arms control's dying flame?

The answer was provided by Edward Shils, then an Associate Professor at Chicago writing in the *Bulletin's* September 1947 issue.[8] After reviewing the impasse at the United Nations, Shils evaluated American arms control policy in its broader defense and foreign policy context, highlighting its necessary link with the emerging policy of containment. Noting that arms control and defense policy had evolved separately since the war, he warned of a bleak future:

> The deterioration due to the atomic bomb will be slow and ruinously entangled with the postwar disorganization of the world economy. As the atomic armaments race gets under way, it will enjoy a more autonomous role as a factor in international tensions, intensifying the hostilities which originally developed from other sources...The present policies of the two states are such as to maximize the frequency of frictions in the future. These frictions will be greatly magnified in significance once an atomic armaments race is under way. Under conditions of an atomic armaments race, the chances of dissolving these frictions by artful diplomacy will be very slight.[9]

Shils went on to argue that good arms policy not only had to be morally sound and politically useful, it had to be practical. The bomb had to be systematically taken into account in defense and foreign policy. If the United States was to pursue a policy of containment (which he personally opposed) it had to recognize that the likelihood of future friction with the Soviets would increase—especially in peripheral areas where social and economic conditions give rise to political instabilities. Since the American atomic monopoly would give way to a nuclear arms race, the result of containment would be an increase in the likelihood of atomic war.

Shils recommended three basic steps towards a more effective security policy: first, the Soviets had to be instructed about the bomb's tremendous force since their policies suggested naivete in this regard. Second, both governments should seek arms agreements outside the United Nations if necessary. Towards this end, Washington and Moscow should establish direct channels of

communication. Third, the United States should recognize that
containment is a military policy only in the last resort.   It is
primarily a political policy with social, psychological and economic
requirements for success.   Therefore, the United States should be
prepared to devote substantial resources to the strengthening of
peripheral areas through foreign aid.

With these recommendations, Shils made a strong case for
integrating arms control and defense planning in a manner that was
not to be practiced for another decade. The bipolar context was not
only recognized, it was regarded as necessitating a bilateral solution
to the problem of avoiding nuclear war.   Although Shils lamented
the lack of consideration of Soviet views in American arms control
planning, his effort to fill this analytic gap exposed the rationalist
bias which he shared with his predecessors as well as with some of
the later Cambridge School.   For Shils believed that the Soviets'
failure to see what Americans saw in the bomb was primarily due to
ignorance regarding the facts as opposed to calculated self-interest,
and that one of arms control's useful bilateral functions would be to
teach the adversary the wisdom of American military perspectives.

The Stability Function of Arms Control

The idea that nuclear arms control might best serve as an
instrument for stability, instead of for political change or propaganda,
also emerged in the 1940s.   As noted earlier the framers of the
Acheson-Lilienthal report believed their ideas would help stabilize
the international system by reducing incentives for surprise attack.[10]
In this sense they saw themselves more as arms regulators than as
disarmers.

Yet they did not suggest in their report, or in later public debate,
that to perform its stabilizing function, arms control had to be
integrated with defense planning and that the two in turn had to be
attuned to the evolving power and interests of the major states. Awe
of the technology itself and the prevailing sense that arms control
might shape international politics rather than the other way around,
led most analysts to focus on the establishment of a multilateral
management regime which would provide for stability at some future
date.

In seeking the stability which a "Grand Design" could offer, few
considered an approach that could serve as a guide to national
security decision-making on a lesser scale. Edward Shils was, in
this respect, in step with the majority opinion of his time.   While he

recognized the danger of unintegrated defense and arms control policies in a nuclear armed world, he believed diplomacy had to create the conditions of peace within which an effective arms control policy could be pursued.   He anticipated the bilateral diplomacy of the 1960s but without its operating premise: that arms control might be successfully pursued in the context of unresolved political friction between the superpowers.   He joined other realists of the later 1940s and early 1950s who called for political settlement as the precondition for effective arms control.[11]

Not everyone agreed.   William T.R. Fox, writing in 1947, urged "middle-run" planning in the arms policy field.[12]   He too believed that the Soviets needed to be brought to the negotiating table so that the issues left from World War II could be settled and a fresh assault on arms control begun.   But he stressed the importance of intermediate steps which could facilitate such an exchange of views and make peaceful co-existence safer in the near-term.   He wrote that "... the prospect for successful control would be much improved by having some of the most obvious targets made a little more difficult to destroy.   It would give the control plan a margin of permissible inefficiency."[13]   This advocacy of selective defense as a near-term contribution to stability and as a hedge against inevitably imperfect arms accords marked the earliest appreciation that there might be a less than absolute solution to the control problem posed by the absolute weapon.

By reflecting on the virtue of applying defense analysis (e.g., reducing vulnerability to atomic attack) to arms control planning, Fox became one of the first to bridge the analytic gap between defense planning and arms control.   In so doing, he emphasized an important point: that much could be done to enhance security and facilitate negotiations by purely national acts and decisions.   This assertion of the importance of unilateral efforts to arms control prospects was not to receive attention from policy-makers for another decade.

Moreover, Fox's "middle-run" considerations suggested that arms control planning should recognize the importance of nuclear weapons for international stability.   As long as other states might develop nuclear weapons, the United States had an interest in keeping them for deterrence purposes.   This was true even though atomic weapons were, in his view, too destructive to be useful in support of foreign policy objectives.   Fox's recognition of the near-term need for nuclear weapons, despite their repulsive characteristics, introduced the "weapons stability nexus" to the arms control field at a time when most arms control thought—and indeed official policy—was still based on a denial of it.[14]

Fox was essentially a realist. Yet in the field of arms control thought, and specifically with respect to the orientation towards near-term efforts, he had the company of a number of social scientists who were building on the work of prewar behavioralists. Some of their work anticipated the interdisciplinary arms control theorizing of the 1950s with its stress on the expectations, motivations, and the general psychology behind strategic decision-making.

For example, Gregory Bateson, Secretary of the Institute for Intercultural Studies, took an anthropological approach to the study of arms races. In an article published in September 1946 he argued that arms control planning should take the socio-cultural characteristics of the opponent into account. Thus he noted that in Russia "preliminary studies indicate that a very high value is set upon achieving one's full strength. It is not the fact that one can beat somebody else that is important but the assurance that one is exerting one's full strength."[15]

Using the work of L.F. Richardson who published in the *British Journal of Psychology* in 1939, Bateson argued that the atomic revolution had decreased the "expense and fatigue coefficients" relative to the "defense coefficients" of states. (The former were defined as factors which diminish the rate of increase in arms; the latter was defined as the multiplying factor which determines the extent to which an action by one side inspires actions by the other.) Bateson believed that this meant there would be a stalemate and an increased chance of surprise attack in a world of more than one nuclear state. Equilibrium or stability would be difficult to maintain. Given that surprise attack was likely to be the pressing issue of the future, he argued that arms control planners ought to try to determine which countries would be most likely to be motivated by weakness, and what could be done to prevent their taking action. He thus anticipated the stability concerns of the Cambridge arms controllers, albeit as a result of anthropological study, not systems analysis or abstract modelling.

Despite the works of these prescient thinkers, the immediate postwar period was not, in general, one in which theorizing about nuclear arms control thrived. As with the field of strategic theory, interest and productivity was limited by widespread confidence in the United States' nuclear monopoly, the immature nature of nuclear technology and extremely tight security restrictions. Moreover, the lack of a tradition of extra-military strategic thought combined with idealism's grip on disarmament literature meant that there were few scholars ready or able to bridge the gap between defense and disarmament objectives as the Cambridge School was later to attempt.

Much of this was to change in the next decade. Not only did the United States and the Soviet Union acquire thermonuclear weapons and sophisticated delivery vehicles, but nuclear options increased. Warheads became relatively cheap. Bombs of various sizes, from atomic demolition munitions and "nuclear backpacks" to one megaton fission devices, proliferated in the arsenals of the great powers.[16] Within the United States, the 1950s also saw great expansion of the arms control community, greater cross-fertilization of ideas within that community, increased public awareness of the nature and effects of nuclear technology, and towards the latter part of the decade, a loosened hold of disarmament premises on arms control thought. This last condition had to do in part with the development of an indigenous school of civilian strategists which accepted as one of its first principles, the nuclear weapons-stability nexus and the role of force in international politics.[17]

Indeed, the close relationship between the development of arms control and strategic theory is one of the salient features of these years. This association between strategists and arms controllers— implying here a somewhat misleading dichotomy—was in large measure a result of their common preoccupation: how to prevent the continuing threat of superpower conflict from becoming a mutually devastating strategic nuclear war. For military strategists such as Bernard Brodie, Albert Wohlstetter, William Kaufmann and a handful of others, the primary objective was no longer to design the best forces for victory but instead to discipline power so that foreign policy and the Atlantic Alliance could continue to be backed by credible instruments of force over the long-haul. For other analysts coming to the issue with a less agnostic view of nuclear weapons, the objective of preventing conflict from spilling over the nuclear threshold was a first priority as well. Their acceptance of the more technical approach of the military planners reflected in part the prevailing frustration over lack of progress in international disarmament negotiations and, in part, an acceptance at last of the political status quo.

However, the essential compatibility of strategists and more traditional arms controllers became threatened by the advance of technology in the latter part of the decade. The advent of ballistic missiles highlighted the problem of extended deterrence, rendering tactical nuclear weapons desirable instruments for NATO commanders, Pentagon officials and civilian strategists at just the time that maintenance of the firebreak—the distinction between nuclear and conventional weapons—was developing central importance for analysts concerned with controlling nuclear arsenals.[18] Although their objectives remained the same—to avoid mutual nuclear annihilation in the event of war—many of the strategists believed that control could be maintained after the threshold was breached while others remained skeptical at best.

In many ways it is useful to think of the 1950s as "The Threshold Decade" in nuclear arms control thought. It was the period when the special place of nuclear weapons was solidified in defense and arms control theory. Before the fifties it seemed as if the deterrent efficacy and, from the disarmers perspective, the military disutility of the Bomb was integral to the device. Combined with our nuclear monopoly, such an assumption made the notion of fine-tuning nuclear weapons policy for the purpose of avoiding war both impractical and uninteresting. But in the 1950s, quantum jumps in atomic capabilities introduced by thermonuclear bombs, advanced delivery technology, and warhead miniaturization meant that finer distinctions in nuclear policy, both with respect to controls and potential use, had to be considered. Thus, one of the first issues that was to absorb arms controllers and military planners was whether or not to distinguish between conventional and nuclear weapons by seeking to establish and maintain a nuclear/conventional threshold even as technological advances worked to blur the boundary between the two.

Related to this question was whether total war could best be avoided by keeping or abandoning nuclear weapons in Western arsenals. From the technical side, disarmament seemed unattainable since fissile stocks were, by the early 1950s, so large that no accounting system could adequately ensure compliance. But it was also true that the ongoing political and military challenge posed by the Soviet Union, and the apparent effectiveness of avoiding war through the maintenance of a deterrent stance with nuclear weapons, soon established the weapons-stability nexus as a premise for arms planning. By the late 1950s, most control theorists were thinking in terms of limited measures or "first steps" to disarmament.

Because of the importance of changes in international, technical and domestic conditions on the development of arms control thought during these years, the remainder of this chapter will be spent discussing these environmental factors. Chapter 6 will deal with the effect of these conditions on individual theorists and their contributions to the development of arms control theory.

International Conditions and Negotiations: The Evolution of Strategic Parity

In general, the 1950s were years in which the bipolar nature of the international system solidified and the gap between the most powerful states and the developing world widened. This structure resulted primarily from the enormous accretion and diversification of Soviet and American power which took place in the period 1949 and 1957. These were the years in which the nuclear arms race took almost classic form as the superpowers contested for ascendancy. It inspired much thought about the dynamics of "the race": whether or not it was one, whether competition leads inevitably to war and, if not, how to capitalize on whatever stability features advances in technology might introduce.

In contrast to the rapid rate of technology change and the new distribution and diversification of power in the international system, the institutional arrangements for conflict resolution remained essentially as they had been in the immediate postwar period. Although the United Nations did embrace new member states emerging from colonial rule and did serve as a sounding board for their collective interest in disarmament, the institution neither reflected adequately the dominance of the superpowers nor offered mechanisms for negotiating bilateral control arrangements. Outside analysts pondered the legal questions involved in changing the U.N. structure or the new initiatives which might be workable within the old. In this respect the arrangements for negotiating controls within the United Nations, which had been so innovative only five years before, acted as a constraint on arms control thinking in the 1950s.

Disarmament Negotiations

By the 1950s, disarmament negotiations within the United Nations had reached a stalemate. The United States had stuck tenaciously to the essentials of the Baruch Plan, enjoying the propaganda victory of having had the U.N. General Assembly endorse it in 1948. The Soviet Union had continued to press for inspection without international management and control, and for maintaining the veto within the Security Council should questions of punishment arise. In addition, each side retained its position on priorities: the United

States favored inspection before a ban while the Soviet Union wanted the reverse.

With the development of the Soviets' nuclear arsenal, the Baruch Plan had become increasingly dated. Still, little was done to change the American approach to negotiations. As was discussed in the previous chapter, there were certain political advantages to the American position which, given United Nations backing, had a ring of moral superiority in a highly competitive international environment.

In December 1953, President Eisenhower did propose a new initiative, an "Atoms for Peace" plan designed to help non-nuclear countries with the development of peaceful atomic programs with the aid of an atomic bank set up by the nuclear "haves." However it was widely viewed at the time as a distraction from the central concern of nuclear disarmament. Indeed, the Soviets viewed the proposed international atomic fuel bank and inspectorate as the Eisenhower Administration's back door to the Baruch Plan.[19] Although negotiations on the proposal were conducted at first on an informal bilateral basis, and international pressure induced the Soviets eventually to cooperate to a limited degree, the Atoms for Peace Plan did not bring about significant reductions in fissile stocks or otherwise broach new ground in the bilateral arms control debate.

After all, as analysts pointed out at the time, the unverifiable quantities of nuclear stocks on both sides made any contributions to an international agency more symbolic than real disarmament. On the other hand, if the arrangements for fissile transfer were accompanied by production cut-offs, the necessary verification provisions and the freeze on the American stockpile advantage would be certain to be rejected by the Soviets. In fact, it has been argued that this very aspect of "cut-off and transfer" made it an ideal joker to introduce in package disarmament schemes from which the United States wanted to reap no more than propaganda benefits. In 1956 when the United States was faced with considerable world pressure to agree to a test ban, the "cut-off and transfer" proposal was re-introduced as part of a package deal.[20]

The Eisenhower atomic pool plan evolved in what was then viewed as a harmless direction compatible with the interests of the major powers: an international arrangement for the limited distribution of technical and material atomic aid to non-nuclear countries under international safeguards. Towards this end, the International Atomic Energy Agency was established in 1956. Not

surprisingly under the circumstances, most aid continued to be given
on a bilateral basis even after the Agency's establishment. [21]

The major effort at international disarmament negotiations
continued to take place within the United Nations framework
throughout the 1950s, although the temperature and apparent progress
in discussions varied considerably with the thawing and cooling of
political relations between East and West throughout the decade.
After the death of Stalin in 1953, the Soviet Union conducted a
"peace offensive" which included a softening of its position in what
had become, as of 1952, combined conventional and nuclear
disarmament negotiations. On May 10, 1954, Soviet negotiators
offered major concessions towards the Western position, including,
for the first time, acknowledgement of the fact that nuclear stocks
had become so large as to be uncontrollable.[22]

The "era of good feelings" which the post-Stalin years introduced
was relatively short lived. As described in the previous chapter, the
United States responded to the Soviet demarche with its Open Skies
proposal in 1955. Heralded at the time by many as a major step
towards realism and innovation in negotiations seriously bogged
down by their own history, the proposal nevertheless became stalled
within a year. American allies were concerned by the bilateral turn
Washington was taking and by the discussion of intrusive inspection
in European aspect which was to get greater emphasis with time.
Similarly, the Soviets were unbalanced by the rather deft return to
the question of wide-ranging inspection. As discussions within the
United Nations evolved, aerial reconnaissance became viewed as a
confidence-building measure (i.e., a tool to aid analysis of the
strategic balance) in the West, and as an anti-surprise attack measure
(i.e., a tool to monitor western-European deployments) in the East.
Although both sides were concerned with warning, the different
orientations—one towards technical aspects of strategic relations and
the other towards Europe—meant that there was precious little
ground for agreement. When the major powers met for a conference
on Surprise Attack in 1958 these differences led to an early
dissolution of discussions.

Towards the end of the decade the Suez crisis, the U2 incident,
and the issue of Berlin among others, brought a chilling wind to all
questions of armaments control. Even the idea of a nuclear test ban,
which arguably had more to commend it to both sides than most
previous official proposals, suffered from the new emphasis on the
exploitation of unilateral advantages. In particular, the rapid growth
in estimates of Soviet missile strength made notions of any

constraints on similar developments in the West appear unwise. Limiting tests, and thus the adaptability of warheads to new delivery technologies, fell as it were, into the "missile gap."

In a fitting end to a decade of fruitless disarmament negotiations, Soviet Premier Khrushchev proposed before the 1959 session of the United Nations General Assembly, negotiations towards "general and complete disarmament." Widely seen as a politically deft, but impractical proposal, the Soviet coup spun international discussion around to square one.

The disarmament negotiations of the 1950s, while inconclusive, nevertheless had great impact on the evolution of ideas about weapons control. The ups and downs of the negotiations themselves inspired controversy and commentary: the Atomic Pool Plan and the Open Skies proposal stimulated thinking about limited agreements and bilateral negotiations; preparation for the Surprise Attack Conference generated studies—particularly at RAND—of the technical requirements of strategic stability; "Atoms for Peace" inspired consideration of controlled information sharing as a stabilizing instrument. Moreover, in the enlivened debate a new group of experts emerged—those journalists and international authorities familiar with the intricacies of current proposals, past positions, and the Soviet negotiating style. Most prominent perhaps were William Frye of *The Christian Science Monitor*, and Hanson Baldwin of *The New York Times*.

Second, the negotiations did begin to delimit that realm in which nuclear restraints or controls might be feasible. It was clear, for example, that efforts at using disarmament for political purposes would squander chances for practical results. More specifically, proposals dependent on intrusive inspection, which itself required significant political concessions from the Soviets, would be unworkable. Limited measures involving less than complete guarantees against cheating began to be considered in official fora and actively promoted in unofficial ones.

Third, the contrast between disarmament proposals and American defense policies and programs threw the question of American security objectives into relief. The new cadre of journalists and civilian analysts probed the discrepancies in official positions on disarmament and defense unmercifully. Thus, for example, Eisenhower's Atoms for Peace, cut-off and transfer proposals were juxtaposed with the New Look and the New New Look prescriptions for increased reliance on nuclear capabilities.[23] The result was more insistent calls for a rationalized security policy in which the objectives of nuclear restraint and national defense might be merged.

Soviet-American Competition

The contrast between defense policy, disarmament negotiations, and the emerging American conception of security was highlighted during the 1950s by the bipolar technical and political competition. With an apparent speed that left many analysts in the West astonished, the Soviet Union had become a serious technological competitor. It had produced an atomic weapon in 1949 and then, in the fall of 1953, thermonuclear weapons.[24] Having acquired this highly complex and revolutionary technology so swiftly, the Soviet Union consolidated a position of perceived parity with rapid advances in the stockpiling of nuclear weapons, industrial recovery, and the development of delivery capabilities.

By 1954 the Soviets had developed a bomber of potential intercontinental range. United States intelligence estimated that it was being produced at an alarming rate, causing fears—especially within the Air Force—of an impending "Bomber Gap" for the late 1950s. On October 4, 1957, the Soviet Union launched Sputnik, becoming the first to test missile technology. The "Bomber Gap" gave way to widespread fears of a "Missile Gap" and a continued Western preoccupation with Soviet capabilities and American vulnerability into the early 1960s. Although both "gaps" were more apparent than real, and the United States was, by strategic military measure, substantially ahead of the Soviets throughout the decade, the *perception* was nevertheless one of unstable strategic parity.[25]

There were essentially three phases in the conditions and perceptions of parity during the 1940s and 1950s, the progression of which proceeded in step with technological advance.

The first phase was the stand-off of the late 1940s in which Soviet conventional superiority in Europe was countered by the atomic capability of the United States. It was balance—but with "the winning weapon" on the American side. Shortly after Eisenhower took office in 1953 he introduced a strategic plan designed to capitalize on this perceived American strategic advantage while offering the prospect of limiting defense expenditures for the long haul. Referred to as the New Look, this plan involved minimal expenditures for conventional forces and reliance on the threat of massive strategic retaliation to deter Communist aggression.

At about the same time as the New Look was being formulated, informed analysts were digesting Soviet nuclear accomplishments and were beginning to predict the emergence of a nuclear stalemate wherein neither side could start a nuclear war without fear of devastating reprisal from the other. During this second phase it was widely believed in military circles that a relatively small number of thermonuclear bombs delivered by long-range aircraft would be sufficient to bring either superpower to its knees. Numerical superiority was widely considered to be a "wasting asset."[26] The assumption was that the primary strategic nuclear targets would continue to be urban industrial centers since the explosive effects and expense of thermonuclear delivery made attacking lesser targets inefficient. The United States maintained bomber bases overseas as well as on the homeland and began the construction of large radar or early warning systems to guard against surprise attack. The distinctive nature of strategic nuclear war was reinforced by the Air Force's monopoly on its instruments and the expected short duration of a thermonuclear conflict.[27]

The third phase of parity emerged in the late 1950s as the Soviets progressed rapidly in delivery capabilities. The natural stability which was believed to have inhered in the earlier situation of parity began to be questioned as strategic nuclear capabilities became more complex and articulated on both sides. The advent of rockets for long-range air attack, the diversification in warhead sizes and the decline in the cost of warhead production made weapons and military bases targettable once again. The development of missiles by the Soviet Union—first of medium and then of longer range—raised the Soviet-American strategic competition to new heights. Not only did it re-introduce the question of superiority, but it raised new problems such as anti-missile defenses, the instabilities of push-button warfare and the potential de-coupling of European from Atlantic defense.

This last question was not so much new as re-emphasized; nuclear weapons development and advances in delivery technology had blurred the distinctions between tactical and strategic war. The issue of disparity between American and European security interests was made more tangible and immediate as Americans pondered measures to control long-range missile developments, at the same time as Europe was being exposed to the new threat of Soviet intermediate range missiles—a problem which was receiving comparatively little attention.

The evolution of competitive parity rendered the problems of stabilizing the strategic nuclear relationship pressing ones. In official circles, the deterrent of Massive Retaliation which was designed for atomic superiority, was joined by a new emphasis on tactical nuclear weapons, especially after 1957, and with a policy of "brinkmanship" in which the advantage, unattainable via weapons superiority, could be achieved through intimidation—that is, willingness to walk to the edge of the nuclear abyss for one's declared position.[28] Both in and outside of the government, military analysts focused on the relationship between strategic stalemate and limited wars. The role individual services could play given the changing requirements of deterrence and defense remained a serious topic which stimulated strategic theorizing and debate throughout the decade. Finally, the problem of extended deterrence introduced for the first time, the possible effects of nuclear proliferation on strategy.

The implications of force relationships for the likelihood of war made strategic planning, including the generation of stability formulae with specifics on force characteristics and declaratory doctrine, a growth industry. Arms control theory developed as part of this industry, embracing many of its central concerns. Both the "bomber gap" and the more widely publicized "missile gap" of the middle and late 1950s unsettled the popular notion that the deterrent stalemate was automatic and that rough parity would mean rough peace. The fear that the Soviets' advanced delivery technology would enable them successfully to overwhelm the United States with a surprise blow shattered the confidence with which most Americans viewed the arms race.[29] In fact, the United States Government responded to evolving Soviet capabilities by encouraging and sponsoring such analyses of the bilateral strategic relationship, as well as by accelerating its strategic programs to ensure that in any measure of overall parity, the West could continue to counterbalance Soviet manpower advantages on the ground in Europe with strategic air power advantages of its own.[30]

This intense interest in the stability of the strategic relationship between the superpowers eventually characterized all nuclear analysis. Indeed, the pursuit of stability fostered by the intense strategic competition of the 1950s, welded arms control to defense in a revolutionary way which was not to be institutionalized until the Kennedy Administration.

The natural critique of the doctrine of Massive Retaliation was its apparent neglect of the need for conventional options and constraints on nuclear use, especially as the superpowers moved into the phase of competitive stability in which both sides were vulnerable and striving for military advantage. The civilian strategists' dual preoccupation with the nuclear threshold and the utility of nuclear force for limited or peripheral conflicts was rooted in the notion that total nuclear war was not in the American interest. Therefore, it had to be decoupled from other military contingencies in which force might be necessary.

These concerns about stability and the nuclear threshold evolved as a response to the rapid rate of technological change and the doctrine of Massive Retaliation—not to the failures of disarmament negotiations in the United Nations. But the underlying judgement that nuclear weapons were categorically different from conventional ones, and that their place in superpower arsenals and doctrine ought to reflect this, was the touchstone shared by both the developing community of "hard" military analysts and the long-established arms control community. Many within the two communities came together in the late 1950s as advocates of "stability before reductions" leaving traditional disarmers on their left and advocates of security through superiority to their right.

In this sense it may be argued that, just as postwar demobilization was a precondition for the development of deterrence theory, so Massive Retaliation was a precondition for the development of the Cambridge Approach to arms control, in which nuclear inhibitions were bound to the logic of deterrence and the "weapons-stability nexus" in the formulation of security policy. Once this relationship between Dulles' doctrine and the Cambridge Approach is recognized, the importance of the differences between the doctrines of Massive Retaliation and Assured Destruction (which was supported by the Cambridge School) are highlighted. In historical context, Assured Destruction had less to do with the advocacy of massive counter-value attacks than with the need for guidelines for sufficiency in strategic forces and for more options at lower levels of military capability.

The Structure of the International System

Bound with the intensifying bipolar strategic competition during the 1950s was an intricate fabric of East-West relations and intra-alliance politics that had important effects on evolving arms control thought. While the complexities of these relationships cannot be discussed in detail, some of their aspects had important impact on arms control thought and should be noted.

First, the competitive nuclear advances of the early 1950s were accompanied by continued frigid hostility between the superpowers. This led a number of concerned theorists to explore new methods of disarmament which might be workable in the absence of any trust or collaboration between parties.   Such creative approaches toward disarmament measures were based on the realization that the openness necessary for assured compliance with nuclear accords was a political impossibility and that, in fact, strategic stability could be improved before the resolution of all political differences.

Second, the loosening of Moscow's position in disarmament negotiations during 1954 and the Soviet leadership's public acknowledgement of the inevitably catastrophic effects of strategic nuclear war shortly thereafter, inspired hopes for an era of better relations and useful rational dialogues between the two adversaries. The belief, cast hard during the 1940s, that the Soviets were impossible negotiating partners thus began to soften.

Third, the recognition that drastic changes in the international system would seriously jeopardize the nuclear stability both sides desired, led American military analysts to adopt as a premise the essentially status quo interests of the contending power blocs. That is, it was believed that neither side would seek to change the essential structure of the international system through war.

The strategic competition between the superpowers and the rate of their peacetime military build-up had other indirect effects on the international system. Alliance systems froze at the same time that the economic and political revitalization of European states were straining these alliance systems from within.   Especially within NATO, allied governments desired greater influence in the play of international politics and greater say about the uses of forces should politics reach "white heat" in the nuclear age. Yet the change in the nature of alliances since the war was unmistakable: what had ceased to hold was the interstate equality intrinsic to the 19th Century relationship when allied collaboration was ultimately conditional upon mutuality of interests.   In the nuclear age dominated by the superpowers, only two states held the ultimate deterrents and made the ultimate decisions.   Collaboration was no longer mutually conditional.   The implicit threat which formerly had worked as a constraint on allied parties was no longer symmetrical.   Especially within NATO, an alliance of free states, the curtailing of political flexibility was painful.   Still, allied states were unlikely to leave NATO if the only alternatives were Soviet domination or neutrality, particularly since it was believed that the latter would lead eventually to the former.

And behind all this was the European's well-hued image of the reluctant American warrior. It was only natural for allies to speculate about where, in the ordering of United States priorities, the integrity of Europe stood. Had the isolationist impulse really disappeared from the collective American psyche? Or perhaps worse: would the American ambition for victory in future conflicts be intolerant of allied interests in nuclear damage-limiting within the European "theater"? Would the global interests of the United States bring war to Europe?

The asymmetry within NATO caused intra-alliance tension and mistrust during the 1950s. Though European leaders—particularly in Britain—sought early on to influence nuclear decision-making in Washington, American leaders quickly made clear that this area was sovereign. On the American side, latent distrust of foreigners was exacerbated by distaste for the Communist movement in France and revelations concerning British nuclear spies in the early 1950s—dramatic news which overshadowed evidence of British nuclear cooperation during the war.

As the strategic competition moved towards perceived stalemate in the 1950s, the problem of extended deterrence became salient. Increasing Soviet capabilities to strike the United States highlighted and compounded the difficulties associated with a strategy of nuclear first use in Europe. Allies sought greater political mobility at the same time as they sought renewed assurances that the United States would be willing to sacrifice its own cities in a nuclear exchange to save Europe's. They discovered during the Suez crisis that their mobility, when it came to force, was slight, in part *because* New York or Washington just *might be* comparable to London or Paris in a crisis involving nuclear exchanges. At almost the same time, the United States acknowledged the essentially hierarchical unity of the Eastern Bloc by failing to support the Hungarian uprising of 1956.

Thus, toward the end of the decade, the very point around which arms controllers were rallying was piercing the heart of European sovereignty: the superpowers' mutual interest in stability. Arms controllers believed this elusive, and in some respects, fortunate stalemate had to be emphasized and indeed reinforced by a weapons restraint policy. But for many Europeans this emphasis on stability was a constant reminder of the superordinancy of American interests within NATO, including the essential American interest in the political status quo despite the division of Germany and European interests outside the NATO bloc.

So it was that from the very earliest consideration of limited arms control measures in the United States, European reaction was testy. There was considerable fear on the one hand that the United States might act unilaterally in such a way that either the extended deterrent would be compromised or the Soviet Union unnecessarily provoked. On the other hand, it was feared that in secret bilateral diplomacy, the superpowers might effect a tacit condominium. For these reasons the first American arms control (as opposed to disarmament) initiative, The Open Skies plan of 1955, received a very lukewarm reception in Europe. The American failure to incorporate the new approach into the United Nations framework had much to do with European ambivalence.

The American leadership was not unaware of these European sensitivities. In fact, the removal of Harold Stassen, Eisenhower's Special Assistant for Disarmament, following his overture to the Soviets concerning aerial inspection in Europe, reflected growing appreciation of the problem. In turn, American initiatives to assist Europeans with peaceful nuclear technology and, in the case of Britain, with nuclear weapons development, were in part compensation for their military and political subordinancy.

Nevertheless, the American orientation was fixed: nuclear aid to allies was not to compromise bilateral stability. Insofar as a French independent nuclear program was more destabilizing than a British one, the former was to be relatively more discouraged. The need to deflect European interest away from an independent nuclear capability, combined with residual belief in American technological superiority, delayed appreciation of the extent to which nuclear assistance programs might be destabilizing through extra-alliance proliferation of nuclear technology. Without much debate, the central assumption of the Acheson-Lilienthal Plan—that "peaceful" and "dangerous" nuclear technologies were essentially indistinguishable—received little attention for most of the decade. It was not until the very end of the decade that arms control analysts began to frame the test ban debate more in terms of the effects on *global* stability than on *East-West* stability *per se*.[31] Following the fate of the test ban, nuclear nonproliferation policy tumbled, as it were, into the "missile gap."

But there were other reasons for what was, in retrospect, a dangerous oversight. In contrast to the essentially frozen bloc politics, the politics of the Third World were heating up in the

1950s. The break-up of old colonial systems resulted in a plethora of new states, a resurgence of nationalism, and the emergence of influential Third World leaders to be courted on the world stage by the competitive superpowers. Aside from exacerbating strains within NATO as European states sought to handle dissolving colonial ties, the new fluidity of the international system heightened the importance of propaganda and world opinion for the formulation of foreign policy and weapons control. It became of great political importance to win the support of new states by offering technical and economic aid and pledging nuclear reductions in the name of global security. Yet the enormous gap between the new states and the technologically advanced, oriented American decision-makers more towards winning friends than toward defense against a potentially proliferating number of enemies. Belief in the impossibility of bilateral defense was thus complemented by a general belief in the implausibility of any third party threat against which defensive preparations might be made.

Such preoccupations of defense strategists and policy-makers meshed on the civilian side, with interest in global technological sharing on the part of scientists still convinced of the benefits of a functional approach to world integration. Despite intermittent warnings from certain members, the scientific community as a whole could continued to believe that a world community could be built from the bottom up without jeopardizing national security.[32] Indeed, Eisenhower's Atoms for Peace Plan, which was a conservative's answer to pressure for disarmament, legitimized and energized the rationalist movement for technology transfer in the name of peace.[33] This is perhaps not surprising for a country whose history has been molded by the intertwining pursuits of expansion, world order, and freedom of action.

Technological Conditions

The preceding description of international conditions suggests that an important element shaping arms control thought during the 1950s was the technological competition between the United States and the Soviet Union. Although some of the features of this competition have been discussed, it is useful to review them in order to clarify and emphasize their impact on arms control thought.

During the 1950s, nuclear science and weapons engineering were young and dynamic fields. Warheads were miniaturized, made more efficient and deliverable, and also much more powerful. Nuclear weapons became relatively cheap. Not only did sources of nuclear materials multiply, but production facilities for uranium enrichment and plutonium production expanded as well. Thermonuclear weapons required little fissile material anyway, being based primarily on the energy release attending fusion of fairly abundant light elements. Atomic scarcity, once the constraint which made use of atomic weapons against military targets inefficient and uneconomical, gave way to atomic plenty—first in fissile stocks and then in a broad range of nuclear capabilities. Warhead miniaturization and the growth in fissile stocks meant that nuclear war could in fact be "returned to the battlefield" in the form of tactical weapons such as the 280mm gun and atomic demolition munitions in portable packages.[34] Thermonuclear miniaturization made ballistic missiles feasible. With the development of solid, as well as liquid propellants, missiles became potentially highly "ready" forces with the capability to be deployed in a wide range of environments.

The combination of nuclear plenty and nuclear diversification meant several things for arms control and defense planning. First, the once obvious technical distinction between conventional and nuclear weapons became blurred as the ease with which nuclear escalation could occur increased and the escalatory ladder was given more rungs. The result was that analysts who acknowledged the undesirability of total nuclear war began to search for ways in which states could opt against starting up the nuclear ladder and, once on, could terminate the climb. Establishing the difference between nuclear and conventional weapons became a purpose of policy rather than the basis of it. Of course, the usefulness of the distinction was dependent on Soviet appreciation of it. The apparent Soviet acceptance in 1955 of the futility of strategic nuclear war laid the basis for later hopes that similar stabilizing understandings could be achieved.

Nuclear plenty and diversification also meant that all three military services could argue the importance of their respective nuclear roles.[35] As pessimism about the ability to defend against missile attacks grew, the logic of deterrence improved the Navy's case for dispersed, mobile, hidden submarines as nuclear weapons launchers. The Army, in turn, benefited from newly evolving concepts of limited war and graduated response since these suggested the need for greater options at tactical levels of engagement. As competition between the services evolved during the fifties over nuclear roles and doctrine, interest in the work of the scientists and strategists was enhanced within the military. This led in turn to a splintering of the scientific community as theoretical nuclear physicists moved back to fundamental research and applied scientists became linked to military efforts through work in weapons laboratories and "think tanks." This shift led to a softening of factionalism within the domestic weapons management community based on improved information sharing concerning weapons developments. It may have also accounted in part for the emphasis on offensive weapons development, since the development of weapons technology was done at the behest of the military—and the most powerful of these was the Air Force's offense-orientated Strategic Air Command. The Air Force lobbied hard for expenditures on delivery capabilities over radar and intercept technologies.

Despite Air Force preferences and influence, the issue of defense was not written off by all analysts. In fact, some of the most prolific arms control thinkers of the 1940s were absorbed by the debate in the early 1950s over continental defense. Men such as Robert Oppenheimer favored the development of tactical nuclear weapons and continental defense *instead of* thermonuclear weapons. They believed the former would buy more defense and security than pursuit of the latter, which, it was feared, would lull Americans into complacency through a false sense of security.[36] For many allied against them, thermonuclear weapons represented the ultimate in unusable and therefore extravagant force. The choice between technological adventure or practical steps to bolster Western defenses brought the arms controllers of the 1940s together with official realists in opposition to the hydrogen bomb. In fact, such considerations inspired George Kennan to raise the issue of a "No First Use" policy as early as 1949.[37]

Following the decision to develop thermonuclear devices, official policy veered toward reliance on their offensive power while many outside the government, including a number of scientists, continued to warn about the need for continental defense to ward off surprise attack. Just as in the late 1950s, surprise attack was conceived during the early 1950s as a significant threat. Nuclear weapons were too inaccurate to have a surgical counterforce role and defenses were too poor to give much warning of incoming warheads. Knowing this, no nuclear state would risk starting a nuclear war without attempting to "win" it decisively on the first go. And just as in the late 1950s, when missile technology raised the specter of collapsed warning time, the early 1950s was a period when warning of bomber attack was to be measured in minutes. There was as yet no DEW line or other early warning mechanism. Such technological conditions, combined with the Administration's emphasis on offensive force, led many arms controllers to be concerned about stability and to advocate improved defenses. As technological advance and American predilections led to a favoring of the offensive, stability remained a unifying concern for arms controllers and strategists. However the defensive solution became not only inadequate but, according to new calculations, dangerously destabilizing.

Finally, the pace of technological change during the 1950s changed the American view of its competitor significantly. Although there remained a certain reluctance to believe that the Soviets were as scientifically capable as the Americans, there was in general, a new respect for their scientific progress. Such advances underscored to many members of the American arms control community, the essential rationality of the adversary. It established the possibility for communication at some level. When both sides began to admit their mutual stake in nuclear stability at mid-decade, the stage was set for bilateral diplomacy aimed at strengthening it.

This shift in weapons control thought from the political objectives and multilateral orientation of the 1940s to the stability objectives and bilateral orientation of the late 1950s brought arms control ideas from the periphery to the center of foreign and defense policy. This in turn exacerbated intra-alliance tensions as the economic and political recovery of Europe led its leaders to challenge American dominance in Europe's political and military affairs. Awareness of the problem of extended deterrence in an age of American strategic vulnerability caused strategists to concentrate less on means of attaining and using nuclear superiority than on controlling conflict at all levels through weapons management techniques.

Domestic Conditions

The new international and technological conditions of the 1950s gave rise to what Samuel Huntington has called a "disequilibrium" in the field of military policy and arms control policy in particular— that is, a period in which conflict existed among the goals of domestic, military and foreign policy.[38] Major changes were taking place in all these areas. Americans desired economic stability at a time when the requirements of defense seemed to be sky-rocketing; they desired the avoidance of military conflict at the same time they and their allies remained extremely dissatisfied with the political status quo—especially in Europe; they desired the elimination of nuclear weapons at the same time that they feared the loss of an adequate, economical deterrent against Communist adventurism.

The turmoil in arms-related public policy gave rise to a broadened arms control community and was in turn exacerbated by it. As Huntington has written:

> During a period of disequilibrium more groups become concerned with the policy area. The area receives more time and energy of general policy-makers...and assumes a larger role in public discussion and partisan debate than it does during periods of stability...[39]

The manner in which arms control's intellectual community grew during these years was affected in turn by the rise in academia of a behavioralist approach toward political questions, the associated persistence and influence of scientific thought, and the consequent emergence of a new elite in the realm of nuclear policy: the civilian strategists.

Methods and Models

The ascendance of behavioralism within academia had far-reaching effect on strategic theory during the 1950s.[40] This theoretical orientation, essentially the disciplined child of rationalism held that human action could best be understood as a product of reason and culture. Instinctual behavior was, by comparison, much less important.

In the realm of international politics, behavioralism challenged traditional theory's reliance upon assumptions and concepts derived from study of the past and terminology which, due to its imprecision, did not allow the testing of the relevance of past experiences for the present. Behavioralists sought to develop a cumulative literature in the field of international relations which would permit heuristic insights on the basis of powerful theoretic frameworks. Approaches and methodologies from a variety of disciplines were adapted to the field of international relations and used as tools for theory-building and associated conceptual breakthroughs.[41]

Behavioralists strived for a scientific approach to international relations in which propositions could be logically or mathematically proved, or were based on "empirical procedures of verification."[42] They attempted to wrest defense policy from what was viewed as the habits of egocentric, ethnocentric, and tradition-bound thought. The fact that American foreign and defense policy had won two world wars but never world peace was blamed on an inability to organize the latter due to preoccupation with unilateral defense requirements. The behavioralists' "scientific approach" was designed to liberate the American strategist from an historic naivete and to instill in him the systemic (as opposed to unilateral) perspective which grand theory could provide.

The behavioralists' desire for scientific rigor and precision gave weight to quantitative methods at the same time that the desire to outline a general theory of politics gave credibility to cross-over works by those schooled in related disciplines. Thus, Oscar Morgenstern, a mathematician, wrote *The Question of National Defense* (1959), the work of Lewis F. Richardson who offered *Arms and Insecurity: A Mathematical Study of the Causes and Origins of War* (Pittsburgh 1960) was widely discussed, and Thomas Schelling, an economist, contributed *The Strategy of Conflict* (Cambridge Mass. 1960).

As a prime example of the new behavioralist approach to international relations, the literature on conflict studies is of particular interest here. An influential economist in this school was Kenneth Boulding, who wrote that:

> ...in order to develop a theoretical system adequate to deal with the problem of war and peace it is necessary to cast the net wider and to study conflict as a general social process of which war is a special case.[43]

This conviction, personally acquired by Boulding during a year of discussion at California's Center for Advanced Study in the Behavioral Sciences during 1954 and 1955, led him to join like-minded colleagues in developing a general theory. *The Journal of Conflict Resolution*, which began publication in 1957, and the Center for Research in Conflict Resolution, established during 1959 at the University of Michigan, were tangible products of this work.

The study of conflict impinged most directly on the subject of arms control in its discussion of conflict *resolutions* wherein cooperation is invoked through skillful bargaining techniques. In this context, the definition of arms control became quite broad. Thus, Boulding defined it "as military cooperation with potential enemies in the interest of mutual security." Thomas Schelling, another leading strategist interested in conflict management, referred to it as "the entire area of military collaboration with potential enemies to reduce the likelihood of war or to reduce its scope and violence."[44]

Schelling in particular relied on the theory of games in his exploration of this subject. Game theory generated models of decision-making based on the concept of the payoff matrix. Parties in the game could gain rewards or punishments based on the positions of all after their "moves" or choices had been made. The mathematicians Oscar Morgenstern and John Von Neumann elaborated the theory in *The Theory of Games and Economic Behavior*. Though their work was designed to be a heuristic contribution to economics—the most rigorous of the soft sciences— the theory had a profound and far-reaching impact on those theorists concerned with arms control. Of particular interest were what were termed *variable sum* games, which involved both conflict and cooperation and offered the opportunity for both parties to gain from the play. This realm of theorizing was rich for those in search of new avenues of weapons management. Of course here, more than in the more general theory of conflict, there was heavy reliance on the rationality of the players—that is the assumption that each would calculate his interests and move on the basis of the best choice. But the theory builders were not policy-makers, coming as they did from deep within various fields of academia, and they frequently noted the limits of their analyses as well as the need to test them.

Thus, arms control theory theorizing gained new impetus in the middle to late 1950s not only because people began thinking rigorously again about methods and purposes of weapons restraint but because the acceptability of contributing unorthodox arms control models had increased. While behavioralists and classicists clashed on university campuses over the value of their respective approaches for established subjects, the relatively new field of nuclear strategy and deterrence theory, oriented as it was to prediction and prescription, thrived on a mixture of the two approaches. In fact, the logic of game theory was congenial to a broad segment of analysts who, considering themselves as traditional realists, were unschooled in its formal principles or fundamentally hostile to them. As Bernard Brodie pointed out:

Many strategic analysts do exceedingly good work in their field without having any great understanding of game theory, though they would unquestionably use some of its concepts. What does matter is the *spirit* of game theory, the constant reminder that we will be dealing with an opponent who will react to our moves and to whom

we must in turn react. It is amazing how little this simple conception
has characterized war plans in the past.[45]

In this "spirit" game theory could be accepted by the defense
community as a tool to enhance the sophistication and realism of
strategic planning even as related rationalist and behavioralist
approaches were deprecated by otherwise conservative military
thinkers.

Such innovation in theoretical approaches to security analysis was
complemented by technological advance in computers which allowed
sophisticated calculations to be made using more variables in a
shorter period of time than traditional methods could accommodate.
The medium of the computer encouraged analysts to seek more data
from more sources when studying the parameters of deterrence.
Mathematicians, physicists, and political scientists were brought
together for the purpose of designing models and software.
Innovation in information processing thus provided the practical
opportunity for cross-disciplinary thought just as behavioralism and
game theory provided the intellectual rationales for it.

Changes in the Scientific Community

The elaboration of new modes of analysis in the social sciences
brought breadth and depth to arm control's intellectual community.
It also brought about a dramatic change in its intellectual leadership.
Science as a method of analysis continued to be revered; but as
nuclear weapons became established as integral parts of strategic
arsenals, nuclear controls appeared less tied to the nature of the
warheads themselves than to the nature of deterrence and its promise
as a peacekeeper. The logic of deterrence and the doctrines spun
out of it, provided rich ground for critiques from widely diverse
disciplines. Whether, and under what conditions deterrence would
work, were subjects in which sociologists, psychologists, and
statisticians felt not only competent but uniquely expert. In this
realm of socio-military thought, those who could integrate such
diverse inputs into comprehensive analysis commanded new
authority. The civilian strategist had become king.

The rise of civilian strategists and their contributions was perhaps
the most startling difference between the 1950s and the 1940s in the
field of arms control thought. The elite status which had once been
reserved for the nuclear physicists who knew the secrets of the
Bomb and the language of its technology was radically transferred to

those who knew the secrets of technical force relationships and the specialized language of deterrence theory. Indeed, representatives of the "soft" sciences tended to look askance at attempts by "hard" scientists to contribute outside their realm of expertise.

Yet there were other reasons for the change in the intellectual hierarchy within the arms control community. There was much demand for policy-relevant approaches to the problem during the 1950s, and on this "hard scientists" were no longer of one group or even of one orientation. The continuation of the Soviet-American arms race, and the persistence of the closed Communist Bloc caused splits among physicists once unified by the concepts of openness and world integration. Many of those nuclear scientists who had been most radical in their appeals for world unity in the 1940s turned away from all notions of control in the 1950s out of fear of hampering the West's ability and will to compete in the inevitable race for technological advantage. They provided expert testimony on the innovations which nuclear technology still had in store, on the dangers of relying on limited means of verification when cheating could be so easily accomplished and so potentially lucrative, and on the dangers of an arms control mind-set for the health of the weapons research establishment. In giving up on disarmament in a politically divided world, nuclear scientists such as Edward Teller became nuclear advocates.

The rest of the scientists concerned with arms control gradually lost interest or otherwise withdrew to the peripheries of the control debate. Some, such as Robert Oppenheimer, lost their security clearances and public stature in the McCarthy era of anti-intellectualism. Their energy was re-directed towards fighting for domestic openness and the maintenance of professional integrity. Others preferred to return to specialized nuclear research, especially in the rapidly developing field of particle physics, while furthering the internationalization of scientific research as a long-term aid to international understanding and integration. After all, theoretical scientists were by definition more interested in their field than in public affairs—more interested in science than in politics. And there was too, a certain conservatism, a desire to be left alone to work without interference. Some, interestingly enough, exercised their continuing concern and interest in disarmament by reading and writing science fiction in which the dangers of science were elaborated but the scientist himself was not only vindicated but heroic.[46]

Several of the relatively few scientists who remained active in the disarmament question did begin advocating "first steps" to disarmament in the late 1950s. However, their advocacy of partial measures was based less on new ideas about arms control than on continued faith that a rationalized and disarmed world community was possible given Soviet scientific progress and the post-Stalin political thaw. In their view, the West had simply to try again with a limited, technically-sound plan, the merits of which would be evident to the Soviet scientific and political leadership. As trust developed, disarmament could proceed in step. Such views, epitomized by scientists such as Linus Pauling, were essentially elaborations of the rationalist approach of the 1940s. Yet the policy which they described, namely a step-by-step approach to arms management, fit well with the trend in the more officially influential and theoretically innovative segment of the arms control community.

None of this is to say that questions of nuclear policy had lost a technical thrust. As has been pointed out, technicians and specialists were heavily involved in discussions of deterrence theory. Civilian strategists relied heavily on technical information in generating their analyses. This was particularly true as they become preoccupied with the *consequences* of technical change. As Ralph Lapp, long-time defense critic and arms control analyst, has noted "one great dividend of the New Look at defense in 1954 was that it stimulated debate about the *use* of nuclear weapons." It did so at just the time when new data on the radiological effects of thermonuclear blasts were raising public concern and renewing public sentiment for their control. Administration officials were thus thrown on the defensive on two fronts; in both, technical judgments were important parts of the debate. But the problem of nuclear control no longer revolved around an arcane technology, the management of which would be *the key* to final solutions. Rather, it revolved around deterrence: the effects of thermonuclear blasts on the survivability of weapons systems; the utility as well as feasibility of passive defenses; the effects of long-run demographic trends on targeting options and survivability. The hard scientists had, in general, become generators of data, important but secondary actors in the strategic debate.[47]

The link which civilian strategists made between the technical and academic communities and the government helped to reconcile private, public, and official thinking on nuclear policy. The preoccupation of private citizens with questions of disarmament and nuclear controls met the official preoccupation with assuring adequate defense. On the one hand, civilian strategists served to funnel new ideas into the government using conceptual models that forced officials to address security questions holistically. On the other hand, they helped to prod private thinking in what may be termed, more policy-relevant directions. The effect was intellectual consensus building; the primary vehicle was the non-profit advisory corporation.

The RAND Institution

The primary bases for civilian strategists during the 1950s were those semi-private institutions created by the military services to advise them on technical and strategic questions. Of these by far the most important was the RAND Corporation, a creation of the Air Force after World War II.

The RAND experiment grew out of an appreciation of the importance of civilian input to the military operation of the allies during the war. Of particular importance had been the form of analysis known as operations research in which scientists evaluated the impact of new technology on military capabilities and methods. Although scientists familiar with technological developments were especially valuable, economists and mathematicians also played important roles in the interdisciplinary and highly quantitative enterprise.[48]

After the war, relations were strained between the military and scientific communities. Nevertheless, efforts were made by most of the services to continue in some form of positive relationship. The Air Force was the most innovative in this respect, perhaps because, as a new organization, it was unencumbered by a tradition of in-house technical studies.[49] Its creation of RAND, which was incorporated as an independent institution under contract with the Air Force in 1948, marked the concrete beginning of what was to be a fantastic growth in interdisciplinary strategic analysis during peacetime.

RAND was at first highly technical in its orientation. But as its staff began to accept the game theoretic approach to strategic analysis, certain of its members began to recruit economists and social and political scientists "... who could study the "utility functions' of consumers and the actual behavior and values of various nations."[50] In 1947, RAND held a conference to attract members of the soft sciences. Although their introduction initially led to disciplinary splits within the organization, the need for impact studies such as the one RAND published on the strategic consequences of thermonuclear weapons, instilled greater interdisciplinary respect between specialists.

The interdisciplinary work at RAND also served to soften relations between civilian scientists and the military as each developed respect for the other's expertise and as the latter came to appreciate the role the former could play in selling its particular orientation or hardware requirements to the public and its political representatives. The Air Force was the first service to reap these benefits as RAND's H-bomb study helped convince the Truman Administration and certain members of Congress of the need for enhanced strategic air power. The Navy and Army benefitted later as the same kind of analysis led to critiques of this approach—even by those associated with RAND.

RAND, and institutions like it, helped to make civilian strategy a profession. The analysts who circulated in this community were paid to think innovatively and to think together. Although they resisted advocacy as best as they could, they could hardly avoid promoting a particular way of thinking about strategy and deterrence. They took behavioralist methodologies, supplied them with technical variables, and wrung out new insights into the requirements of security in the nuclear age. Influenced both by the military and its requirements and by the public for whom they published and testified, their focus was upon maintaining national security by making strategic nuclear war unattractive and unnecessary for the major powers. Their premises included the practical necessity of nuclear weapons for deterrence and the superpowers' mutual interest in the avoidance of total nuclear war.

Of course, it should be noted that while RAND played a unique role as link between private and public thought on strategic questions, the community of civilian strategists extended to many who were not privy to government secrets during these years. Access to government secrets made it easier to be innovative and authoritative, but it was not necessary for general participation in debate on deterrence questions. Indeed, the prominence of the civilian strategic community brought with it a swelling of public information on nuclear issues. Not only did the strategists generate their own literature, thereby furthering the strategic debate already taking place on many campuses, but they also served as news-makers when testifying before Congress. A cadre of well-informed journalists developed during the decade, the members of which helped to interpret doctrinal changes and to discuss the implications of technical developments for the general public. They in turn helped to publicize and thereby focus growing public concerns over weapons effects so that these became issues with which public officials and strategists had to deal.

It has been said by a number of informed observers that all of the central concepts related to modern strategy and arms control flowed directly from work done at RAND during the 1950s. While this might be true in a policy sense—many practitioners of defense policy under McNamara were hired from RAND—it is less true in the intellectual sense. For example, as will be shown in the succeeding chapter, ideas about how to use arms control to reduce the risk of war during periods of superpower mistrust and hostility were generated by analysts and scholars in the late Truman Administration, long before associates of RAND addressed this flip side of deterrent strategy. Analysts at RAND stretched strategy to meet arms control concerns, but scholars on campuses from a variety of intellectual traditions were stretching international relations to meet the contemporary problems of deterrence and arms restraint as well. Thus, complementing the professional strategists at RAND, were those civilian strategists who, remaining scholars, trained a new generation of security analysts through individual teaching and publication. Their base was not the advisory corporation but the institutions of "peace research" or "war studies" on university campuses.

Finally, it should be noted that, in contrast with the 1940s, most innovative arms control thinking occurred outside the government bureaucracy. There were several reasons for this. First, as has been mentioned, advanced strategic and arms control thought was theoretical and interdisciplinary. Although steps had been taken to introduce new positions for nuclear specialists at high levels within the Executive Branch, the general lack of staff support and the *ad hoc* nature of their mandates made comprehensive analysis and planning difficult. Integrative strategic work, especially on arms control, was, not surprisingly, oriented more toward description and prescription than theoretical speculation and innovation.

An example, in the late Truman Administration, was the Acheson Panel on disarmament which, it will be recalled, was tasked with assessing the future of arms control given the stalled discussions within the United Nations. Although it's report was described in the previous chapter as insightful and prescient in a number of respects, the ideas it contributed were of a general nature, aimed at encouraging new thinking rather than providing a new and coherent policy framework. The Stassen group brought in to design new arms control methods for the Eisenhower Administration in 1955 did attempt to design a new approach, but its size, lack of bureaucratic leverage, and preoccupation with immediate policy initiatives in an essentially conservative administration inhibited original and wide-ranging thought. In addition, the requirements of secrecy meant that groups such as Stassen's and Acheson's could contribute to the "market-place of ideas" only to a limited extent. Thus the "new" approach embodied in the Open Skies proposal, which in fact did not originate with Stassen's group at all, inspired public discussion of limited measures as an approach to disarmament but lacked explanatory theory or heuristic framework. Stassen's group became essentially the executor of negotiations on overflights rather than a long-range planning group.

The need for a government organization geared to arms control planning in an age of rapid and often secret technological change became evident to a number of arms control analysts during the 1950s. Despite public concern with nuclear weapons effects and widespread preoccupation with controls, arms control thought was lagging behind increasingly complex and arcane strategic theory. Lack of government sponsorship was blamed by some, but the problem was not well recognized until hearings were held by Senator Hubert Humphrey's Subcommittee on Disarmament after mid-decade. These hearings brought together people and ideas from private and public realms, and generated greater support for limited arms control measures, particularly a limited test ban. An actual government think tank on arms control was not established until 1961 when the Arms Control and Disarmament Agency (ACDA) was created.

Conclusion

The 1950s offered a stimulating environment for arms control thought. Technological advance was rapid, but those believing themselves competent to address the consequences of these changes increased in number. Improved information processing, and the epistemological debate on university campuses led to a new effort to integrate knowledge for the purpose of managing force in the modern age. "Peace research" thrived and became institutionalized.

Interdisciplinary programs were established with a view towards making theoretical developments policy relevant. The National Planning Association, the National Academy of Sciences, the RAND Corporation, and a plethora of other private and public "think tanks" provided bases from which the academic entrepreneur could contribute new ideas and be assured of wide exposure within and outside of the government.

The integrationist thrust provided by changes in the intellectual community received a boost from the public's re-awakened concern with nuclear effects towards the end of the decade. Congressional hearings on disarmament broadened the audience for arms control planning, stimulated policy planning within the government and, perhaps most importantly for arms control thought itself, provided a forum for the exchange of ideas and thus, consensus building. As the nation sought direction, ideas were exposed to the test of policy relevance; outmoded or impractical ones tended not to be bought.

> What the Humphrey Subcommittee accomplished in the two years since it was created, was to snatch the subject down from the clouds, and to bring the Congress, the press, and the public face to face with the technological environment that surrounds the problem of arms reduction and arms control in the year 1957.[51]

Indeed, Adlai Stevenson's proposal for an H-bomb test moratorium made during the 1956 presidential campaign has been traced to the testimony presented before the Subcommittee.[52] His campaign not only advertised the arms control problem, it challenged the domain of the experts and served to further intellectual consensus building in a policy-oriented direction.

Such bridge building between segments of the weapons-management community was facilitated by the growth in fissile stocks which convinced many of the impracticality (if not undesirability) of complete nuclear disarmament. Furthermore, the intelligence and evident rationality of the Soviets, as demonstrated by their ability to compete in the nuclear field, combined with the political assessment that the basic Soviet ideology and global distribution of power was unlikely to change, led others to reject notions of avoiding war through nuclear supremacy or political conversion of the Russian people. The middle ground between disarmament and a nuclear offensive stance became a managed nuclear security program, the limiting boundaries of which would be conceived and maintained via arms control planning and policy. In this light, arms control offered Americans the prospect of maintaining a hand in the ordering of an international community conducive to American interests at the same time as it soothed concern about the instruments upon which the United States was coming to rely in this effort. In its scientific orientation, and in its concessions to both the expansionist and isolationist impulses, the Cambridge Approach, which evolved out of the 1950s intellectual climate, was a peculiarly American solution to superpower status. It was the perfect complement to a foreign policy of containment.

Notes

1. Hewlett and Anderson, *The New World*, p. 357. Oppenheimer later advocated discussing the bomb with all allies before using it against Japan [*Ibid.*, p. 367.]
2. Robert J. Oppenheimer, "International Control of Atomic Energy," *Foreign Affairs* (January 1948).
3. See Chapter 4, pp. 97–99.
4. James Conant, *My Several Lives*, p. 487.
5. Jacob Viner, "The Implications of the Atomic Bomb for International Relations," *Proceedings of the American Philosophic Society*, Vol. 90, No. 1 (January 1946): 53–58.
6. Oppenheimer, "International Control," p. 42.
7. *Ibid.*, p. 48.
8. Edward Shils, "American Policy and the Soviet Ruling Group," *Bulletin of the Atomic Scientists*, Vol. 3, No. 9 (September, 1947): 237–239.
9. *Ibid.*, p. 237.
10. See Acheson's comments in Hewlett & Anderson, *The New World*, p. 548.
11. See Hans Morgenthau, "The Conquest of the United States by Germany," *Bulletin of the Atomic Scientists*, Vol. 6, No. 1 (January 1950): 21–26; and "The H-Bomb and After," *The Bulletin of the Atomic Scientists*, Vol. 6, No. 3 (March 1950): 76–79.
12. William T.R. Fox, "Atomic Energy and International Control," in William F. Ogburn, ed., *Technology and International Relations*, pp. 102–125, esp. pp. 118–125.
13. *Ibid.*, p. 114.
14. For a definition of the term "weapons-stability nexus," see Chapter 2, p. 24.
15. Gregory Bateson, "The Pattern of an Armaments Race, An Anthropological Approach—Part I," *Bulletin of the Atomic Scientists*, Vol. 2, No. 5/6 (September 1946): 10–11.
16. Oral history session with Dr. Theodore Taylor conducted under the auspices of the Nuclear History Program, Spring 1989.
17. For an excellent recent essay on the development of this body of thought, see Marc Trachtenberg, "Strategic Thought in America, 1952–1966," *Political Science Quarterly*, Vol. 104, Number 2 (Summer 1989): 301–334. Trachtenberg points out the fundamental conceptual conflict between the idea of using thermonuclear weapons to threaten

escalation and the absurdity of an all-out war in which both sides have second strike postures on pp. 301–302. Trachtenberg notes also the fallacy of considering the strategic community as rigidly divided during the period.

18. An excellent oral history conducted by Robert Wampler under the auspices of the Nuclear History Program illuminated this period. The participants included General Robert Goodpaster, Professor Robert Bowie, and General Robert Richardson.

19. An interesting argument can be made that at least some officials within the Republican Administration, including Eisenhower himself, conceived of the Atoms for Peace Plan as a sincere effort at a limited first step toward arms control. See Henry Sokolski's unpublished paper, *Eisenhower's Atoms for Peace Plan: The Arms Control Connection* (Washington, D.C.: The Wilson Center International Security Studies Program, The Smithsonian Institute, July 6, 1983).

20. See William R. Frye, "Characteristics of Recent Arms Control Proposals and Agreements" in Brennan, *Arms Control*, pp. 68–85.

21. Interview with Charles Van Doren, United States Arms Control and Disarmament Agency, Washington, D.C., 1978.

22. *Ibid.*, p. 75. This was reflected in their downgrading of prohibition of possession (as opposed to use) of nuclear weapons to a later stage of their plan.

23. See Mary M. Simpson, "News and Notes," *Bulletin of the Atomic Scientists*, Vol. 10, No. 3 (March 1954): 106. The New Look and the New New Look are described in the following section.

24. It is arguable that the Soviets were in fact the first to test a deliverable thermonuclear device. In any case, American analysts were concerned that the Soviets had employed a thermonuclear process in their test that would have given them an edge in the miniaturization of warheads and therefore in the development of nuclear-tipped missiles. See Fred Kaplan, *Wizards of Armageddon* (New York: Simon & Schuster, 1983), pp. 114–121.

25. Colin Gray, *Strategic Studies and Public Policy*, pp. 274–288.

26. Clifton M. Utley, "Atomic Superiority—A Wasting Asset," *Bulletin of the Atomic Scientists*, Vol. 7, No. 3 (March 1951): 75–76.

27. The roles of other services were conceived as "mop-up" ones. Belief in the primacy of the strategic equation for the outcome of war was affirmed by the famous B-36 debate of the early 1950s. In this controversy the Air Force's arguments for primacy of strategic air capability prevailed over the arguments, essentially from the Army, that the next war should be decided by relative conventional strength since thermonuclear weapons were better for terrorizing than for military purposes.

28. It may be argued that tactical nuclear weapons were always conceived as part of Dulles's doctrine and Eisenhower's New Look defense posture. However, tactical nuclear weapons did not receive an important place in strategy until the "New New Look" of 1957.

29. For government analysts privy to intelligence information, the Soviet achievement was not a startling revelation. In fact, a pessimistic bias in estimates of Soviet intentions had lent ideas of transitory inferiority and thus international instability a degree of plausibility unwarranted by the facts themselves. Since information on the closed Soviet state was limited and poorly distributed even within the Government, projected Soviet capabilities were based on potential production schedules given first-strike intentions. Such worst-case estimates seemed more prudent that relying on "negative" intelligence (that is, the lack of evidence that the opponent was achieving his maximum potential).

30. See Kaplan, *Wizards of Armageddon*, pp. 160–166.

31. See for example, David Inglis, "The Fourth Country Problem: Let's Stop at Three," *Bulletin of the Atomic Scientists*, Vol. 15, No. 1 (January 1959): 22–25.

32. The First International Conference on Atomic Energy was held in Geneva from 8–20 August 1955. While most reports recorded exhilaration at the new freedom of information exchange, a dissenting view also emerged. Two physicists, Frederick Seitz and Eugene P. Wigner, pointed out that the United States divulged much more information than the Soviets, and that the Soviets only shared information and techniques about technology which had long been described in open American literature. The authors went on to recommend a certain reserve on the American side in the future. See the authors' letter under the title, "On the Geneva Conference: A Dissenting Opinion" in the *Bulletin of the Atomic Scientists*, Vol. 12, No. 1 (January 1956): 23–24.

33. The Geneva Conference held in August 1955 to share information on an international basis among nuclear scientists was a direct spin-off in the scientists' view of this conservative program. See Eugene Rabinowitch, "About Disarmament," *Bulletin of the Atomic Scientists*, Vol. 13, No. 8 (October 1957): 280.

34. The best data series on the deployment of nuclear weapons in Europe since World War II is in the collected works of Phillip Karber and his research associates, Ian Snyder, Michael Yaffe and Diego Ruiz-Palmer, completed under the auspices of the multi-national Nuclear History Program during 1989 and 1990.

35. The best discussion of interservice rivalry during the 1950s is the now classic essay, "The Origins of Overkill: Nuclear Weapons and American Strategy, 1945–1960" by David Alan Rosenberg, *International Security*, Vol. 7, No. 4 (Spring 1983): 3–71.

36. Oppenheimer initially rested his opposition to thermonuclear development on the belief that early designs would not work. However he joined many scientists in believing that no policy decision could long prevent the scientifically possible from being accomplished. Therefore when he realized theoretical advances would make it work, he changed his mind about the H-bomb.

37. George Kennan, *Memoirs 1925–1950* (Boston: Little, Brown & Company, 1967), pp. 471–500.

38. Huntington, *The Common Defense*, pp. 7–14.

39. *Ibid.*, p. 8.

40. For a good contrast of behavioralism and other approaches see James E. Dougherty and Robert L. Pfaltzgraff, Jr., *Contending Theories of International Relations*, pp. 379–381.

41. Perhaps the most significant work on war and peace published out of this school was Quincy Wright's voluminous work *A Study of War* which was first published in 1942 with a second edition edited by Karl Deutsch in 1955 (New York: Appleton-Century-Crofts).

42. Hedley Bull, "International Theory: The Case for a Classical Approach," *World Politics* 18 (April 1966): 361–377.

43. Kenneth E. Boulding, *Conflict and Defense, A General Theory* (New York: Harper & Row, 1962), p. viii.

44. *Ibid.*, 339; Schelling, "Reciprocal Measures for Arms Stabilization" in Brennan, *Arms Control*, p. 169.

45. Quoted in Herzog, *The War Peace Establishment*, p. 46.

46. Arthur S. Barron, "Why Do Scientists Read Science Fiction?" *Bulletin of the Atomic Scientists*, Vol. 13, No. 2 (February 1957): 62–66.

47. James Killian, a scientist from MIT, was named Special Assistant to the President for Disarmament in 1957. His influence was largely responsible for the shift toward limited technical negotiations in the late Eisenhower period. While the shift was important from a policy perspective, it was based less on theoretical insight than on recognition of practical opportunities for a limited accord upon which experts might agree.

48. See Fred Kaplan, *Wizards of Armageddon*, pp. 52–53; and Bruce L.R. Smith, *The RAND Corporation*. (Cambridge: Harvard University Press, 1966), pp. 1–66, for discussion of the origin of RAND and the use of operations research.

49. Smith, *A Peril and a Hope*, p. 3.

50. Kaplan, *Wizards of Armageddon*, p. 67.

51. Jerome H. Springbarn, "The Humphrey Sub Committee; Was it Worth It?" *Bulletin of the Atomic Scientists*, Vol. 13, No. 6 (June 1957): 22.

52. *Ibid.*, p. 225.

6

Arms Control Theorists of the 1950s

Introduction

International, technological and domestic conditions described in the previous chapter constituted the context for the development of the Cambridge Approach to Arms control. The likely persistence of nation states for the foreseeable future and the likely continuing hostility and ideological incompatibility of the Soviets were no longer widely debated. The bipolar structure of the system had not only solidified, it had become elaborated as both sides organized hierarchical alliance systems competing for allegiance in the Third World.

The technological competition between the superpowers contributed to these developments but it also demonstrated to many Americans the sophistication of their opponent. Thus, the rationalism of the 1940s, which had led to arguments for multilateral agreement on an open world, began to take new direction: towards secret negotiations for the purpose of organizing a stable, bilateral world order. What remained, and continued to attract, was the notion that peace could be organized through the exercise of reason and logic and not simply derived from technological competition.

Nuclear weapons had endured. On the one hand they had, in fusion form, become so horrific as to confirm their status as weapons of mass destruction. On the other hand, they had become so integrated into military arsenals and plans that they appeared tantalizingly conventional in their tactical forms. And it was this latter quality that made nuclear weapons unique. They were not only horrible, they were, in their lower yields, so apparently manageable that one could convince an opponent—and oneself—that they were intended to be used. This tension, inherent in the concept of deterrence, was critical to the development of a new approach to arms control.

For at the same time as nuclear weapons became widely accepted as a necessary evil, lax management of them came to be considered by many strategists as the most likely cause of war. It came to be recognized that mutual acquiescence to the political status quo could stem, not only from joint satisfaction with it, but also from joint

168

appreciation of the risks of changing it. If the risks were sufficiently reduced for one side by the acquisition of a significant nuclear advantage, war might ensue. Such logic led to acceptance of the weapons-stability nexus: keeping nuclear weapons to prevent their use while controlling changes in their stocks and deployment to avoid general nuclear war.

What then, were the implications of these developments for arms control thought? The most dramatic and salient result was that theorists began to consider objectives other than nuclear disarmament. The question became, not whether to have a nuclear arsenal, but what kinds of nuclear weapons should be included in it to preserve Western security without provoking general catastrophe.

Next, given that nuclear technology had to be countenanced for stability's sake, how might the technology be managed so that its evolution would not jeopardize the strategic balance, leading one side to take advantage of a presumed superiority? Whereas the first issue was one of static superiority—finding a balance that might endure political and economic stress given known technological parameters, the second issue was one of dynamic stability—finding ways to make certain that the static balance would not be disturbed by scientific breakthroughs or technological momentum in uncontrolled military fields. The latter was not just a question of numbers. It was conceivable—in fact hoped and expected—that numbers might eventually be meaningless in the stage of stalemate marked by "saturation."[1] It was more a question of qualitative change: how to ensure that a scientific breakthrough on one side would not inflame the nuclear fabric of peace.

These attempts to organize stability generally post-dated reconsideration of arms control methods. In the early years of the decade, at the height of the Cold War, arms control thought evolved slowly and often subtly. Analysts began to speculate about new methods of pursuing nuclear peace in the absence of an open world and foolproof inspection. The focus was on techniques; ideas clustered around "partial measures." Some advocated political first steps involving integrated foreign and arms control policy, while others suggested limited arms management initiatives involving integrated defense and arms control planning. With the latter came the earliest literature on "comparative risk" and "sufficient verification": a discussion of what was *necessary* to ensure *adequate* compliance with agreements among sovereign states *given the alternative risks* attending an unrestricted arms race.

This work on arms control methods was mostly done by scientists and scholars on university campuses who had followed multilateral disarmament negotiations and had become discouraged by them. The later, detailed work on stability designs was mostly done by strategists and weapons specialists associated with the military. Working together and sharing ideas, they gave collective birth to the Cambridge Approach to arms control by the end of the 1950s.

The purpose of this chapter is to discuss the contributions of specific individuals who, in this decade, developed the concepts and methods characteristic of the Cambridge Approach to arms control. The limits of space and subject matter require that only those ideas both directly relevant and systematically presented be given attention. Furthermore, the work of some analysts will be excluded if only because it did not differ markedly from the work of those who, in the judgement of the author, presented their ideas most consistently, powerfully and innovatively.

Finally, no attempt will be made to link theorists together in an effort to determine direct influences or otherwise to substantiate connections between earlier and later contributors. Detailing personal associations of this kind would inevitably be incomplete and misleading. It would also suggest influence in many cases where there was none. In this study it is assumed instead that ideas offered and exchanged in debate became part of the intellectual "goods" of the time. The point of the following analysis is that many of the ideas bought and sold in the golden age of arms control policy—the 1960s and 1970s—were marketed much earlier.

This chapter is divided into two parts. In the first, ideas relating to the methods of arms control will be addressed, while ideas relating to stability will be the subject of the second. Although this sequence may seem backwards from a logical perspective, it is historically correct since ideas on new arms control methods pre-dated ideas related to the Cambridge Approach to arms control objectives.

It should be noted here that, with respect to sources, the following chapter relies heavily on the *Bulletin of Atomic Scientists*. There are several reasons for this. First, the *Bulletin* (as it will be referred to throughout), was devoted during these years to following, not only the affairs of scientists, but also the broader debate on nuclear controls. Although the biases of its editors are apparent, their opinions were drawn and elaborated in response to articles published from a wide range of sources—some favorable, others diametrically opposed to the editors' positions.

Second, the *Bulletin* not only published articles from regular contributors, it solicited from many theorists who were not otherwise publishing but were known for their strongly held and influential views. In addition, the editors gathered articles originally published elsewhere and organized them according to themes, with commentaries solicited and attached. By so doing, they not only captured a public debate in enduring form, but contributed to it. The *Bulletin* was therefore a unique publication—especially during the early 1950s when ideas concerning arms control and disarmament invoked feelings of futility, exasperation, hostility, or widespread apathy. It was the precursor of journals, published in the 1960s and after, which devoted themselves to questions of national security and arms control. Eventually these later journals eclipsed the *Bulletin's* role in the development of the Cambridge Approach and the arms control literature generally.

New Methods of Arms Control

New approaches to the arms control problem evolved in response both to the lack of progress in United Nations discussions and to the changing perception of the nuclear threat after Soviet acquisition of the atomic bomb in 1949. As the importance of effective bilateral diplomacy increased, the nature of leverage changed: American analysts were coming to realize that atomic secrets could no longer buy a Soviet place at the negotiating table, and that future efforts to reduce the likelihood of nuclear use would have to be based on the mutual interests of the superpowers.

Still, dissatisfaction with the multilateral route to controls did not bring an immediate revolution in arms control thought. In the first place, it was hard for those steeped in the history of the disarmament debate to give up on established institutions and methods. The United Nations had, after all, promised so much not so very long ago. Many concerned with the nuclear question set their sights on improving the United Nations structure through Charter revision at the United Nations Review Conference to be held in 1955. Their intellectual effort was addressed more to legal improvements of the multilateral mechanism than to innovation on the theoretical plane.[2]

In the second place, most analysts concerned with nuclear diplomacy recognized that the early 1950s represented a nadir in Soviet-American relations; to them it was not apparent that bilateral disarmament negotiations would be any more productive than the multilateral ones had been. Such political realists only went so far as to suggest that negotiations on outstanding political issues might eventually facilitate arms agreement. Without political solutions, seeking arms reductions was just milking the venom from an angry snake—the effect at best temporary, the danger palpable.

But there were others who began to think in new directions, who favored searching for technical solutions which represented the lowest common denominator between the two powers. Theirs was an effort to frame a limited accord *given* political antagonism. Of these, a number began to consider unilateral methods of arms regulation to reduce the threat of nuclear war.

Bilateral or Unilateral Methods?

Consideration of new arms control methods and initiatives began in earnest after the Soviet atomic test in 1949. Within the government, officials were seized with the immediate question of whether or not to develop a thermonuclear bomb to regain technological superiority. In considering this choice, a few informed scientists argued for negotiations before development. As Dr. Hans Bethe put it:

> I thought the alternative might be or should be to try once more for
> an agreement with the Russians, to try once more to shake them out
> of their indifference or hostility by something that was promising to
> be still bigger than anything that was previously known and to try
> once more to get an agreement that time that neither country would
> develop this weapon.[3]

Bethe believed bilateral negotiations were not only desperately necessary but feasible. In his view, the Russians might be "brought to reason" because of the horrendous nature of the weapon in store. And if they could not, if negotiations should fail, security could be assured by hedging the bet: pursuing scientific research on the H-bomb in parallel with the diplomatic effort. The implicit belief was that the risks of negotiating an accord in a politically hostile environment could be reduced by vigorous scientific work in the relevant technology.

What Bethe favored was a limited, bilateral arms control initiative at a time of extreme international tension. His aim was not to reduce arsenals but to channel the technological race away from an enormously destructive course in which neither side, in his view, could have an interest. This assumption that the superpowers shared an over-riding interest in an arms accord, together with implicit calculation of relative risks—the notion that the risks of competitive H-bomb development were greater than the risks of negotiating control in the absence of security guarantees—set him apart from the majority of arms control thinkers of the time.

And yet his primary purpose was not the stability or nuclear balance so emphasized by the Cambridge Approach; indeed the concept of mutual deterrence was not yet understood or widely accepted. Instead, his purpose was to reduce the destructiveness which inhered in the technological race, for he could conceive of no rational military purpose for a weapon of such extravagant force. In his view, it was easier to ban such a technology before its development than to do so after that technology had a place in military arsenals. This view was, in turn, based upon a critical assumption about the arms race: Bethe joined Robert Oppenheimer and many other scientific advisors at the time, in believing that the Russians were largely imitative in their nuclear program. Although Oppenheimer did not favor negotiations, he agreed with Bethe's classical liberal view that the United States could, by example and moral force, "set the pace" of the adversary's program.[4]

Most official opposition to the H-bomb was not, however, framed in terms of its impact on arms control negotiations.[5] Men such as AEC Commissioners James Conant and Robert Bacher, Soviet expert George Kennan, and AEC Chairman David Lilienthal, opposed its development primarily on the grounds that it would further imbalance the American military posture. They believed a major weapons decision of this kind had to be considered in the context of both overall structure of the United States' defense posture and the constraints which economic considerations placed on it. For this reason, Lilienthal in particular, wanted the issue brought before the American people in the hopes that public pressure would force the Congress and the military to choose between H-bomb development and tactical fission systems.

However such a move would not have benefitted the opponents of thermonuclear weapons. The public was, at the time, quite willing to leave questions of defense—nuclear and conventional—to the expertise of the military. In 1949 and early 1950, the deepening of the Cold War left many suspicious of the Soviets and fearful of their aggressive intent. Secretary of State Dean Acheson took the persuasive position that the Soviets were likely to develop the H-bomb in any case and, should the United States forgo its development, would then be in a position to blackmail Washington in future negotiations. In short, he feared a reversal of the situation of leverage upon which American diplomacy had rested for so long.

Acheson's assumptions were fundamentally different from Bethe's. He believed political competition and hostility overshadowed mutual concerns about technological development, and that the arms game was not necessarily one of "follow the leader." The public was well-primed for such an argument, especially when backed by the military judgement that a qualitative leap in nuclear capability would not only redress a growing Soviet threat, but could spare the expense of countering it with conventional means.

Still, even after Truman's decision to continue research and development on the thermonuclear device, hopes for control did not disappear from official circles. On February 2, 1950, Senator Brian McMahon proposed an arms control plan with bilateral objectives and a multilateral cover.[6] Accepting the H-bomb decision as dictated by "severe realities," he nevertheless argued for "moving heaven and earth" to stop the arms race. Specifically, he recommended a package deal in which a new control plan would be devised and presented to the Soviets with the dual challenge that it be made clear to the Russian people, and that it be negotiated at a United Nations meeting in Moscow. In exchange for this cracking of the Iron Curtain, the Soviets would have the opportunity to share in an economic aid program, the funds for which would be drawn from the American military budget ($50 billion over five years) and distributed to all governments willing to divert proportionate amounts from military to "constructive" purposes. Although the mechanisms for this control scheme were new, the objectives were old: Senator McMahon sought to open up the Soviet Union by combining a new mode of leverage with bilateral arms control diplomacy.

McMahon's proposal did draw attention to the negotiating impasse in the United Nations, and it did suggest that the United States might profitably help to overcome it with a bilateral initiative, but it was heavily criticized for being too simplistic and naive. In a biting review, William W. Kaufmann, one of a developing school of civilian security analysts associated with RAND, argued that no progress in arms regulation was going to be possible until the Soviets had a greater stake in the status quo. The argument was not over the obsolescence of the Baruch Plan or the need for a new initiative with bilateral orientation, but rather over the timing and sophistication of the proposal, given the subversive and expansionist nature of the Soviet system.[7]

Kaufmann's critique, published after the outbreak of the Korean War, was characteristic of the times. Whereas the Soviets had been considered to be ideological, stubborn, and evasive negotiators since the opening of the United Nations disarmament discussions, they were, by the 1950s, generally considered impossible. The latter view was given intellectual substance by Nathan Leites in a powerful book, *The Code of the Politburo*, published in 1951.[8] Leites asserted that the Bolsheviks were ideologically incapable of compromise with "the enemy" and would cooperate only in an effort to control or subvert their negotiating partners.

The arms control implications of these observations were drawn by Edward Shils in a review of the book written for the *Bulletin*:

> The possibility of international control of atomic energy, which experience itself has now shown to have been a vain hope, is now also shown to be unreconcilable with the deepest Soviet convictions concerning the nature of the political universe.[9]

In Shils' view, Leites had refuted the notion that negotiations—even when tied with generous economic aid—could lead to useful controls or a liberalization of the Communist regime. In fact, there could be no collaboration even on the basis of mutual interest. If there were temporary changes in Soviet attitudes leading to a relaxation of tensions, it would always be a change of tactics, not of objectives.

Such pessimistic views were characteristic of the times. As late as the summer of 1954—over a year after the death of Stalin—a broadly representative symposium to consider "Alternatives to the H-bomb" concluded that a joint (Soviet-American) search for improved security was ruled out by the "implacable hostility of the enemy."[10]

Similar negativism marked the product of the disarmament panel, briefly discussed in Chapter 4, which was established by Acheson late in the Truman Administration. The Panel of Consultants was composed of Robert Oppenheimer (Chairman), Vannevar Bush, John S. Dickey, Allen W. Dulles, and Joseph Johnson (with McGeorge Bundy as rapporteur). Set up to review disarmament prospects in light of the United Nations stalemate and current world events, the Panel submitted a report in January 1953 which, it will be recalled, colored the future of arms regulation as far from bright.[11]

In assessing the reasons for lack of progress in international arms negotiations it concluded that:

...there can be little doubt that the principal cause of difficulty, here as in so many other places in the postwar world, has been the nature of Soviet politics and the behavior of Soviet representatives.[12]

It called the United Nations negotiations a "propaganda contest" and concluded that no disarmament agreement was possible since "... it is hard to make progress in the limitation of armaments when there is a high level of tension in the international political situation." Moreover, "even if present tensions should eventually decrease, there would remain divergences too deep for trust or friendship." The Panel, and Leites, agreed that "... their (the Soviets) hostility may be so deeply rooted that they simply cannot understand the idea that agreement might be of benefit to both sides."[13]   In retrospect, one contributor to the Panel put it this way:

> It was very clear that you could not negotiate with the Russians much about anything and that nothing was harder to negotiate about than disarmament, and if you put these two things together it just was the bleakest picture in the world of getting anything effective down that line.[14]

However, for those on the Oppenheimer panel, pessimism about disarmament negotiations during the early 1950s did not necessarily mean nothing could be done about arms regulation.   Unwilling to give up on the prospects for regulating arms and avoiding nuclear devastation, a number of these same analysts began to consider how unilateral acts and "inter-locking moves" by both parties might contribute to international security.   As the Panel's report stated in 1953:

> It is important to understand that an arms race is not something either black or white-either totally unlimited or firmly regulated by international treaties.   The problem of arms policy is to develop the kind of strength which may be needed to reduce the Soviet danger while at the same time keeping to a minimum the danger of a catastrophic resort to atomic weapons on both sides.   In such an effort there are useful steps which fall far short of a treaty of arms regulation.   Any development which gives us freedom to reduce our own commitment to the use of atomic weapons will tend to decrease the possibility of an atomic war.   So too will measures which combine a defensive character with a deterrent effect upon the Soviet Union.   For it is always possible that a real decrease in the sharpness of the arms race itself might be achieved by acts and not by treaties.[15]

This broad approach to regulating the arms race was a sharp break with the past. Having accepted the importance of nuclear weapons to the defense of the West, the panelists dismissed disarmament. Having accepted Soviet hostility and non-cooperation for the foreseeable future, the panelists were skeptical that there could be productive negotiations even on a bilateral basis. Instead, the panelists argued for an arms policy that combined vigorous attention to defense requirements with equally vigorous attention to the "transcendent dangers of the weapons themselves."[16] They accepted the concept of welding arms control to defense policy in the nuclear age.

The Recommendations of the Oppenheimer Panel: Another Look

The Panel's recommendations were insightful, provocative, and prescient of the Cambridge Approach. Although its members were quite general about the objectives towards which a regulatory arms policy should be addressed, they were forceful and relatively specific about the new methods or instruments which a regulatory approach might employ. After touching briefly on the first, the following analysis will concentrate on the second.

Limited Measures. The members of Acheson's panel believed that the basic objective of any nuclear arms limitation should be to eliminate, not the weapons themselves, but the capability of either side to strike the other with "direct and crippling blows." They noted that it had become apparent since 1945 and 1946 that a decisive atomic attack would require accurate delivery of atomic bombs in considerable numbers; therefore, effective regulation would not require disarmament—a goal which besides being impossible to attain, was in their view, unnecessary. They described their limited objective as follows:

> ... much would be achieved if it should be possible to get a reduction in the size of stockpiles and bombing fleets such that neither side need fear a sudden knockout from the other. Such a reduction would not give assurance against the use of atomic weapons but it would give protection against the danger of a surprise knockout blow, and this is the danger which is so critically important in its political meaning for both the United States and the Soviet Union.[17]

They believed that

> ... any scheme of arms regulation which is to have a chance of
> acceptance by the Soviet Union must take into account the depth of
> the Soviet attachment to the principle of the Iron Curtain.

Moreover, while inspection was considered necessary to effective
control, it was important:

> ... in the interest of political reality, that such inspection *do as little
> violence as possible* to a principle which seems to stand near the
> center of the Soviet system—the need for a closed society.[18]

The panelists were clearly convinced of the importance of
proposals limited both with respect to weapons reductions and
political purposes. In acknowledgement of the controversial nature
of their opinion they wrote:

> It is possible to argue, of course, that there can be no real safety until
> we have an open world, and the argument has force, but to accept it
> entirely would be to deter all hope of arms regulation until after a
> revolution had occurred in Russia—and perhaps still further, for it is
> far from clear that a new Russian revolution would bring an open
> society. For the present, it seems better to take some account of the
> Iron Curtain.[19]

Unwilling to accept the old notion, promoted as recently as
McMahon's proposal, that American purposes should be to win the
hearts and minds of the Russian people, they advocated making arms
control a bilateral, intergovernmental, politically status quo policy.
While technological outcomes were the immediate objectives of
the Panel's approach, its members had only a vague concept of the
bilateral military relationship toward which defense and arms control
policy should be aimed. They suggested that neither side should
have the capability for a surprise attack, but they stopped short of
designing a bilateral solution. Their recommendations, heavily
weighted toward denial of a Soviet capability to achieve a knockout
blow, included for example, improvement in the American effort at
continental defense. They raised specific concerns about the
emergence of a relationship of mutual assured destruction:

> If the atomic race continues, therefore, we seem likely to have within
> a relatively few years a situation in which the two great powers will

each have a clear-cut capacity to do very great damage to the other, while each will be unable to exert that capacity except at the gravest risk of receiving similar terrible blows in return. And this situation is likely to be largely unaffected by the fact that one side may always have many more weapons than the other ... It is always conceivable that a world of this kind may enjoy a strange stability arising from general understanding that it would be suicidal to "throw the switch." On the other hand it also seems possible that a world so dangerous may not be very calm, and to maintain peace it will be necessary for statesmen to decide against rash actions not just once, but every time. In particular, since the coming of such a world will be gradual and since its coming may or may not be correctly estimated in all countries, there is a possibility that one nation or another may be tempted to launch a preventive war "before it is too late," only to find out that the time for such a blow has already passed.[20]

While the Panel looked with foreboding at this potential course for bilateral military relations, it did not offer a detailed counter-design for bilateral stability. The panelists merely suggested that some restriction on offensive capabilities beneath "saturation" levels would be desirable. Indeed, their bias toward unilateral prescription was captured in their more general objective: to increase American "freedom of action" through a regulatory arms policy. That is, they sought to structure the American defense posture such that resort to nuclear weapons would be less necessary. That meant both discouraging Soviet attack and improving tactical military capabilities so that lower levels of force might be available.

The panelists believed that such a limited approach would be more realistic than the detailed disarmament schemes both sides continued to advocate publicly, and would eventually result in agreements which would be easier to negotiate and to maintain:

This somewhat more robust sort of scheme would be characterized by a basic agreement to reduce all major forms of armament well below the point where they threaten destruction to other major powers; such an agreement should be designed to provide wide margins of safety. In keeping with these wide margins, the scheme could get on with a relatively simple system of inspection, designed to prevent any major violation from going unnoticed but not pretending to guarantee against relatively minor and inconclusive breaches of the agreed levels.[21]

Bilateral or Unilateral? Given Soviet technological advance, political intransigence and fundamental hostility, how did the Panel hope that arms control could be pursued? The foregoing discussion suggests that the panelists were primarily interested in guiding American decision-makers towards a frame of mind in which the dangers of nuclear weapons were better appreciated. Arms control in this sense meant self-discipline, and involved spending money on unfamiliar and historically unattractive systems of defense (radar and interception) to enhance deterrence. It also meant spending money to increase the American freedom to choose not to go nuclear—for example by raising the nuclear threshold through increased conventional capabilities.

For such decisions to be made,the American people would have to be edged out of their complacency. They would have to be told, with candor, about the grave dangers of the nuclear arms race as well as the challenge which the Soviets posed. The panelists were advocating a government effort to re-invigorate the arms policy "contract" which was rooted in the immediate postwar period but which had been allowed—even encouraged—to whither under the heavy blanket of atomic secrecy. It was, in their view, imperative that the public understand why defense was terribly necessary but also necessarily disciplined with respect to its structure and composition, not just its cost.

Yet the panelists went further. First, they hinted that the American approach might have a bilateral angle. They pointed out that past American nuclear policies had aggravated the technological race, heightened the likelihood of nuclear war, and increased the chances that its conduct would be divorced from political considerations. Such was the nature of a first-use policy.[22] While moving from here to a "balanced and acceptable" international limitation might be a terribly complex effort, still it might be achieved "by a series of interlocking actions that are not formally embodied in a treaty." In this effort, the United States would have to take the initiative—not just because of the "rigidity and totality of commitment" represented by its military posture, but because of the implacable hostility and political rigidity of the adversary.

Second, they did not dismiss negotiations with the Soviets completely:

Even negotiation, which seems so remote, so unmanageable at present, and unlikely in the immediate future, is not to be wholly dismissed. The dangers of the arms race are at least as great for the Soviet Union as they are for the United States, and the passage of time may well increase the pressure on the Kremlin for serious consideration of alternatives to its present policy. It would be unwise to neglect the possibility that negotiation may become feasible in the reasonably near future. It seems important that American policy should not permit the continuance of a situation in which our own rigidities would inhibit us from creating an opportunity to negotiate.[23]

Moreover, until negotiations became possible, it was important that the United States leadership seek ways of at least communicating with its Soviet counterpart. In the panelists' view, this primarily meant "active listening" on the American side for changes in the Soviet attitude towards controls—a change which might attend Stalin's succession or the advance of the arms race itself. But communication was also important to prevent serious Soviet miscalculation involving either "the importance" of nuclear weapons or the dangers which inhered in American uncertainty and speculation regarding Soviet intentions and capabilities. Though the Soviets were deemed unlikely to be candid or particularly cooperative in bilateral exchange, the panelists believed that:

... even the most practiced deceiver tells more than he intends, and we are persuaded that it would be good to have a continuous record of the way the Kremlin sounds in communication on this subject.[24]

The Oppenheimer Panel's report embodied thinking which differed sharply with the past. By downgrading the importance of disarmament and the multilateral United Nations discussions, it brought arms control out of an intellectual wilderness, shaping and taming it to the requirements of American defense and foreign policy. In so doing, its theorists introduced a regulatory approach to arms policy which foreshadowed, in a number of respects, the Cambridge Approach which was to follow. Where their design differed most dramatically from the latter was in the realm of stability scenarios—especially the effect of defensive systems employed by both sides.

Where it most clearly coincided with the Cambridge Approach was in its advocacy of an arms control process integrated with defense planning: its pursuit via "interlocking actions"; of tacitly recognized technological outcomes given certain political realities (especially the closed nature of the Soviet system); its associated interest in using unilateral capabilities for security in a weapons restraint environment (as opposed to comprehensive guarantees arranged within a treaty); and in its stress on the importance of *continuous* bilateral communication to avoid miscalculations of capabilities and intent.

In the details of some of these points lay certain differences between the two approaches. For example, the Oppenheimer Panel believed the unilateral capabilities which were necessary to hedge against Soviet duplicity or misadventure could only be adequately ensured if the American people were constantly informed about arms control and defense planning and thus remained party to the entire approach. The Cambridge Approach, designed at a time not of public complacency, but of public agitation inspired by the test-ban debate and missile gap debates, embraced no philosophy of arms control in a democratic society. Second, the Cambridge Approach explicitly favored not just "active listening" to Soviet views on the bilateral military relationship, but communicating American conceptions of stability and formulas for its achievement to the adversary. Of this, the Oppenheimer Panel was quite skeptical:

> We are inclined to emphasize the value of listening for sounds from Soviet representatives rather above that of any communication that the United States might be able to make, at least at the beginning. It is far from certain that we have it in our power at present to make ourselves understood in the Kremlin...[25]

Despite these important differences, the Oppenheimer Panel's report was strikingly close to the Cambridge Approach with respect to its attitude towards arms policy. However, it had almost no impact on the course of official policy. The incoming Eisenhower Administration took hold of one of its recommendations—the need for candor with the public—and turned it into a program for impressing the public with the peaceful potential of nuclear technology. This reflected a different calculation of the American public's capability to handle the complexity of the technological, military, and political challenges it faced. Fearing that disclosure of the facts would result less in informed public debate than public hysteria, officials in the new Administration accepted the motives for "candor," but concluded that the need was for assertion of leadership and for new initiatives to dispel public concerns and to motivate Americans to the challenges of the nuclear age. One of the results was the Atoms for Peace proposal of 1953. In the continuing atmosphere of nuclear secrecy, however, the Oppenheimer Panel's report did not come to light until years later.

The Contributions of the Unofficial Community

Still, consideration of new approaches to the arms control problem was being carried on in private circles. Several physicists, political scientists and lawyers, despairing of disarmament prospects in the politically hostile context of the early 1950s, argued for "first steps" which addressed the political problems making arms restraint impossible. For example, Leo Szilard, a physicist long active in the issue of nuclear controls, called for a nuclear free zone in Europe.[26] He reasoned that Europe would remain vulnerable to a Soviet atomic attack regardless of American promises to retaliate, and if aggression should occur, the destruction in the theater would inevitably be massive. This put the Europeans in a politically and militarily untenable position which offered but one solution: release of European governments from the Atlantic Pact. Szilard suggested that in place of the formal alliance, bilateral assurances of respect for individual countries' neutrality should be offered, except in the event the Soviet Union attacked the United States with atomic weapons. Europe would then be able to arm conventionally while remaining removed from nuclear war. Szilard believed this would be more politically viable for the Allies—since they would not have to trade the reduced probability of nuclear war for massive destruction should deterrence fail—but it would remove the most important area of conflict in East-West relations. After all, he reasoned, in the event of war, the United States could not keep Europe. Either it would be lost through unwillingness to resort to nuclear use or it would be destroyed by atomic weapons. Without nuclear weapons in Europe, the primary threat to the Soviet Union would be removed and they would have no incentive to use nuclear weapons there. In the ensuing political atmosphere, de-fused by a return to mobilization strategies on both sides, the prospects for nuclear disarmament would be, in Szilard's view, considerably improved.

Hans J. Morgenthau, a professor of international politics, also believed the resolution of political issues was a precondition for disarmament.[27] Leaving the technical and military feasibility of H-bomb development to "the experts," he argued for a resolution of European questions through negotiations.

However, as the early 1950s unfolded, Morgenthau became primarily concerned with continuing official disregard of the bipolar structure of the international system, the advent of which had been heralded in the military realm by the Soviet atomic explosion in 1949 and in the political realm by the defection of China that same year. Instead of developing a foreign policy appropriate to the condition, the United States had been pursuing the elusive goal of quantitative superiority in the military realm while hiding politically within the mythical world of traitors, spies and internal subversion. The dangers of these illusions brought him to call, in October 1954, for greater attention to the *prevention* of atomic war since developments in its destructiveness no longer made it an instrument of rational policy.[28] While not labelling his recommendations "arms control," he nevertheless advocated certain unilateral steps which the Oppenheimer Panel had identified: active defense and target multiplication to enhance deterrence, and improved conventional capabilities in case of war.

Although both Szilard and Morgenthau were disenthralled with American attempts to regain military superiority, and therefore considered new bilateral efforts to prevent nuclear war, their preoccupation with the political divisions between East and West set them apart from those who contributed more directly to the Cambridge Approach. Morgenthau and Szilard acknowledged— indeed insisted—that arms control could not achieve political ends; but they did not conclude that outstanding political issues ought to be considered the "givens" of arms control planning and policy. As others were seeking to integrate weapons constraint and military policy, they were arguing for integration of defense policy and foreign policy to enhance the realism of both.

Interim Solutions: Adequate Verification and Comparative Risk

Most of the theorizing about limited measures, which might be more properly called "arms control" in the Cambridge sense, was done by those more exclusively preoccupied by the disarmament problem during these years. David F. Cavers, a professor of international law at Harvard University, took the position that there was mutual interest in disarmament negotiations, and therefore a basis for dialogue which did not exist in the political realm. In his view, official policy ought to embrace negotiations without waiting for political detente. Cavers turned his attention to an interim plan for control which would be suitable for the period following the Soviet atomic test but before the development of significant "peaceful" programs on either side.

He reasoned that during this period, which would last for perhaps twenty years, low demand for non-military nuclear energy would limit the need for the large-scale facilities and fissile stockpiles which posed such problems for control agreements. In fact, the central danger in his view was the growth in stockpiles of fissionable materials. The longer these were allowed to develop, the more difficult it would be to provide acceptable assurances in any arms control agreement against prior stockpiling of weapons. Acknowledging the impossibility even at that time of air-tight controls, he posed the following test for an arms control design: "... will the plan prevent the accumulation of enough bombs to give the nations possessing them a substantial advantage in case of war?"[29]

Cavers concluded that if the United States and the Soviet Union were immediately to place all their dangerous materials and facilities for nuclear development at an international location, the residual, unverifiable nuclear capabilities on each side would not be enough to give either state a significant nuclear advantage in case of war. Therefore, he proposed that such a depository be established and that it provide storage for reactor components, fuel, and explosive parts. Further, it would be left completely undefended; that is, vulnerable to knockout blows from both sides. Simply put, the significant nuclear weapons capabilities of each side would be held hostage by the other while internationalized nuclear energy development would continue unhampered. In making this recommendation, he explicitly rejected the concept of a "strategic balance" in nuclear capabilities endorsed by the earlier Acheson-Lilienthal Plan.[30]

Cavers' plan incorporated a design for stability to be achieved through limited measures. However, it was only in these latter characteristics that it anticipated the Cambridge Approach. Cavers' stability was to be based not on nuclear deterrence but on the denial of significant nuclear capabilities to either side, thus depriving each of a decisive win using atomic instruments. His aim was not so much to prevent nuclear war (though he probably hoped this would result) as it was to slow the arms race and to limit the destructiveness of war should it occur. He wanted a breathing space to allow time for the development of feasible plans for disarmament. To repeat, Cavers, central concern was with the threat posed by the growth of fissile stocks on both sides—a problem which the pursuit of peaceful nuclear purposes would only exacerbate. As a legal expert, his focus was not on stability but on verification of reductions and adequate security guarantees.

However, by acknowledging the futility of disarmament efforts and by advocating limited bilateral measures to cope with the nuclear threat in a politically divided world, Cavers was, as was the Oppenheimer Panel, breaking new ground in 1950. Where Cavers made his contribution in the early 1950s to the network of ideas characterizing the Cambridge Approach was in his discussion of "adequate verification" of control measures—this is the notion that there can be an insignificant margin of error in an advantageous control scheme in the nuclear age. Later in an article published in 1955, he also pointed out that agreements based on mutual interests could best be *enforced* by the threat of breaking them. At the same time he made explicit nuclear arms control's relationship to outstanding political questions—a view that was implicit in the Cambridge Approach and directly contrary to Morgenthau's position:

> It is often said that agreement on arms control must await a general political settlement. What is less often recognized is that arms control implies the settlement of political issues, at least to the point that warfare is not to be used to resolve them ...[31]

The key, of course, was to make sure that there remained sufficient national military capabilities to enforce the political stalemate. Still, Cavers held out for the positive effects of long-term arms control on political discord:

> As these tough political problems are examined with the needs of arms control in view, the happy suspicion grows that it may be easier to settle a dispute as a means to achieving some larger and independent purpose than it would be to resolve it wholly on its own merits.[32]

Cavers' notion that an insignificant margin of error could exist in arms control agreements could not have emerged in the early postwar period when the possession of only a few nuclear weapons was considered a decisive capability. But by the early 1950s he had company in his views.

In 1951, two physicists who had worked on the Manhattan Project at Los Alamos and had moved on to the Argonne National Laboratory at Chicago published an article proposing, as Cavers had, a limited interim control scheme. Unlike Cavers however, David R. Inglis and Donald Flanders were planning for that period of time after the re-arming of the West but before the deployment of tactical nuclear weapons—an interim in which Western dependence on atomic weapons could be lessened.

Inglis and Flanders were critical of official disarmament policy, including its political thrust:

In the domain of atomic energy ... we seem to have no plans, except possibly to re-offer the proposals already made, for the acceptance of which our main reliance would seem to lie in the possibility of internal change within the Soviet Union.[33]

They proposed that the West consider basing its arms control initiatives on the mutual interests both sides had in avoiding nuclear war. They believed a first step was possible in which stability would be achieved by an "adequately verifiable" cap on deployments below "saturation" levels. Their ultimate aim was still disarmament, but their immediate objectives were much less ambitious:

An ideal atomic control scheme would eliminate competing stockpiles entirely, as the Baruch proposal aimed to do. Now that competing stockpiles exist it may be too late to seek such an ideal solution except as the result of a long evolution. A first step in that direction might be an agreement that tolerates the existence of opposing stockpiles limited to a size well below saturation. The situation would still be dangerous, but less so than with unlimitedly increasing stockpiles.[34]

What Inglis and Flanders had in mind was a rudimentary kind of stability in which neither side would have the capability to overwhelm the other in a surprise strategic blow. It was believed that without such capability, neither side would initiate nuclear use for fear of retaliation. On the other hand, once "saturation" was possible by either or both sides, the temptations for first use might become uncontrollable:

The prospect of atomic destruction is indeed too grim to permit us to stop negotiations, or even to stop thinking about the problem, after trying with only one scheme ... there are other less far-reaching aims which, if achieved, would greatly reduce the threat. Perhaps the minimum aim worth striving for is to limit the growth of stockpiles to a point well below saturation, which would have the two-fold effect of keeping the temptation for atomic surprise attack within bounds and of maintaining the possibility of eventually establishing fully effective control.[35]

In making this argument, the authors gave the bilateral military objectives of arms control policy a new twist: they began advocating a particular level of nuclear capability for the adversary. Moreover, they made explicit for the first time, the questionable

desirability of nuclear disarmament. For in the context of their train
of thought—what measures of verification were both feasible and
adequate in a politically hostile state system—disarmament might
raise insoluble problems:

> Today's is an especially distrustful world, and no atomic control
> scheme is worth discussing that will not operate in spite of mutual
> distrust.   Under these circumstances the possession of fissionable
> materials by both sides rather than by just one may be advantageous
> in initiating agreement. There is serious uncertainty in the ratio 0/0.
> But if the sizes of the opposing stockpiles are not too disparate (and
> do not greatly exceed the ultimate saturation), there may be less
> danger to either side if an agreement is made that permits each side to
> keep a declared amount in comparison with which the error in
> estimation of the actual amount is not decisive. Thus it seems that
> serious consideration should be given to the technical and political
> feasibility of such an approach, among others.[36]

The authors believed this group should work in cooperation with
other government agencies, should assess risks, debits, and credits of
various control schemes and suggest new ones with a view to their
political success. This required the participation of scientists, but
also,

> ...men versed in politics, statecraft and perhaps also mass psychology
> and other specialties, since any technically sound results must be put
> into a form that has the best prospect of acceptance in spite of world
> tensions.[37]

This was because they believed the framing of effective agreements
would require "attempts to maximize the desirability to both sides
..."[38] The authors' premise, that mutual interests had to be the basis
of workable accords, had not only taken them beyond the
multilateralism of the Baruch approach, but it had led them to a
bilateral orientation necessitating the kind of sweeping analysis
which, coming largely from RAND, eventually characterized the
Cambridge Approach.

Finally, where would such limited or interim measures lead us?
The authors' view was as long-range as it was unspecific:

> The chief hope would seem to lie in gradual mellowing of the Soviet
> Government with growing maturity. This is quite conceivable in the

course of a half-century or so, if the atomic crisis can be held off that long.[39]

Cavers, Inglis, and Flanders left aside the question of how large an international inspectorate would be required to carry out their proposals. Given the Soviet penchant for secrecy and their consequent reluctance to entertain proposals involving an intrusive presence, this angle was critical. Although these theorists assumed such presence would be small, they were not explicit in this regard, and one can only guess that they believed total war would be limited to the strategic nuclear realm and that adequate verification need only limit itself to ensuring that decisive strategic attack would be impossible.

James R. Newman proposed a limited agreement in 1954 in which he tried to specify verification requirements under contrary conditions.[40] He suggested preventing capabilities for surprise attack via agreed levels of atomic and conventional capabilities. Yet he too did not believe an agreement had to be air-tight. The verification need only ensure that the agreed level was being maintained. In arguing the point, Newman made explicit the connections between adequate verification and its objective—the avoidance of total war, which he envisaged as both conventional and nuclear:

> It is assumed ... that a very large inspectorate would be needed for each country and that would seriously hamper the conduct of internal affairs, government and private. These assumptions are unjustified. The several inspectorates need not be large. A small group of inspectors, at key points, can keep major production activities under surveillance. It is not important to know everything; it is important only to know important things. It is important to know if a country is mobilizing. If an international agreement fixes levels of armament production, levels thought to be adequate for defense but inadequate for waging war, it is important to know whether the levels are being adhered to.[41]

Newman went on to identify the critical indices of mobilization: steel production, electric power, ship building, etc. He concluded that "the inspectors need not concern themselves over leaks; their task is to look for floods."[42] War mobilization would be a flood; therefore the notion that there could be hidden preparation for major war was, for Newman, absurd. Newman's proposal was bilateral and limited: a "practical alarm system which would give weeks or months of warning of a planned attack, rather than minutes or hours." Yet it was based on an image of future hostilities that was even then becoming obsolete—the notion of the "broken-backed war." In this conception, the nuclear aggressor would initiate general war through an attempt at surprise nuclear attack followed by "mop up" operations using conventional forces. Major aggression would therefore be based upon a mixture of strategic nuclear offensive power and mobilization capability. Although this concept of war was largely out of date, the point made in Newman's analysis was significant: in order to determine what constituted "adequate verification" one had to specify what would constitute significant compromise of the bilateral stability which one was sanctifying in an accord.[43] The lack of attention to this problem in the early 1950s was related to the immaturity of stability concepts and uncertainty over the nature of any nuclear war.

Conclusion: The Emergence of Limited Approaches

The work of the Oppenheimer Panel and, in private circles, the efforts of Cavers, Inglis and Flanders suggests that analysts were beginning to see the benefits of limited, bilateral arms control measures before there was clear understanding of, or consensus about, the objectives that would justify these measures. Despite their differences, however, certain themes ran through all their proposals.

First, there was a sense of urgency common to these analyses derived from fear of rapid technological change. Cavers was preoccupied by the growth of fissile stocks which threatened to render any accord unverifiable and thus unworkable. Inglis and Flanders feared that growth of fissile stocks would lead to widely deployed tactical nuclear systems, which, once integral to Western arsenals, would be too critical to the defense structure to make control politically feasible. The Oppenheimer Panel, privy to the knowledge that the abundance of fissile stocks was already a reality for both sides, stressed the political and military dangers which would attend the technical achievement of "saturation" capabilities while concentrating on the dangers involved in an undisciplined American nuclear build-up. As a result, all these analysts proposed initiatives to contain the technical developments which they feared, with varying degrees of concession to Soviet interests and proclivities: Cavers suggested an international depository of nuclear stocks vulnerable to either side; Inglis and Flanders called for arms control proposals that addressed Soviet concerns and which would codify—indeed bless—a certain nuclear capability for both sides; the

Oppenheimer Panel took the lesser, but no less forward looking position, that the United States ought to de-emphasize offensive systems while attempting to communicate or at least actively listen to the nuclear concerns of the other side.

Second, these new approaches specifically rejected using arms control to achieve political results. Either they believed it could not be done, or that it would take too long and would be too dangerous to try without simultaneously pursuing the nuclear problem. Instead, they argued for limited measures based on mutual interests in containing the technological threat. These interests were believed to exist despite political hostility, and could be realized in arms accords because the latter did not need to be foolproof to provide adequate security. The risks involved in concluding them could be less than those involved in unrestrained technological advance.

Third, there was remarkable agreement on the need to integrate arms control and defense policy and to rationalize the arms policy process. This was made most explicit in the works of the Oppenheimer Panel and of Inglis and Flanders. In setting forth this domestic objective, they appreciated the unilateral characteristics of arms management policy which became so imbedded in the Cambridge Approach: the need to think of defense planning in the nuclear age as as much an exercise in self-discipline as an effort at energetic competition.

Finally, there was a renewed appreciation of the "proper" objective for arms control policy: nuclear stability. This goal, lost in political and technological winds since the Acheson-Lilienthal report, had become pinned down once more—albeit now with a bilateral orientation. Although the widely-shared sense of urgency meant emphasis was placed on what might constitute feasible first steps to technological containment, there was a vague appreciation of the fact that whatever accord might be reached ought not just slow the arms race and the potential for nuclear destruction, but actually make nuclear war itself less likely.

However, for the most part, it was assumed in the early 1950s, that a nuclear freeze would be more stable than competition toward "saturation." There was, as a result, less effort expended on designing agreements which would act simply to brake technological advance. Still, these analysts were beginning to explore the problem of preventing nuclear war, and their earliest ideas in this respect deserve some further exploration. Following this, the contributions of the strategists of the late 1950s will be discussed.

Early Stability Theory

It will be recalled that in the period from 1950 to 1954, the concept of deterrence and its requirements were only beginning to be understood. Whereas the decisiveness of nuclear weapons had been considered during the 1940s as inherent in the mere possession of even a few of them, in the early 1950s it was believed inherent in the unexpected and well-placed use of a limited arsenal. Their advantage lay in strategic use against cities—causing cities to, in effect, "kill themselves" with fire storms and instantaneous destruction. Even though relatively slow bombers would deliver them, the image of destruction "out of the blue" was similar to that of the later missile age since there was no effective warning system either on the American continent or in the form of surveillance of Russian facilities. Moreover, since arsenals were still believed to be relatively small—especially on the Soviet side—attack was expected to be as decisive and quick as possible to prevent any chance of retaliation by the victim. This meant that all nuclear weapons would be maximized—that is, used against major population and industrial centers without warning.

By the end of 1953, the premises upon which calculations of stability were based were being challenged by technological developments. It had become apparent that the supply of weapons-grade materials had not only become large, it had become so abundant that it seemed clear that scarcity of weapons materials would no longer be a problem for either side, no matter how fast the arms race. Moreover, given unlimited supply of nuclear warheads, weapons would be targeted against the adversary's cities, but more importantly, his launchers, thus jeopardizing the victim's retaliatory capability. Whereas Cavers began in 1954 to address these problems by proposing a standstill plan for nuclear offensive systems to ensure "balance of destructive capabilities," most analysts recommended boosting defensive systems themselves through direct or indirect methods.[44]

Perhaps one of the most innovative proposals in this respect was put forward by David Inglis in several articles published in the *Bulletin* during 1954 and 1955. In essence, Inglis proposed placing international controls on thermonuclear tests in order to slow the development of offensive capabilities and to allow defensive techniques to catch up. He believed that atomic developments up to that point had proven that testing improves the versatility and ease of delivery of these weapons and that, this portended continued supremacy of the offense. A thermonuclear test-ban would not stop stockpiling, but it would make these weapons old-fashioned relative to prospective means of delivery while defensive measures (radar screens and interceptor missiles) could be developed unhampered by the agreement.[45]

Integral to Inglis' proposal was an appreciation of the problems of deterrence unusual in non-governmental analysis of that time. It was based on a critique of the recently proclaimed policy of Massive Retaliation. Whereas most analysts centered their critiques around the implications of such a doctrine for the conduct of limited war, Inglis turned his attention to the strategic relationship.

> Massive retaliation requires surviving the initial attack well enough to mount the retaliatory offensive. Anything more anticipatory than this is not retaliation but "preventive attack" ... Our policy of massive retaliation then requires some measure of defensive capabilities, or that the enemy attacking force be short of completely overpowering. The potential aggressor needs to be convinced not only that we have the offensive capability of penetrating his defenses and laying waste his land; it is just as important that he be convinced that he cannot forestall our retaliatory attack by a crippling surprise blow. Thus, even within the limited framework of our policy of massive retaliation, what he can do to us and in particular our launching sites is quite as important as what we are prepared to do to him.[46]

This last statement was crucial to understanding Inglis' support of a test-ban. His advocacy of this arms control measure was derived from a concern that the relationship of bilateral strategic forces might result in nuclear war even after both sides had the ability to obliterate each other. This was because Inglis recognized that it was not just the capacity to launch an offensive attack that ensured stability, but the capability to devastate the attacker after receiving a counterforce blow.

Thus Inglis took arms control thought one more step beyond the "weapons-stability nexus." Nuclear weapons were not only necessary, they had to be capable of a particular mission in order to prevent nuclear war. That mission was to strike second—a feat not so easy to accomplish and one which a well thought-out arms control policy could help ensure. In 1954, Inglis' unusual appreciation of the delicacy of the strategic balance was recorded in the following passage:

If we proceed with the unlimited arms race, both sides will presumably develop rapidly on toward the era of the complete "push-button" war. We will develop the capability of delivering, after allowing for losses in penetrating the defenses, several times as much destruction as will be required to destroy all important targets. We thus need be sure that only a modest fraction of our retaliatory force can escape the initial attack. On the other hand, the Russians will presumably also be capable of destroying our important installations several times over, so the initial attack is apt to be relentlessly thorough and it will perhaps not be likely that a sufficient retaliatory force will be missed and take off. The apparent desirability of making an attack will be continuously and sensitively subject to the whims of judgement concerning this delicate balance.[47]

Inglis' solution to the nascent era of saturation was to control the development of offensive systems. Arms control would thus be used for the limited bilateral purpose of stabilizing the arms race by channelling technological developments in relatively non-threatening directions. Important to his argument were the assumptions that hydrogen bombs could be made small enough to be placed on bombers, and that both sides would eventually have the capability to attack launchers themselves—thus jeopardizing the integrity of deterrent forces. Inglis was on the verge of understanding the distinctions between counterforce and countervalue targeting, first and second strike capabilities, and the role arms control could play in affecting both sides' incentives and choices in these regards. For, as he put it, an H-bomb test ban

... treats both sides alike, and while putting a gentle lid on their *absolute* military strengths leaves their anticipated *relative* strengths, which is the important consideration, approximately unchanged.[48]

But there was another facet of stability that Inglis believed a test ban would help to ensure: the exclusively bilateral relationship of nuclear deterrence. He not only recognized the bilateral structure of the international system, believing arms control should accept it and work within it, but he argued that arms control should be used to preserve it for stability's sake:

There is another argument which should make the H-bomb test ban proposal attractive to the two present H-bomb powers, and that is that it will prevent the H-bomb race from becoming a many-sided affair, for no other powers can independently develop H-bombs without making test ... In the era of traditional weapons, a "third force" was considered a stabilizing influence because it could by careful statesmanship maintain a balance of power and perhaps prolong the peace. But with the tremendous premium on surprise attack provided by atomic weapons, although the magnitude of the prospective retaliation is a strong *rational* deterrent, the danger is that some statesman will act irrationally as statesmen have been known to do in the past, and it takes only one mistake to destroy civilization as we know it. The rise of more H-bomb powers will have as its main effect the introduction of more statesmen with the power to make the fatal mistake.[49]

Within Inglis' test ban proposal was also the assumption that this measure need not compromise what has been termed "dynamic stability"—the maintenance of disincentives for either side to attempt aggression based on the temporary advantage achieved through technological breakthrough. In Inglis' conception, dynamic stability could best be augmented not by intrusive inspection designed to give warning, but by national technical means aimed at ensuring retribution. In the first place, the Lucky Dragon incident and the United States' detection of the first Soviet atomic explosion constituted evidence of the feasibility of distant monitoring. Therefore, Inglis believed observance of the ban could be adequately ensured. Second, the absence of restrictions on research and development of new warhead designs or testing scenarios plus both parties' continuation of vigorous armaments efforts in other fields, would deter attempts by either party to take advantage of a breakthrough. Neither could be sure, once the accord was abrogated, that its relative position would be significantly enhanced. Indeed, it might be significantly worsened:

With the very primitive type of arms limitation provided by the H-bomb test ban proposal, the direct advantage is, of course, not so great as with more substantial disarmament, but it is an advantage of the same sort. A violation would presumably mean that the unlimited arms race would be on again, test and all. The test ban is proposed in order to reduce the attractiveness of sudden aggression, not for the sake of saving effort on armament. With the test ban, each side would in the interests of complete preparedness want to think what tests it would like to make were it not for the ban, so as to be ready to enter the unlimited arms race quickly if the other side should commit a violation. If each side is convinced that the other is not napping, neither is nearly as apt to declare aggressive intentions by violating the test ban before finishing the development and production

of a crucial new weapon than it would be to make a surprise attack
with the completed weapon. Aggression would thus seem much more
inviting without the test ban.[30]

Inglis thus posed the stability question: could the long-term
absence of aggression best be assured with a test-ban or without?
His conclusion in favor of one rested on the concepts of dynamic
and static stability: A test ban would prevent a potentially inequitable
advance toward the missile age without denying either side the
armaments efforts necessary to deter unilateral assertion of a
presumed advantage—be it acquired via a scientific breakthrough or
low-level cheating. Who, after all, could be assured that the advance
would not be matched or bettered by the opponent—especially if the
absence of complete inspection left each side with a healthy measure
of secrecy in its laboratories? Indeed with a test ban, each party
would be maximizing its capability to enforce the measure by a
vigorous research effort in the field of warhead design—an effort
that might not get so much public support and attention if the
rationale for it were not so clearly underlined by the need to enforce
a treaty preserving a relative nuclear balance.

By posing the arms limitation argument as he had, Inglis threw
into question the benefits of disarmament, the benefits of enforced
openness or internationalized nuclear research (i.e., the loss of a
national enforcement capability or a measure of secrecy in national
armament efforts), as well as the advantages of unrestricted
competition. He got to this provocative position by way of
deterrence theory and an unusual appreciation of rapid changes still
underway in nuclear technology. In his method of analysis and
attitude towards arms control, he anticipated the Cambridge Approach
by at least six years. He differed from it in his advocacy of
improved defenses, which he believed would be necessary to ensure
retaliatory capabilities. But the capability to retaliate required not
only that the United States have the ability to withstand attack, but
that its force be able to penetrate Soviet defenses "to lay waste" in
retribution. He did not examine the possibility that competition in
non-nuclear defensive capabilities combined with a qualitative cap on
offensive systems might in itself be destabilizing. The development
of extensive radar systems, supporting accurate missiles with high
explosive warheads on the defensive side, could lead one party to
believe it could launch a massive attack, put its improved defenses
on alert, and evacuate its cities in preparation for the counter-blow
from relatively slow and vulnerable bombers. After the exchange,

the aggressor could foresee, given adequate preparations, a clear position of superiority. It was certainly arguable that defensive systems needed greater emphasis if the arms race was going to remain stable, but where arms control might fit in shaping the race remained problematic.[51]

Inglis' approach to stability through arms control was innovative, but different in its discussion of static balance than that of the Cambridge Approach. It will be recalled that the latter rested on the calculation that a robust, stable stalemate had to affirm the fear of nuclear retribution from the victim. In other words, nothing should compromise the ability of either side to visit terrific destruction on the other. The populations of each should, in effect, be held hostage to the forces of the other. In this light, the development of defensive deployments could be a problem if they interfered with effective retaliation, while the development of offensive technology could be good to the extent that increasingly small, transportable, and easily protected delivery systems could be armed with hugely destructive warheads. For eventually the point would be reached where an attacker would have to expend a large percentage of its force in an attempt to waste a relatively small percentage of its victims' retaliatory capability. Then the victim would still have a capability to visit huge destruction against the attacker's population.

Second, the Cambridge Approach was based on an appreciation of the problem of the nuclear "threshold," an issue which Inglis' test-ban proposal did not directly address. The problem was one of nuclear escalation from local skirmish to strategic nuclear war. In a situation where both sides had unlimited access to fissile stocks, and thus the capability for widespread deployment of tactical nuclear systems, what would prevent a battlefield skirmish from turning into a mutual atomic catastrophe? Although arms control solutions to this problem were hotly debated among adherents to the Cambridge Approach, all of them accepted the problem as a real one—that there was the possibility of nuclear escalation and that it would be triggered by first nuclear use. Conventional and tactical nuclear weapons were considered, therefore, intrinsically different no matter how comparable their effects.

In the mid-1950s, arms policy analysts both in and out of government circles were addressing these two stability problems. In the following section it will be shown that theorists were contributing key concepts of this approach earlier than has generally been recognized.

The Structure of the Strategic Debate in the 1950s

The utility of a threshold between conventional and nuclear use, as understood within the Cambridge Approach, was based on several assumptions.   First, it was assumed that the technologies of traditional and atomic weapons were distinguishable, making abstinence from nuclear use politically and militarily significant. Second, it was assumed that this distinction ought to be enhanced as an object of arms policy because gradations between conventional and nuclear forms of force at low levels could conceivably blur the choice about whether or not to "go nuclear."   Third, it was assumed that neither side had an interest in crossing the nuclear threshold because of fear of escalation to mutually devastating central war. Appreciation of these aspects of the escalatory problem and, therefore, the need for arms control theory to embrace a concept of the threshold and seek in practice to raise it, took considerable time.

To begin with, the unconventional nature of nuclear technology, so well appreciated after its devastating and decisive first use, was challenged only three years after Hiroshima.   In 1948, a British scientist, P.M.S. Blackett, wrote a controversial book in which he asserted that atomic weapons were not revolutionary in their effects, but were, in fact, comparable in some ways to the incendiary bombs dropped during World War II, and therefore might not be decisive in any future conflict.[52]   Although Blackett received commendations from some quarters for his detailed and sophisticated analysis, he was heavily criticized by most American analysts for failing to appreciate the instantaneous destruction inflicted by nuclear weapons—a quality that made notions of defense against their use seem absurd.   However, Blackett's conclusions were also discounted for political reasons.   He was widely considered to be a member of the radical left, with certain Communist sympathies.   This association significantly compromised his argument, since he was suggesting exactly what the Soviets were officially proclaiming at the time: that nuclear weapons were not all that special.

By the early 1950s, however, atomic weapons were being labelled as "conventional" by members of the American security establishment themselves, including those formerly critical of Blackett's thesis.[53]   As the United States demobilized and came to rely increasingly on tactical nuclear systems for the defense of Europe, it was insisted that low-level nuclear capabilities were essential to a credible Western defense given Soviet manpower advantages on the ground.

The reasons for this change were fully discussed in the preceding chapter. However it should be recalled here that few analysts at the time were considering the implications of tactical nuclear retaliation because it was assumed that the Soviets could not match the American tactical arsenal due to a lack of sufficient fissile stocks.[54] For example, Robert Oppenheimer favored using nuclear technology for the defense of Europe, opposing development of thermonuclear weapons in the belief that research and development resources should be spent instead on tactical nuclear systems. He argued that the unconventional nature of nuclear weapons was critically tied not to the technology itself, but to effects of nuclear weapons on certain targets. Thus he believed, at least until 1953, that nuclear weapons policy could be tailored such that strategic use would be deterred but tactical use would be countenanced in combat.[55] Lingering technical innocence led men such as Major General James M.Gavin to declare that tactical atomic bombs were of great use to combat forces since "... lingering radioactivity following an air burst at, say, two thousand feet, will not last more than a few minutes."[56] Similarly, Bernard Brodie who had stressed the deterrent qualities of the atomic bomb so effectively in 1946, argued forcefully for a new stress on the military utility of nuclear weapons for a conflict such as the Korean one:

We have thus far given the Chinese every possible assurance that they could intervene with impunity ... We should be publicizing right now the fact that strategic bombing does not necessarily mean mass slaughter.[57]

By 1953 and 1954 however, the scope and complexity of the debate had changed. American officials' observations that nuclear weapons had become practically conventional ran up against public outcry and allied anxiety over their contemplated introduction into the Korean conflict.[58] It was becoming obvious that there would be no scarcity in nuclear materials to hamper tactical nuclear developments on the Soviet side. Moreover, the announcement of the doctrine of Massive Retaliation in 1953 pointed up for a number of critics, the inadequacy of American preparations—both with respect to doctrines and hardware—for deterrence and repellence of limited aggression.[59] While some argued that tactical nuclear weapons could be used in limited conflicts without provoking bilateral strategic war, others were more skeptical.

There ensued a debate on limited war, a discussion of how best to deter and to respond to aggression, at a variety of levels. And while there emerged a broad consensus on the need for a politico-military posture increasingly described as "graduated deterrence," there remained considerable difference over the best methods of limitation under varying circumstances—by targets, types of weapons, geography, etc.—and whether or not such limitations could or should be codified by international agreement.

A thorough discussion of the rich debate on limited war is beyond the scope of this study. However, it is important to note two of its features which significantly affected the development of the Cambridge Approach to arms control. First, the arguments over tactical nuclear use were informed by a desire to avoid strategic nuclear war over less than vital interests. Given the potential gradations of nuclear capabilities on both sides, the increasingly global (i.e., geographically unlimited) dimensions of the policy of containment, and the game-theoretic estimate that effective limitations would have to be simple and easily recognizable by both sides, it became increasingly appreciated by military analysts that the only barrier to strategic nuclear war which had the potential to be *certain* would be nuclear abstinence at tactical levels in peripheral conflicts.

Second, within this assessment there remained considerable debate in the mid-1950s over the defense of Europe. Here, two vital interests clashed: the desire to reinforce bilateral strategic stability, which logically dictated unilateral American control of nuclear instruments and a high threshold for nuclear use in Europe, and the need to assure Europe of its adequate defense, which required assurance of American intent to go nuclear if necessary. The more American analysts suggested the need to raise the threshold in Europe or to inspire conventional expenditures by allies, the more they feared allied interest in independent nuclear capabilities and a weakening of deterrence in the theater—both destabilizing results. However to the extent they encouraged forward-based tactical nuclear deployments in Europe under exclusive American control, the more likely it became that any conflict in Europe would escalate to strategic (intercontinental) war. For that matter, the more the American effort to stabilize the bilateral strategic relationship via acquiescence to offensive capabilities on both sides, the more heightened were European anxieties. On the one hand, if the bilateral strategic relationship was stabilized by effective measures based on *mutual* interests of the superpowers, American superiority would be compromised, making the assurance of escalation weaker.

But the more Americans were certain of their nuclear supremacy, and relied upon it for nuclear deterrence, the more likely would be American tactical nuclear use in Europe, with the attendant prospect of devastating the allies in order to protect them.

These issues were not resolved in the 1950s and, in fact, remain unresolved today. They involved complicated discussion of American security interests, technological change and deterrence theory. And while those associated with the government and "think tanks" such as RAND had certain advantages in generating authoritative analysis, it ought not be assumed that they had exclusive domain over the field or that they, for that matter, were not preoccupied by the arms control implications of their work. In a sense, what the Oppenheimer Panel prescribed in 1953 became a reality: the majority of defense analysts both in and out of government became absorbed by the problem of weapons management—the dual appreciation of the need to keep nuclear weapons for deterrence and defense, and the need to limit their utility to avoid the catastrophe which they alone could threaten. Whether analysts got to this point via traditional concern with nuclear strategy or by way of frustration over disarmament became, in any fundamental sense, irrelevant. The Cambridge Approach— biased in favor of deterrence over defense—was a subset of the strategic consensus which emerged from this period and claimed within its membership contributors from both military and disarmament backgrounds.

The Cambridge Approach: Early Contributions to Stability Theory

Earlier it was argued that David Inglis and Donald Flanders were among the first arms control theorists to recognize the problem that increased fissile stocks would pose for intrusive, multilateral arms control methods. This led them to propose in 1951-not a disarmament agreement but a limited accord to cap nuclear deployments enforced largely by national means. However, they were also beginning to realize, earlier than most, what effects abundant fissile stocks might have on nuclear stability. They feared the intractable problems which might result from excessive political dependence on tactical nuclear systems in the West.[60]

Strategic Stalemate and the Threshold. In 1952, a few months after their "deal before midnight" was proposed, Inglis re-emphasized the political problem posed by dependence on tactical nuclear defenses:

> The advent of tactical atomic weapons apparently increases the political difficulties of attaining some sort of atomic control much more than it influences the technical difficulties ... The changes in potential international political attitudes toward atomic control when nations have come to rely on tactical atomic weapons for their ground defense may be enormous and decisive. So long as atomic weapons were confined to their original strategic role, there was the hope that the two sides would each prefer not to start an atomic war and feel obligated to maintain force of conventional arms sufficient for its estimated needs. As soon as atomic weapons become mixed up with field warfare such a neat separation of the categories no longer exists. Even in "small" wars of attrition, of which we now have examples in progress perhaps as part of a pattern, there will be strong temptation to use atomic weapons. With tactical atomic weapons in use, small ones, larger ones, far from cities, nearer to cities, and with conventional bombing of facilities in cities being taken for granted, there will be no clear-cut dividing line. One result of tactical atomic weapons will be to make all-out atomic war seem more imminent, and the search for control schemes more urgent even from the fairly short-range point of view.[61]

Inglis believed 1954 would be the critical year. By this time conventional forces could be strong enough that the United States would be able to "negotiate from strength" the abolition of atomic weapons before either side became excessively dependent on them. As 1954 came and went, Inglis turned his attention to controls on offensive strategic nuclear systems through a test ban.

In March 1951, Clifton M. Utley, a news commentator of the National Broadcasting Company, agreed with Inglis' assessment of the tactical nuclear problem but took it a step further. Calling American atomic superiority a "wasting asset" he linked his argument against tactical nuclear defense of Europe (then being popularly supported) to the prospect of Soviet tactical nuclear capabilities and the emergence of a "balance of terror" at the strategic nuclear level:

> Either Russia will catch up on us in the production of atomic weapons, or, if she doesn't, if we maintain our present lead by speeding our atomic progress at the rate she speeds hers, our margin of superiority will be constantly less effective as a deterrent capable of keeping Russia from making war.[62]

Therefore in Utley's view, atomic superiority could not be relied upon to deter a Russian attack on Western Europe, and a significant conventional ground defense in Europe was necessary.

This connection between the effectiveness of the extended deterrent and the emergence of strategic stalemate motivated analysts such as Inglis, James Killian and A.G. Hill to reach a conclusion quite contrary to Utley's. They prescribed additional efforts on defensive measures at the strategic level to make the nuclear defense of Europe credible once bilateral offensive stalemate was reached.[63] They reasoned that a ban on missile development would permit the development of a "metastable equilibrium" at the strategic level in which defense and offense were balanced, depriving each side of the assurance that it could successfully launch a strategic blow. In contrast to a "balance of terror" in which both sides threatened annihilation through offensive retaliation alone, such a state would make deterrence more credible, and put it on a sounder basis in Europe, since damage could then be limited if war should occur.

Such reasoning led to support of a thermonuclear test ban on the grounds that it would prevent the advent of the missile age, and with it, a perhaps insurmountable boost to the offensive side of the nuclear equation. This issue: the desirability of bilateral competition into the missile age, formed the crux of the early test ban debate in strategic circles; it was in this context that the first views prescribing a bilateral relationship of assured destruction were presented.

The Emergence of the Concept of Assured Destruction. Before the debate in the mid-1950s over the impact ballistic missiles would have on deterrence, there was a growing appreciation that defense against nuclear attack was impossible. Of course such an assessment was made immediately after the war by Bernard Brodie. However, the early assertion was based on the qualities of the weapon itself, not its mode of delivery. Brodie's assertion became a subject for debate in the early 1950s when civilian analysts, including respected disarmers, began suggesting that, while nuclear effects were terrible, a defense against their carriers was possible and might reduce the effects of a nuclear strike to at least tolerable levels, permitting in turn a retaliatory blow.

Against this argument were those who believed defensive measures could never adequately protect against well-planned aggression. A particularly forceful argument was made by Hornell Hart, a professor of sociology at Duke University.[64] Culling as much information as possible from open sources, he graphically demonstrated that expected increases in Soviet offensive capabilities were likely to overwhelm expected improvements in all forms of passive and active defenses, and that even with maximum effort in the defensive field, the United States would be unable to survive a massive blow without national paralysis.

Then, in the Tenth Anniversary Symposium organized by the *Bulletin* in 1956, three articles were published which, at one time, lay the intellectual basis for what became the Cambridge Approach's counter-design for stability.   Richard L. Meier, in a piece entitled "Beyond Atomic Stalemate," used the principles of game theory and "gamesmanship" to derive seven propositions which, in his view, offered maximum prospects for survival in the nuclear age:

- "It is far easier to maintain a standoff between two superpowers than between three or four."   (The principle of nuclear bipolarity.)
- "The unilateral publication of much information now kept secret would reduce the chances of fatal error." (The importance of communication and signalling.)
- "There should be no dependence upon nuclear weapons for small skirmishes or incidents." (The principle of a high nuclear threshold.)
- "Foreign policy should aim at preventing large-scale conflagrations, even revolutions, in every part of the world." (The importance of maintaining the political status quo.)
- "An international police force would be useful for containing small-scale threats to the peace which are irrelevant to the short-run policies of the superpowers."   (The demotion of multilateral peace-keeping instruments to the service of bilateral balance.)
- "When superweapons have been mounted in hidden launching sites up to saturation levels, it appears to be no longer possible to   negotiate disarmament   at   the   nuclear   level."   (The fundamental divergence between arms control and disarmament thought.)
- "An important proportion of conventional armament today is directed to the defense of home territories from attack with conventional weapons, or for counterattack to opponent's home territory.   Virtually the whole of this is unnecessary." (The obsolescence of the concept of the "broken-backed war").[65]

In the one sweep of his analysis, Meier had consolidated those views previously articulated in the stability debate, which underpinned the Cambridge Approach to deterrence. Moreover, he added the significant twist that not only should arms control not be aimed at political change in the Soviet Union, but that it should accomplish quite the opposite. For in the world of bilateral stalemate, rational action, and therefore the internal stability of both major powers, was a vital mutual interest.

In the second piece in this symposium, C.W. Sherwin introduced the salient stability argument so important to the Cambridge Approach, the concept of mutual assured destruction.[66] For Meier, stability was "due to occur" as a simple result of saturation. In Sherwin's argument stability was by implication much less automatic.

Sherwin began with a remarkable assertion. Turning disarmament theory on its head, he proclaimed that nuclear weapons were the technical instruments which might at last offer the prospect of long-lasting global peace. He chided revolutionary scientific thinkers for their preoccupation with outmoded political concepts, and called them to speculate instead about unconventional solutions based on the new technology.

The new technical tools which made Sherwin's design feasible were "small, light, cheap nuclear weapons" and "small, very fast, airborne delivery vehicles." Their existence in societies characterized by concentrated wealth made strategic war a very risky business. This led Sherwin to pose the question: "Can strategic war become so dangerous and risky that it will be useless as a tool of national policy—even for oligarchies or dictatorships?"[67]

Sherwin believed the answer to this question was positive, and he based it on an analysis of the modern costs and benefits of warfare:

> The power of new weapons, and the nature of present day economies, combine to make certain that "counter-economy" warfare will be highly efficient in the future, whereas the counter-force (strategic) warfare will remain a moderately inefficient operation, provided the natural advantages of defense against the latter are fully exploited. If this is true, war becomes a game in which both sides can expect, with very high probabilities, very great net losses ...

The strategic weapons carriers, on the other hand, are everything the cities are not. Compared to cities, they are *small*, *...light*, *...mobile*; furthermore, they can be widely *dispersed* over the continents or on or under the seas, and can be *protected* from blast by special buildings or underground shelters. Finally, they can be manned by a very small fraction of the population...

> All these natural advantages can, I believe, keep counterforce strategic warfare relatively inefficient, in spite of the weapons revolution, particularly if active defense of the weapons carriers' bases is properly developed. It is here that active defense becomes truly significant...[68]

The implications for deterrence of the counter-economy efficiency of modern war were developed by Sherwin on the basis of theoretical work done by Warren Amster of the Convair Corporation.[69] Sherwin defined deterrence "... as a method of forcing good (or more accurately, rational) behavior through the fear of self-destruction." He then applied Amster's theory of "security" in order to derive prescription:

> The key function in Amster's theory is one he calls "security." It is calculated as follows: *Blue* calculates how many weapons he can expect to have left should *Red* make an all-out attack against his forces. Then, *Blue* divides this number by the number of weapons he thinks he needs to launch against *Red's* economy to produce losses which are adequate for deterrence. *Red* makes similar calculations to estimate his own security. If the so-calculated "security ratio" of *Blue* is one, then even after suffering an all-out counter-force attack (the most dangerous thing that can happen to a nonaggressor), he will have enough forces left for an effective counter-economy retaliation. Note that if an economy is very cheap to destroy, the nonaggressor does not need to have many weapons left to be adequately armed for the purposes of this strategy. If one side's "security ratio" is zero, it means that this side can expect to be disarmed by an all-out counter-force blow. This is, of course, a very dangerous and unstable situation.[70]

According to Sherwin, Amster went on to explain that each side required "an optimum and not a maximum force. Larger or smaller forces actually *reduce* security." Furthermore, the optimum level would depend on the extent to which forces were invulnerable and cities exposed. The greater both these factors, the smaller the optimum force need be. In any case, an arms race need not develop.

Amster's "security theory" embraced Meier's notion of strategic cooperation between adversaries, and gave it theoretical substance. As Sherwin explained:

Four estimates of "security" are involved. Each side estimates its own security, and also estimates what it thinks the other side's security is. These four numbers (all based, in part on opinions and incomplete intelligence) are combined in the theory to calculate the "stability" of the system. If all four security numbers are near unity, the system has maximum stability. Each side is then unafraid of strategic attack, and believe the other side also is unafraid. Suppose however, that *Red* believes that *Blue* has inadequate (or unconvincing) information about *Red's* capabilities; *Red* may then suspect that *Blue* is underestimating *Red's* security. The theory shows then it is in *Red's* self-interest to convey certain information to *Blue*, to correct this error and reduce the disagreement between their security estimates. This information must not go so far, however, as to give Blue significant help in either his offense or defense.[71]

Given such security arrangements, what were the purposes of nuclear systems and how would they be used if deterrence failed? Apparently, Amster defined three purposes: "1) to prevent the start of strategic war; 2) to stop such a war should it start; and 3) failing this, to carry out a predetermined amount of destruction of the attacker's country."[72] The doctrine of employment would be one of proportional counter-economy retaliation, prompted only by strategic attack.

The purpose of the measured response is not to *win*, but to prove to the attacker that his losses are likely to be incredibly large, in the hope that by this demonstration the war will be stopped before both sides are irreparably destroyed. For example, if one side accidentally launched a weapon, the strategy (publicly announced in advance) would call for retaliation by one weapon, not a hail of weapons.[73]

And what about the problem of extended deterrence? Sherwin introduced his article by acknowledging its central concern with strategic stability; but he suggested that:

... if one can produce stability against the occurrence of large "strategic" wars, one had reason to expect that the "small war" will not spread beyond certain bounds. Conversely, if strategic instability is allowed to persist, the slightest perturbation on the boundary could precipitate a "large war."[74]

Moreover, if a limited war started spreading toward the edges of areas covered by the "umbrella of deterrence,, the policy of "measured retaliation" could contain it before a strategic nuclear disaster would occur.[75]

Sherwin went on to support his and Amster's arguments with game theoretic analysis:

> In a system of this type, strategic warfare ... becomes a special type of non-zero-sum game-one in which both sides have a probability of great loss. Von Neumann and Morgenstern show in their work on the theory of games, that a two-person non-zero-sum game is equivalent to a three-person zero-sum game, with a hypothetical third player pocketing the net losses of the two real players (or vice versa). The perfectly rational players, assumed in the game theory, will not play such a game unless the two real players (who effectively form a coalition against the third party) expect between them to win at least half the stakes. When the probable net loss exceeds half the total stakes, the coalition of real players refuses to play at all with the hypothetical third player. When the odds in favor of large losses are great enough, presumably even not entirely rational players will refuse to play. In the deterrent era, military applications of game theory will be concerned not so much with how to *win* games, as with how best to *avoid* playing. It is a new kind of game.

> Between nations, this situation is new and untested by experience. The nearest analogy is two powers forced to cooperate by the threat of a third power. Alliances generally last as long as both sides feel that the threat of the third power is more dangerous to them than any alternative. *In the new situation, the "third player" is a creation of military technology which cannot enter into an alliance.*[76]

Sherwin noted that there still existed the problem of technological breakthrough. However, he believed that if there was a "safety factor" built into the system, one could expect stability to last for a fairly long period of time. In fact, he believed that a technological breakthrough might someday be found which would permit the United States to assume the position of "supreme defense" in which the American economy and armed forces would be invulnerable to military attack from any other state-be it rational or irrational. But he could foresee nothing that would provide this opportunity in any reasonable period of time.

Finally, Sherwin argued that the condition of stability, which he was describing, was implied by the new technology but not automatically derived from it. Rather:

... the new technology, and the nature of our economy, are pushing the great powers toward this state; but ... only deliberate and skillful exploitation of all natural advantages can place them in the ... "Deterrent State" (the condition of maximized stability).[77]

Still, the obvious logic of the proposal was, he believed, an important advantage over other stability designs. He argued:

... if a strategy based on rational exploitation of deterrence is not obvious enough to be eventually adopted by the leading nations, then it is scarcely a very safe mechanism to preserve peace. If the system appears to be so marginal that it can be successfully obstructed by entrenched interests of the leaders, the electorate, or the military, then it is not good enough, it is simply has to be so obvious and so (relatively) cheap that no group can prevent its implementation, for example, by insisting on the attainment of some irrelevant political and military goal.[78]

Sherwin's proposal provided the central stability argument which was missing from Meier's strategy for peace in the age of nuclear stalemate. Sherwin succeeded in turning the problems of the nuclear age inside-out: the centralized nature of the economy, the political difficulties associated with civilian defense, the awesome proliferation of unverifiable offensive launchers on both sides, and the "overkill" qualities of thermonuclear weapons, became advantageous rather than threatening to the peace. Together, Meier and Sherwin provided a counter-design to the metastability for which balanced offensive and defensive capabilities were being advocated.

It was left to the third article in the symposium to argue for the relevance of Sherwin's article to the strategic debate in the late 1950s. Sherwin based his analysis on public information available in 1956 and on a theoretical analysis originally authored by Warren Amster in 1952. In "Design for Deterrence," Warren Amster brought his and Sherwin's analysis up to date.[79] He pointed out that the advent of the missile age further supported the stability design which he and Sherwin had outlined. The new technology might have made the defense of cities feasible were it not for the widespread effects of fall-out—a problem increasing recognized—and the political and economic difficulties of providing protection everywhere it might be desired. Besides, "... present experience indicates that shooting down a streaking missile will probably be possible, but not reliable enough when the life of a city is at stake."[80] He concluded,

... deterrent strategies would be most effective when a retaliatory threat is frankly directed against cities. There isn't much choice in this because retaliation won't work well against a hidden underground missile force. Even if retaliation were attempted against missile bases, a great many cities would be victims of hits or fall-out. This situation implies that we may some day have to hold foreign cities as hostages to insure the survival of our own. Naturally we would expect other nations to do likewise with us.[81]

This last point was one which set him apart from Meier. Amster believed that this stability game was one which could adjust to many players, each having a National Protection Force providing counter-economy offense and hard target defense. In short, the exclusive bilateral nuclear relationship need not hold if nuclear war was to be prevented. In the long-term, however, Amster hoped and expected that the components of the National Protection Force would be regarded merely as peacekeeping machines and not really weapons at all. While states in the game might continue for some time to look for new, shinier, and more automatic versions, "the deterrent capabilities of missiles may one day be taken for granted and no longer attract attention."[82]

The logic of these collected arguments from the *Bulletin's* Symposium was powerful and attractive. It suggested that the United States could "go with the flow" of technological development and diversification in the name of peacekeeping and in the interest of providing that "safety factor" in Sherwin's system otherwise known as redundancy. All that was necessary was to make sure that the strategic systems deployed fit the technical parameters of second-strike counter-city deterrence and not first-strike counterforce ones. Luckily in Amster's view, technological trends in themselves favored the former.

The design thus presented was remarkably similar to the policy of assured destruction articulated during Robert McNamara's tenure at the Pentagon. However, the latter was far more a force acquisition guideline than an employment doctrine; indeed, it was never clear just what relationship McNamara's concept would have to the conduct of war as opposed to the preparation for it. Amster and Sherwin were, however, very clear on this: in no case would an offensive system be targeted against another; retaliation was to be solely against cities—otherwise the weapons would become considered politically and military useful which, intrinsically, they were not.

For all the force of this argument, it was weak on the problem of extended deterrence. How was Europe to be defended? Meier believed that conventional forces might be necessary, but that if bilateral detente evolved out of stalemate, they might actually be reduced. He failed to recognize the complexity of the problem. Sherwin on the other hand, edged around it by noting that the superpowers would have an incentive to "damp down" small wars in the interest of avoiding a big one; yet he failed to suggest how the integrity of Western Europe would then be maintained. One might surmise that he believed that Europe would have to be defended with conventional weapons. But what if the conventional conflict was inconclusive? Would NATO remain unified if the United States refused to engage its nuclear arsenal (thus condemning its homeland) as Europe lay prostrate before it? On the other hand, what if the Russians were losing? What would prevent a totalitarian state from using nuclear weapons in an attempt to force a draw?

Amster solved the problem by including in his analysis an implicit argument in favor of nuclear proliferation. Apparently there was nothing wrong, from his perspective, in ensuring the defense of the West by providing allies with their own National Protection Forces. Sherwin countered that there was: it would introduce too many players, and thus too great a likelihood of miscalculation. No one had a solution.

The "Classic" Contributions of the Strategic Community

In 1980 Colin Gray, a well-informed strategic analyst, wrote:

Contemporary arms control theory was an invention of the strategic studies in the period 1958–1960. International cooperation and even collaboration in the joint management of the strategic balance was rediscovered as an area of activity worthy of urgent attention."[83]

Whereas Gray's second sentence was in large measure true, the first was not. As the foregoing analysis has demonstrated, almost all the central features of modern arms control theory had been developed prior to 1956.[84]

Moreover, the evolution of arms control (as opposed to disarmament) thought in the early to mid-1950s followed the course of more general strategic theory, and in some cases anticipated it. That this would be so is, upon first impression, quite surprising. During the early 1950s many members of the community of civilian strategists had access to government secrets about technological change, Soviet capabilities, military deployments, and targeting information through secure government "think tanks." Moreover, they had a close, collegial atmosphere—especially at RAND—which was conducive to the kind of stimulating exchange of views that produce revolutionary theoretical works.[85]   One would have expected virtually all the strategic ideas of the 1960s—including those concerning arms control—to have been produced by RAND associates.[86]   In fact they were not.   A considerable portion of the strategic literature on limited war for example, was written by political scientists in academia, while most of the central strategic issues were raised and explored within the arms control literature out of concern about increased potential for nuclear war at a time when the risks associated with it were growing.

Upon reflection, the coincidence of private and officially-informed literature is not that surprising. In the first place, the central motivating factors for the course of debate were not classified secrets but public knowledge.   It was Dulles' articulation of Massive Retaliation and the experience of the Korean War which inspired most of the discussion of limited wars; it was the growth of fissile stocks on both sides—a development not classified by 1953 and evident to many scientists before that—which inspired discussion of the implications of diverse and abundant offensive delivery systems for the conduct and deterrence of nuclear war.   And the technological development of missiles was discussed in the public literature as early as the 1940s.   Thus Inglis, for example, was writing about "the delicate balance" in the *Bulletin* at approximately the same time as Albert Wohlstetter was discovering the same problem at RAND.   Moreover, Inglis' further point—that arms control ought to be pursued in the service of preserving this delicate balance—was hardly a popular idea and, "buried" in a disarmament journal, it received little attention at the time.

In the second place, the mode of analysis which carried most force in discussion of stability relations was game theory, a method well known outside government circles and indeed embraced by the rising behaviorist leadership on university campuses.   Thomas Schelling's work on strategic bargaining, originally published as successive articles in *The Journal of Conflict Resolution* beginning in June 1956, structured as it was around the theory of games, the "strategy of conflict" and allegorical reference to decision-making within families, traffic jams, and tribal groups, was consistent with the work of Sherwin, who used remarkably similar techniques to illustrate remarkably similar issues in 1956.

Third, recognition of the gap between technological evolution and disarmament prospects had been identified by 1950 both inside and outside the government. American intellectuals were sensitive to the need to ground nuclear weapons policy to a security program which would be supportable over the long-term by the American public. This was, after all, one of the central rationales behind the New Look policy—to provide long-term defense at reasonable cost. But the New Look did not go far enough in its search for public support; it neglected the popular insistence on nuclear restraint, a problem evident to many strategists but especially to those long occupied with the problem of establishing nuclear controls.[87] Thus, the peculiar American security "contract" which prescribed a balanced approach to arms policy involving both limits on nuclear use and adequate defense against Communist hegemony, dictated that nuclear theorists, be they garbed in military, quasi-governmental, or arms control coats, stomp the same broad path in search of credible, policy-relevant goals. Broad consensus on security policy was thus, not surprisingly, "in the works" shortly after the Baruch consensus met with bankruptcy at the end of the 1940s.

Nevertheless it is true that most of the "classic" arms control literature did emerge in the late 1950s and early 1960s. It achieved its status in part because its authors were plugged into the strategic debate and strategic community of the time. But the time was also ripe for policy-relevant theory: the problem of surprise attack remained, the pace of technology had slowed, and a respect for Soviet interests and capabilities had become both earned by the adversary and politically viable domestically. Moreover, Eisenhower's Open Skies proposal of 1955, and subsequent official efforts at technical discussions on selected issues, lent a new credibility to limited measures even as official policy remained wrapped around bulky and infeasible plans for disarmament.

In addition, the cohesion and rigor of the "classic" works, such as *Strategy and Arms Control* by Thomas Schelling and Morton Halperin, *The Strategy of Conflict* and *Arms and Influence* by Schelling and the original *Daedalus* volume on arms control, *Arms Control, Disarmament and National Security* (especially the chapters by Robert R. Bowie, Donald Brennan, and Henry Kissinger) surpassed those of the earlier efforts. Especially on the problems associated with strategic stability and extended deterrence, the classic arms control literature relied heavily on the work of RAND associates. This work stood apart from the rest, not just because of the advantages mentioned earlier (access to secrets, professional associates, etc.), but also because the sponsors of their work (the Air Force) would support lengthy, theoretical and speculative "think pieces" on relatively arcane subjects.

This was very important to the depth of the work on arms control and strategic theory published later in public form. For in the early to mid-1950s it was difficult to earn a living as a strategist if one was not affiliated somehow with the government. Schools devoted to strategic studies were just coming into their own and they tended to draw faculty whose interests were divided—for example between political science, physics, or law and national security policy. Thus, what non-governmental contributions were made tended to be short, occasional articles rather than books—especially in the field of arms control, a subset of national security studies even more dominated by interdisciplinary theories. Contributions in this form tended to have less detailed reasoning than the products of RAND study groups which, when they appeared in consolidated form before the public, had a depth and an elegance unmatched anywhere else.[88]

The late 1950s were important years for the establishment of the objectives and premises of the Cambridge Approach. If the collected works of these "civilian strategists," as they came to be called, did not constitute an "invention," they did, in many cases, become definitive for the field, and served as the body of work most salient in the minds of those who adhered to the Cambridge Approach in the early 1960s.

Logic and symmetry would dictate that a lengthy analysis ensue on the contributions of civilian strategists to the arms control paradigm of the Cambridge Approach. However, the course of the strategic debate, and the contributions of major theorists such as Bernard Brodie, Albert Wohlstetter, James King, Robert Osgood, Herman Kahn, and Thomas Schelling have been discussed thoroughly in excellent books recently published.[89] Here it will suffice to point out certain contributions to the strategic debate which had special relevance for the emerging arms control paradigm.

Judging by the influence with which he has been credited and the longevity of his works, the single greatest contributor to the development of the methods of modern arms control was Thomas Schelling. Schelling, as most of the civilian strategists, was an economist by training. He came to the subject of arms control by way of his interest in bargaining. His first work of relevance to the subject, "An Essay on Bargaining" was published in *The American Economic Review* in June 1956.[90] In it he discussed both

> ... explicit bargaining and the tacit kind in which adversaries watch and interpret each other's behavior, each aware that his own actions are being interpreted and anticipated, each acting with a view to the expectations that he creates."[91]

He noted that the subject covered traditional economic concerns but also problems ranging from "... the threat of massive retaliation to taking the right of way from a taxi."[92]

The insights which Schelling offered were provocative and wide ranging, from the notion that a weakness can be made a strength ("the power to constrain an adversary may depend on the power to bind oneself"), and that relative abilities to communicate may be important ("asymmetry in communication may well favor the one who is ... unavailable for the receipt of messages ..."), to the roles of secrecy and precedent can play in the conduct of negotiations.[93] Schelling developed the implications of his analysis for the problem of limited war in an article, "Bargaining, Communication, and Limited War," published during 1957 in *The Journal of Conflict Resolution*.[94] Here, Schelling explored further the principles of tacit bargaining, especially in the case where the parties' preferences with respect to outcomes conflict, and underlined the importance of limits which are distinct, recognizable, and preferably established in advance by the adversaries.

Schelling's interest in the subjects of bargaining and conflict led him to question the applicability of insights derived from zero-sum games to non zero sum-games involving elements of cooperation. In "The Strategy of Conflict" published in *The Journal* of *Conflict Resolution* in 1958, he posited another "ideal-type" game, the one of pure cooperation where all sides attempt to play to a mutual "win."[95] Casting aside classical non-zero sum calculations as too abstract and symmetrical, he sought to expand the theory by considering the roles which coordination, threats, promises, and acts themselves can have on the play. In so doing, he derived the notion of the "strategic move," thus giving theoretical support for the kind of unilateral approach to arms control which the Acheson panel had prescribed long before:

> If the essence of a game of strategy is the dependence of each person's proper choice of action on what he expects the other to do, it

may be useful to define a "strategic move" as follows: A strategic move is one that influences the other person's choice, in a manner favorable to one's self, by affecting the other person's expectations on how one's self will behave. One constrains the partner's choice by constraining one's own behavior.[96]

In early 1959, Schelling gave a paper at a conference on "International Relations in the Mid-Twentieth Century" at Northwestern University in which he related his theoretical insights specifically to the problem of international relations.[97] This was a very important paper in that it not only specified the contribution he was making, but the limits which the analysis had for the conduct of policy. He pointed out that there were two general realms for a theory of conflict based on realism (that is, taking conflict as a given in human affairs): the realm in which participants are studied in all their complexity—rational and irrational behavior, motivations, etc.; and the realm in which the participants are viewed as rational, conscious and artful. This latter field of study in which players seek to win, he termed "the strategy of conflict." Its study he believed, could provide a *benchmark* for the understanding of actual behavior by establishing "correct" behavior in given circumstances.

If we confine our study to the theory of strategy, we seriously restrict ourselves by the assumption of rational behavior-not just of intelligent behavior, but of behavior motivated by a conscious calculation of advantages, a calculation that in turn is based on an explicit and internally consistent value system. We thus limit the applicability of any results we reach. If our interest is the study of actual behavior, the results we reach under this constraint may prove to be either a good approximation of reality or a caricature. Any abstraction runs a risk of this sort, and we have to be prepared to use judgement with any results we reach.[98]

Not only did Schelling explicitly deny any identity between his theoretical construct and "truth," but he stressed its bias: toward the "exploitation of potential force" rather than the "application of force" in conflicts. He clearly and explicitly disconnected his discussion of strategy in "games" from the military usage of the term.[99]

Schelling went beyond the methods of "cooperation in conflict" to discuss stability more directly in his work on surprise attack. Here he addressed what has been termed "static stability," crediting C.W. Sherwin and Warren Amster for their previous methodical approach to the problem.[100] Elaborating on their logic he wrote that "...

schemes to avert surprise attack have as their most immediate objective the safety of weapons rather than the safety of people."[101] But Schelling added a perceptual twist that was to be characteristic of the Cambridge Approach: "The surprise-attack problem, when viewed as a problem of reciprocal suspicion and aggravated self-defense, suggests that there are not only secrets we prefer not to keep, but military capabilities we might prefer not to have."[102] And, since there are of course capabilities which, by the same logic, we would prefer the other side not to have, the subject was one which involved both unilateral moves and negotiation.

Schelling spent 1959 at RAND where his work influenced and was influenced by, the ideas of theorists such as Bernard Brodie, Daniel Ellsberg, Malcom Hoag, Herman Kahn, Albert Wohlstetter and William Kaufmann. Of course, Wohlstetter's analysis of the delicacy of the strategic balance was critical to the arms control paradigm that was emerging, for it established the notion that strategic stability was not simply derived from stalemate but had, instead, to be engineered. His article, "The Delicate Balance of Terror," published in *Foreign Affairs* during 1959, provided a tightly reasoned rationale for pursuing limited arms control instead of comprehensive disarmament or even simple reductions.[103]

William Kaufmann, also of RAND and influential on the work of Schelling, had begun by 1954 to prescribe strategies suitable to the realm of action between diplomacy and all-out war. Based on the presumption that neither side wanted annihilation but rather a contest, he argued for raising the nuclear threshold by preparing for a conventional defense of Europe, limiting the nuclear deterrent to the role of counter-city retaliation, and the employment of tacit bargaining and "signalling" in support of national security.[104]

Toward the end of the decade, Kaufmann began to move toward a position tolerating limited counter force nuclear strikes. His concern was with the defense of Europe, a problem which appeared easiest to solve by composing the American arsenal of both a "strategic reserve" of nuclear capability and a potential for limited hard-target capability. In attempting to resolve the NATO riddle in this manner, he built upon the analyses of counter-force and intra-war bargaining done by Brodie, Andrew Marshall, Joseph Luftus and Nathan Leites at RAND.

Conclusion

By 1959, it was evident that the thrust of modern nuclear arms control thought, based as it was on deterrent logic, was being affected more by the theoretical developments in military strategy than by the evolution of disarmament thought.   Indeed, the community of disarmament theorists had become dispersed and divided at approximately the same time that the strategic community was coalescing and achieving a measure of theoretic unity.   The objectives and premises of the arms control and disarmament communities were diverging drastically, though the policy objectives of the two seemed coincident.   What emerged in the late 1950s was a broad but shallow consensus in support of limited measures.

This split between arms control theorists and disarmers did not go unrecognized by participants in the theoretical debate.   In 1959, Arthur Lee Burns wrote a politically path-breaking article which specified the points of divergence between the two schools with considerable force.[105]   However, much effort was expended on denying it—especially by a number of the new arms control strategists who chafed at the charges that their efforts were morally compromising.   Thus, Donald Brennan would testily write in the introduction to the book which he himself would dub the "Bible" of the Cambridge Approach:

> ... *there are no basic differences in the morality of the authors.* This fact bears on a false dichotomy that certain extremists have been trying to create-that of "disarmament *versus* arms control." The point of view of this book (as with most students of these affairs) is that "arms control" is a generic term that includes the possibility of literal "disarmament" among other possible cases.   In the recent past, unfortunately, a few writers have been attempting to create a new meaning of their own for "arms control," a meaning that seems to embrace only limited and rather special forms of arms control. These writers hold that "arms control" (in their limited sense of the term) is a distinctly wicked doctrine, and those who advocate it (as opposed to "disarmament") are made to appear as immoral proponents of the continuation of the arms race.[106]

Yet Brennan at the same time went on to enumerate the goals of arms control strictly in terms of the requirements of deterrence, the approach being thought of:

...as oriented toward improving the national security of each of the nations involved by adjusting at least some armament capabilities and uses to those "actually" desirable in the light of the intentions, actions, and adjusted capabilities of the other nations.[107]

He went on to conclude in his chapter, "The Setting and Goals of Arms Control," that the elimination of all war was beyond present capabilities.[108]

As arms control theory moved into the 1960s, it thus reflected both consensus as to interim requirements (limited measures) and deep divergence over the "end game" (elimination of war and the dissolution of nuclear arsenals versus perpetual deterrence). What bound the theorists was a desire to avoid a devastating nuclear war through the pursuit of realizable arms limitations; but what divided them were the limiting problems of the weapons-stability nexus on the one hand, and the riddle of post-attack scenarios in Europe on the other. The Cambridge Approach recorded the temporary resolution of the former in its acceptance of mutual deterrence, but hedged the latter as theorists grappled with the side of strategy Schelling had not addressed: employment doctrine. Thus, while the principles of an arms control approach to national security policy were reflected in the McNamara era, so were its equivocations and uncertainties as graduated deterrence, mutual assured destruction, limited warfighting capabilities, and tacit bargaining were all pursued. It is not surprising that the Cambridge Approach—as a consensual paradigm for national security policy—had within it the seeds of its own destruction.

Notes

1. See Chapter 5, pp. 140–143.
2. See for example, Grenville Clark, "The Practical Prospects for Disarmament and Genuine Peace," *Proceedings of the American Philosophical Society*, Vol. 97, No. 6 (December 1953): 645–651.
3. U.S. Atomic Energy Commission, *In the Matter of J. Robert Oppenheimer* (Washington, D.C.: United States Government Printing Office, 1954), pp. 329–330. Dr. Bethe opposed the development of the H-Bomb before the Korean War. After the war broke out he went to work on the weapons project at Los Alamos despite continuing reservations.
4. Gilpin, *American Scientists*, pp. 98–102.
5. Enrico Fermi and Isador Rabi, members of the General Advisory Committee to the Atomic Energy Commission, did join Bethe in support of negotiations. They opposed the H-Bomb on strongly ethical grounds. As

they wrote in their minority annex to the GAC report, "It is necessarily an evil thing considered in any light" (as quoted in the U.S. Atomic Energy Commission's *In the Matter of J. Robert Oppenheimer*, pp. 79–80). However, after the "minimal decision" was made to proceed with the development of the fusion device, a few influential members of the State Department opposed testing it and favored negotiations. For a penetrating analysis of the "minimal nature of the H-bomb decision," see Warner R. Schilling, "The H-Bomb Decision: How to Decide Without Really Choosing," *Political Science Quarterly* (March 1961): 24–46.

6. See *Congressional Record*, Vol. 96, No. 25, pp. 1534–1537.

7. William Kaufmann, "Disarmament and American Foreign Policy," *Foreign Policy Reports*, Foreign Policy Association (1 September 1950): 89–90.

8. Nathan Leites, *The Code of the Politburo* (New York: McGraw Hill, 1951).

9. Edward Shils, "The Bolshevik Elite: An Analysis of a Legend," *Bulletin of the Atomic Scientists*, Vol. 7, No. 3 (March 1951): 77–80.

10. This symposium was organized by the *New Leader* which ran articles from June-September 1954. The articles were reviewed by Alan Sympson in the *Bulletin of the Atomic Scientists*, Vol. 11, No. 1 (January 1955): 35–37.

11. McGeorge Bundy, "Early Thoughts on Controlling the Nuclear Arms Race: A Report to the Secretary of State, January 1953," *International Security*, Vol. 7, No. 2 (Fall 1982): 3–27. Oppenheimer was then Director of Princeton's Institute for Advance Study, Bush was with the Carnegie Institute of Washington, Dickey was President of Dartmouth, Johnson was President of the Carnegie Endowment (and as with Dickey, a former State Department official with background in disarmament negotiations).

12. *Ibid.*

13. *Ibid.*, p. 7.

14. Atomic Energy Commission, *In the Matter of J. Robert Oppenheimer*, p. 95.

15. *Ibid.*, p. 18.

16. McGeorge Bundy, "Early Thoughts on Controlling the Nuclear Arms Race," p. 17.

17. *Ibid.*, p. 26.

18. *Ibid.*, emphasis added.

19. *Ibid.*

20. *Ibid.*, pp. 11–12.

21. *Ibid.*, p. 26.

22. "... the United States had decided to use (the atomic weapon) to keep its control wholly unshared, to make as many as possible, to plan for their use and to base that plan centrally on the concept of an immediate and devastating strategic blow at the center of hostile power. The decision to conduct this operation would at present be uniquely American ..." [*Ibid.*, p. 14].

23. *Ibid.*, p. 18.

24. *Ibid.*, note 24.

25. *Ibid.*, note 24.

26. Leo Szilard, "Shall We Face the Facts? An Appeal For a Truce Not a Peace," *Bulletin of the Atomic Scientists*, Vol. 5, No. 5 (May 1949): 269–273.

27. Hans J. Morgenthau, "The H-Bomb and After," *Bulletin of the Atomic Scientists*, Vol. 6, No. 3 (March 1950): 76–79.

28. Hans J. Morgenthau, "The Political and Military Strategy of the United States," *Bulletin of the Atomic Scientists*, Vol. 10, No. 8. (October 1954): 323–325.

29. David F. Cavers, "An Interim Plan for Control," *Bulletin of the Atomic Scientists*, Vol. 6, No. 1 (January 1950): 13.

30. See Chapter 4, pp. 99–104. In brief, the Acheson-Lilienthal Plan recommended a distribution of sensitive nuclear facilities among states in accordance with the distribution of power in the international system at the time of the agreement so that these internationalized facilities would be vulnerable to national seizure should the agreement be abrogated by any one state.

31. David F. Cavers, "The Challenge of Planning Arms Controls," *Foreign Affairs*, Vol. 34, No. 1 (October 1955): 65–66.

32. *Ibid.*, p. 66.

33. David R. Inglis and Donald A. Flanders, "A Deal Before Midnight," *Bulletin of the Atomic Scientists*, Vol. 7, No. 10 (October 1951): 306.

34. *Ibid.*

35. *Ibid.*

36. *Ibid.*

37. *Ibid.*, p. 317.

38. *Ibid.*, p. 317.

39. *Ibid.*, p. 306.

40. James R. Newman, "Towards Atomic Agreement," *Bulletin of the Atomic Scientists* Vol 10, No. 4 (April 1954): 121–122.

41. *Ibid.*, p. 121.

42. *Ibid.*, p. 122.

43. *Ibid.*

44. David F. Cavers, "International Control of Armaments," *Annals of the American Academy of Political and Social Science* 296 (November 1954): 119.

45. David R. Inglis, "Ban the H-Bomb and Favor the Defense," *Bulletin of the Atomic Scientists*, Vol. 10, No. 9 (November 1954): 353.

46. *Ibid.*, p. 355.

47. *Ibid.*

48. *Ibid.*, p. 356.

49. *Ibid.*

50. *Ibid.*, p. 355.

51. James R. Killian, Jr., among others, argued vigorously for improved defenses without specifying a need for a cap on offensive systems. However, he argued that arms control might be facilitated in an environment of balanced defense and offense since both sides would have warnings and defense in place in the event of treachery. See for example, his article, co-authored with A.G. Hill, "For a Continental Defense," *The Atlantic Monthly* (November 1953).

52. P.M.S. Blackett, *The Military and Political Consequences of Atomic Energy* (London: Turnstile, 1948).

53. Gray, *Strategic Studies*, p. 169.

54. During a television program entitled "Armed Forces Hour" on 4 June 1950, General Lawton Collins, Army Chief of Staff stated that "... we don't believe the enemy would have these (tactical) weapons because there is a limit to his industrial capacity and his research and development field."

55. Robert Gilpin, *Scientists*, pp. 117–118.

56. Major General James M. Gavin, "The Tactical Use of the Atomic Bomb," *Combat Forces Journal*, January 1951, reprinted in *Bulletin of the Atomic Scientists*, Vol. VII, No. 2 (February 1951): 46.

57. Kaplan, *Wizards of Armageddon* p. 49.

58. On 30 November 1950, Truman mentioned the possibility of nuclear use in Korea, prompting a hurried visit by Britain's Prime Minister Clement Atlee and an announcement that the West was not "trigger happy."

59. This problem had been a concern of George Kennan, among others, during the 1940s when Brodie's original analysis held considerable force and the United States had a monopoly of atomic weapons but no doctrine for their strategic use and no low-level nuclear capability. For his early analysis of the problem see his *Memoirs 1925–1950* (Boston: Little Brown & Company, 1967), pp. 431–500.

60. Inglis and Flanders, "Deal Before Midnight," pp. 305–306, 317.

61. David R. Inglis, "Tactical Atomic Weapons and the Problem of Ultimate Control," *Bulletin of the Atomic Scientists*, Vol. 8, No. 3 (March 1952): 83.

62. Clifton M. Utley, "Atomic Superiority: A Wasting Asset," *Bulletin of the Atomic Scientists*, Vol. 7, No. 3 (March 1951): 75.

63. This was Inglis' position, although he was skeptical that defense could ever truly "catch up," David Inglis, "National Security With the Arms Race Limited," *Bulletin of the Atomic Scientists*, Vol. 12, No. 6 (June 1956): 196–201. It was also the view of Richard Leghorn and others. See Richard S. Leghorn, "Controlling the Nuclear Threat in the Second Atomic Decade," *Bulletin of the Atomic Scientists*, Vol. 12, No. 6 (June 1956): 189–195 and James R. Killian Jr. and A.G. Hill, "For a Continental Defense," *The Atlantic Monthly* (November 1953).

64. Hornell Hart, "The Remedies *versus* the Menace," *Bulletin of the Atomic Scientists*, Vol. 10, No. 6 (June 1954): 197–205.

65. R.L. Meier, "Beyond Atomic Stalemate," *Bulletin of the Atomic Scientists*, Vol. 12, No. 5 (May 1956): 147–153.

66. C.W. Sherwin, "Securing Peace Through Military Technology," *Bulletin of the Atomic Scientists*, Vol. 12, No. 5 (May 1956): 159–164.

67. *Ibid.*, p. 159.

68. *Ibid.*, pp. 160–161.

69. Sherwin records the paper as "The Design of a Deterrent Air Weapon System," but without further citation.

70. *Ibid.*, p. 161.

71. *Ibid.*, p. 162.

72. *Ibid.*, p. 161.

73. *Ibid.*, p. 162.

74. *Ibid.*, p. 159.

75. *Ibid.*, p. 161.

76. *Ibid.*, pp. 161–162.

77. *Ibid.*, p. 161.

78. *Ibid.*, p. 164.

79. Warren Amster, "Design for Deterrence," *Bulletin of the Atomic Scientists*, Vol. 12, No. 5 (May 1956): 164–165.

80. *Ibid.*, p. 165.

81. *Ibid.*

82. *Ibid.*

83. Gray, *Strategic Studies*, p. 295.

84. Thomas Schelling underscored this point during a conference organized by the American Academy of Arts and Sciences in January 1990.

85. Fred Kaplan, *Wizards of Armageddon*, pp. 51, 62. RAND analysts shifted from one project to another and "raided" study groups for the purpose of gaining skills and insights to be applied to a related problem.

86. *Ibid.*, p. 11. Kaplan writes, "... the catch phrases of the popularized strategic debates of the 1960s and 1970s—counterforce, first strike/second strike, nuclear war-fighting, systems analysis, thinking about the unthinkable, shot across the bow, limited nuclear options—would all have their source the strategists of the RAND Corporation of the 1950s."

87. This requirement was masked by public apathy at the time, and it may have been hoped that the United Nations negotiations, based as they were on a "Majority Plan," long backed by the America public, would satisfy the domestic interest in restrained reliance on weapons and mass destruction.

88. None of this is meant to depreciate the obvious point that RAND had, at one time or another, attracted the participation of some of the best and most imaginative thinkers of the time, in large part because of the very advantages which it offered.

89. See *inter alia*, Laurence Martin, *Strategic Thought in the Nuclear Age* (Baltimore, The Johns Hopkins University Press, 1979); Fred Kaplan, Wizards of Armageddon; Jerome H. Kahan, *Security in the Nuclear Age* (Washington, D.C.: The Brookings Institution, 1975).

90. Thomas Schelling, "An Essay on Bargaining," *The American Economic Review*, Vol. 46, No. 3. This essay was subsequently included as a chapter in his book, *The Strategy of Conflict* (Oxford: Oxford University Press, 1963), pp. 21–52.

91. Thomas Schelling, *The Strategy of Conflict*, p. 21.

92. *Ibid.*

93. *Ibid.*, pp. 22, 26.

94. Thomas Schelling, "Bargaining, Communication and Limited War," *The Journal of Conflict Resolution*, Vol. 1, No. 1, March 1957, pp. 19–36.

95. Thomas Schelling, "The Strategy of Conflict," *The Journal of Conflict Resolution*, Vol. II, No. 3, September 1958.

96. *The Strategy of Conflict* (Oxford: Oxford University Press, 1963), p. 160.

97. *Ibid.*, p. v.

98. *Ibid.*, p. 4.

99. *Ibid.*, p. 3.

100. *Ibid.*, p. 7; see also Schelling's *Surprise Attack and Disarmament* (RAND Corporation Report, P–1574, 10 December 1958, 1574).

101. Schelling, *The Strategy of Conflict*, p. 7.

102. *Ibid.*, p. 231.

103. Albert Wohlstetter, "The Delicate Balance of Terror," *Foreign Affairs* (January 1959): 211–235.

104. See William W. Kaufmann, ed., *Military Policy and National Security* (Princeton: Princeton University Press, 1956). Of course, Kaufmann was not the only one making these arguments: James King, "Nuclear Weapons and Foreign Policy 1: Limited Defense," *The New Republic* (1 July 1957): 18–21; "Nuclear Weapons and Foreign Policy: Limited Annihilation," *The New Republic* (15 July 1957): 16–18. Also by the same author, "Nuclear Plenty and Limited War," *Foreign Affairs*, Vol. 35, No. 2 (January 1957): 238–256.

105. Arthur Lee Burns, "Disarmament or the Balance of Terror?" *World Politics*, Vol. 12, No. 1 (October 1959): 132–145. Burns in fact credited Warren Amster's work, *A Theory for the Design of a Deterrent Air Weapon System* (San Diego: Convair-General Dynamics Corp., 1955), with first establishing the basis for this split—see this Chapter, pp. 207–212.

106. Brennan, *Arms Control*, pp. 9–10.

107. *Ibid.*

108. *Ibid.*, pp. 19–42, *passim*.

7

The Cambridge Approach
Revisited and Reviewed

The Theoretical Joining

The two projects on arms control organized in Cambridge during 1960 brought together a wealth of ideas, many of which are accurately and inspiringly preserved in the rapporteur's reports and collected papers of the Summer Study of Arms Control. The participants were generally well known to each other, even though some were relatively new to the emerging field of security studies. The names of most of them remain well-known to security specialists to this day.

A careful reading of the literature which the participants in these seminars produced dissuades the analyst or historian from describing the group as a "school." Brennan's volume contained proposals ranging from unilateral disarmament to a moratorium on controls pending change in the international political context.[1] Minutes of the Summer Study disclose the divergent views which inspired the books by Schelling and Halperin and by Frisch.[2]

Yet these projects did clarify the premises and objectives of the participants. In the process a dominant orientation and a cohesive set of concepts emerged. Although the approach has been discussed in chapter 2, it is useful to review its four basic principles:

1. Arms control should be considered and implemented within the context of the contemporary international strategic environment.

Most of the contributions to both projects began with acceptance of the existing politico-military setting within which arms control had to operate. It was presumed that neither Superpower was so dissatisfied as to be willing to risk nuclear war in order to change the status quo and that no lesser powers had the capabilities to do so. This belief translated in practical terms into an endorsement of the bipolar system, lending a certain logic to the pursuit of bilateral arms control schemes—albeit with intermittent reference to the problems which Communist China (and western allies) presented to the negotiating and implementing of them. That nuclear weapons may have played some role in containing Soviet aspirations for international systemic change led the new arms controllers to believe that nuclear weapons not only could not be abolished but possibly should not be. They thus recognized what has been called here the "weapons-stability nexus"—that is that nuclear weapons were necessary for deterrence and that changes in policies relating to them could critically affect the likelihood of war. Participants tended to associate arms control with international "security arrangements" instead of "reductions" or "disarmament."[3]

As a consequence of the perceived weapons-stability nexus and status-quo orientation, the new arms controllers demoted inspection from its former position as a policy objective which, if successfully achieved, would change the international political structure or, if unsuccessful, would demonstrate the contrary need for greater exertion in defense efforts. Inspection became instead an instrument with both positive and negative features: a means by which agreements could be maintained within the limits of acceptable risk and as a confidence-building tool which might help to maintain a plateau of military effort on both sides.

With respect to the negative aspect, the policy question had thus become relative not absolute: given that neither side trusted the other, that technology would undergo constant change in service of military ends, and that military information and communication between adversaries would be incomplete, what was *necessary* to know about the adversary's strategic program to ensure compliance with an accord, and would the inspection system give *adequate* evidence of *significant* violations? On the positive side the question became one of unilateral efforts: given mutual interest in a particular accord, what inspection measures could be included which would allow each side maximum opportunity to demonstrate its compliance with the agreement—especially in times of crisis or rapid technological change?

Inspection had become a complicated regulatory function integral to an arms agreement and to its subsequent implementation over a period of technological change.[4] Moreover, since the anarchic international system required that enforcement be left to national means, adequate inspection was perceived as tied to the overall military posture; any gaps in monitoring capabilities could be reduced in significance by the American deterrent, which would make capabilities achieved by the opponent's evasion or cheating insufficient. The feasibility of inspection and enforcement were not, therefore, set values for any accord but rather linked to the degree of redundancy or "safety" built into both sides of the military equation.[5] The question became not "do we have the capability to detect any cheating in a particular arms agreement" but rather "do we have adequate military capability to render any undetectable cheating in the agreement militarily useless?"

The majority of the theorists extended this logic to conclude that an "optimum" strategic force structure had both an upper and lower limit. The upper limit could be delimited using criteria of assured destruction, although some scholars emphasized the need for redundancy and limited "no cities" options as well. The lower limit could be derived from consideration of both those capabilities necessary for nuclear deterrence and the adequacy of conventional forces for preserving a high threshold in time of conflict. Both limits would be designed to ensure security in an arms control environment characterized by the absence of trust, imperfect information, and the will to evade limits on the part of the adversary.

Viewing the stability relationship in such systemic terms, the Cambridge arms controllers believed improved communication could be a means of reducing the necessary "safety factor" built into both sides' arsenals. Information exchanges would clarify the motives behind any party's increased military spending. If a boost in one party's defense budget were advertised as only an effort to enhance redundancy or second-strike capability, the adversary might not feel the need to compensate and might even take actions to reduce the threat which had precipitated the first party's insecurity. Cooperation in threat adjustment could lead to situations in which non-threatening forces would be provided to an opponent to increase his confidence in his own deterrent, rendering misperceptions, miscalculations, and disruptions of the arms control environment less likely.[6]

2. Arms control must be primarily addressed to the problem of containing the threat which nuclear weapons pose to strategic stability.

The majority of the analysts perceived the problem of surprise attack as the most pressing and urgent. They therefore emphasized measures to prevent bilateral strategic nuclear war and not techniques of limiting war once it had occurred or reductions in military expenditures.[7]

The question of arms control priorities was directly connected to the assumption that "first steps" had to be related to the givens of the strategic environment, not to the logic of the theory itself. In theory, arms control was conceived by some, especially Schelling and Halperin, as a broad instrument bound to issues of strategy in all its facets.[8]   However, attention to contemporary circumstances suggested that first steps deal with resolution of the primary threat: bilateral strategic instability arising from accidental war or preemptive attack. Broad agreement among participants would be facilitated if such contentious problems as post-attack scenarios, including questions of proportionate retaliation or limited counterforce strikes, and long-term objectives, such as ensuring a non-nuclear world, could be skirted.

The Cambridge arms controllers extended their bilateral strategic orientation to analyses of nuclear proliferation: they perceived the proliferation threat as primarily one of catalytic war. Aside from the question of China, however, the problem received little attention. For example, most of the participants believed that the crux of the test-ban issue rested on its effect on the strategic equation. Indeed, discussion in the Summer Study seminar on the utility of a test-ban concentrated on the test ban's probable effects on strategic arsenals, explicitly leaving the proliferation question as secondary. Donald Brennan and Morton Halperin's analysis of the test-ban specifically stated that the question of its desirability rested first on its effects on strategic stability and, if this was answered positively, only secondarily on its global effects.[9]   There were even intimations of the view that nuclear proliferation might not be dangerous.[10]   In Richard S. Leghorn's chapter, "The Pursuit of Rational World Security Arrangements," the proliferation issue was not discussed at all.[11]

The participants in these study projects agreed on certain fundamental requirements for "static" strategic stability. Dalimil Kybal was one of those in the Summer Study who made the point most forcefully: "the critical parameter in counterforce exchanges is the ratio R of the number of weapons expended by a force to the number of weapons killed."[12]   He and others agreed that parity in numbers was not of critical import; more so was the parity that ensured that both sides could strike second. With the presumption of a weapons to target ratio greater than one, the Cambridge arms controllers favored some form of finite or positive deterrence involving bilateral assured destruction capabilities. This was based on the generally-held belief that a strategic nuclear attack of any magnitude would be an inappropriate response to an extreme non-nuclear provocation. Thus, strategic nuclear arsenals only needed to be directed against strategic attack or "extreme nuclear provocation" by the adversary. To deter this, invulnerable second-strike weapons-systems were favored for both sides and the concept of allowing or even giving the Soviets second-strike forces was raised and not strongly contested.[13] However, there was no agreement on whether the stance which the United States should seek would be one of actual parity or maximum superiority within a stable balance.[14]

Indeed, the "best" size for the American arsenal was widely debated. Some analysts felt that in an arms control environment (i.e., wherein both sides are cooperating to achieve stability) the optimum force ought to be dictated strictly by its capability to inflict "adequate" retaliatory devastation on the enemy, with the exact specification left to politico-military determination.[15] Others believed the optimum force might well be set at "punitive" rather than "suicidal" levels.[16] Still others believed that some additional measure of capability might be necessary to overcome an attack which was partially counterforce, to resist blackmail or to limit war if it should occur through accident or miscalculation. These situations might require a limited defense or counter-force capability. However, in all assessments, the stability of the system depended on positive missile-to-target ratios.

The divergence within the arms control projects over the feasibility and desirability of comprehensive versus limited accords reflected the lack of agreement on the requirements for "dynamic" stability. Those advocating comprehensive accords sought to define the desired end-state while proposing limited arrangements to be achieved as first steps. These were not all, or even largely, disarmament schemes.[17] However, they did suggest the need to specify the situation of equality towards which both sides would move, solving the problem of the arms race by defining an agreed end-state. Advocates of comprehensive measures criticized independent limited measures as inadequate, risky, and thus prone to failure. Limited measures would, in this view, simply re-channel competition to uncontrolled military fields.

The advocates of independent limited measures were skeptical of the feasibility of specifying end-states, preferring to use limited measures (including unilateral weapons decisions) for limited ends—one of which might be to channel technological developments in stabilizing directions. Those of this persuasion looked upon unhampered research and development in military fields as a positive feature of an arms control environment; such research would provide added insurance   against unilateral break-out by the opposition. Implicit in these arguments was the assumption that both the technological and the strategic nuclear advantage was with the United States at the time, and that American interests might best be met by an arms control approach that left unspecified the magnitude of the strategic edge in a bilateral relationship of "essential parity."[18]   This last issue was raised by Brennan as a subject deserving greater attention in the future.[19]

3. Arms control as a critical element of national strategy must not compromise American capability to use force in support of its interests; rather it must seek the contrary: to tailor force to interests in order that the credibility and utility of the military force structure might be maximized.

The emphasis on the problem of strategic nuclear stability did not eclipse all questions of limited war. Indeed, the Cambridge arms controllers achieved a broad consensus on what was needed to develop conventional capabilities to deter and to respond to less than total conflict.   The majority of the participants went beyond opposition to strategic counterforce or war-fighting capabilities to oppose the use of tactical nuclear weapons for limited war.   Brennan emphasized this point in his chapter on the "Setting and Goals of Arms Control":

> An issue that is much less dead (than the question of limited strategic nuclear war), but seems to be rapidly dying, is the use of a response intermediate between conventional forces and a strategic nuclear strike, namely, tactical nuclear weapons and limited nuclear war.   Close analysis of limited nuclear war appears to indicate that it would be militarily disadvantageous if used by both sides, at least, in most cases where it might be employed.   In addition, it would be highly dangerous and would be likely to produce undesirable political effects, such as hastening the spread of nuclear weapons to other countries.[20]

This assessment, underscored by the inclusion of Henry Kissinger's chapter reconsidering limited nuclear war in Brennan's volume, combined with the general bias against comprehensive agreements, suggested the need for improved conventional capabilities, and thus a raising of the nuclear threshold:

It should be noted, however, that in the absence of a comprehensive arms-control program, an extremely good general-war capability might be required in the event of a failure of Type C deterrence (deterrence of extreme non-nuclear provocations), simply to persuade the enemy that it is unmistakably in his interest to refrain from transgressing the HE-nuclear boundary when the subsequent HE war begins to go badly for him. This last might be called "escalation deterrence"—preventing the scale of initially limited conflicts from growing to disastrous proportions.[21]

4. The arms control process is intrinsically important and offers both a new sphere for the pursuit of strategic ends, and a long-range hope for accommodation with the adversary.

The Cambridge arms controllers generally agreed that there was value in the arms control process itself (including negotiations, self-discipline regarding military procurements, doctrine and tacit signalling or confidence-building measures). This belief derived from the participants' systemic orientation toward stability: in order for mutual understandings about an optimum security arrangement to evolve— especially in the non-comprehensive realm of controls—it was essential for the military capabilities of both sides to reflect a consistent set of stability objectives over time. This, combined with continuing efforts at information sharing and communication regarding "strategic images," would lead to an increased stake for both sides in the system, improved conditions for inspection (given the increased jeopardy involved in threatening the breakdown of a control environment through low-level cheating), and perhaps eventual political accommodation.

In addition to these specific points, certain historical themes emerged during the Cambridge discussions of 1960. The Cambridge arms controllers discussed political openness as a policy objective. Yet in schemes organized around the concept of mutual deterrence, they depreciated such political pursuits in favor of ensuring the cooperativeness, rationality and internal predictability of the adversary.

Second, the issues of secrecy and public support for arms control received rather scarce attention. The analysts discussing arms control in 1960 seemed to recognize public support for arms control and defense measures as important, although not controlling. If anything, the concern was with overselling controls, not with public ignorance.

For example, there occasionally seemed to be an implicit distrust of public opinion in so far as it might impute a special morality and virtue to international agreements. Making too much of limited measures could doom the "experiment" of arms control which, at least according to Schelling and Halperin, would inevitably be deeply enmeshed in the politics of the Cold War.[22]   The Cambridge arms controllers therefore gave only passing attention to the responsibilities of political leaders in shaping attitudes towards the nuclear problem.[23]

The Cambridge arms controllers believed that secrecy in reaching arms agreements was advantageous for a variety of reasons— particularly for improving prospects of reaching accords on sensitive matters   and   for   reducing   the   propaganda   significance   of negotiations.[24]   However   when   combined   with   a   bilateralist orientation, reference to the need for secrecy or "privacy" had rather disturbing implications for allies. Schelling and Halperin made this astonishingly explicit in their book on the subject:

> There is also the important possibility that the main participants in arms . control negotiations are embarrassed and inhibited by the presence of allied countries or countries to which they have military commitments.   Secrecy may eliminate some of the obstacles to plain speaking and to drastic proposals. ... If our definition of arms controls is broad enough to include all the possible forms of military collaboration between the United States and its main enemies, there may will be understandings reached, or even explicit agreements, that must be kept from certain other countries.   For example, agreements about preventing the spread of weapon technology, or even of nuclear weapons, or agreements involving delicate political settlements, might well have to remain secret.   The peculiar status of relations between the U.S.S.R. and China is a potent reminder that we are not the only major country that may occasionally wish to be less than wholly candid with its allies.[25]

Given the importance of propaganda and secrecy concerns in the Cambridge arms control framework, it is remarkable that so little attention was paid to the problem of ensuring domestic support for an arms control program of admittedly mixed purposes conducted by complex, secretive, and tacit bargaining.

Critiques in Perspective

The lack of attention to the problem of designing an arms control approach sensitive to democratic requirements and processes was one of the critical failings of the Cambridge Approach. Though ultimately damaging to the viability of the theory, this oversight was perhaps understandable. The public's general interest in disarmament was evident, indeed pressing. And in the past the public had seemed willing to be led.

There existed, after all, the historical relationship between authoritative pursuit of arms control and defense measures which has been termed the security "contract." This was not, obviously, a formalized agreement but rather a tacit understanding which had evolved out of the earliest postwar years. The American public had established a record of apparent ambivalence on the issue of nuclear controls which was based on a deferral of the issue to the expertise of national leadership. In a complicated interplay throughout the 1940s and 1950s, the public was exhorted to sacrifice for the military purpose of countering Soviet aggressive designs and inspired by proposals promising openness or disarmament. And while journalists and a few military analysts commented on the juxtaposition of the Baruch Plan and conventional de-mobilization in the 1940s, the Atoms for Peace Plan and the tilt toward tactical nuclear solutions for Europe, the Open Skies proposal and Massive Retaliation with its implicit contemplation of first use, the package disarmament schemes (including a test-ban) of the late 1950s and the New Look re-emphasizing tactical nuclear defense in the later 1950s, the public— including many arms control analysts—accepted the apparent duality. They did so because both the nuclear threat and the Soviet threat were real, intermittently tangible, and arguably increasing. Hiroshima was followed by the Lucky Dragon, revelations concerning strontium-90's long-term genetic effects, and American vulnerability to "push-button" war. Fear of Soviet subversion in Europe was followed by the Korean war, and a Soviet nuclear build-up which, after Sputnik, threatened to overcome American military supremacy.

In determining the balance which had to be achieved in the effort to contain both the nuclear and Soviet threats, the government had been granted unprecedented secrecy and authority. Yet the warning, made explicit in the Oppenheimer Panel's report in 1953—that candor had to complement policy initiative if the balance between military build-up and restraint was to be solid and enduring—was left largely unappreciated. One may credit American leadership for bringing the country prosperously through a troubled age when public volatility might have led to destabilizing swings in military capability or will. However the long-term effort to exercise nuclear deterrence was jeopardized by the poor rationalization of disarmament and defense objectives and the lack of an effort to bring the American people "on board" as the Oppenheimer Panel had suggested.

As the 1950s moved into the 1960s, nuclear secrets and scientists' expertise were replaced by the deterrent logic and the expertise of scientific strategists. Moreover, defense and arms control policies were officially joined so that the objectives of both would be complementary. Yet the rationale for the change, which was embedded in the Cambridge Approach, and the nature of the sophisticated calculations involved, were never clarified for the public.

Rather than appreciating this potential weakness in their stability designs, the advocates of the Cambridge Approach assumed a free hand in nuclear affairs when there was none. That their design might be too complex for domestic appreciation was a flaw tolerable in theory but not in practice. If the approach was to work, the challenge it presented for a democratic system had to be accepted and met. Indeed, as the Cambridge Approach became accepted by policy-makers during the 1960s, this theoretical gap proved a central policy weakness: while American officials sought to educate the adversary to the requirements of stability, they neglected both candor with the American people and the kind of mass educational effort in nuclear affairs which Sputnik had inspired in the sciences. As a result, the public was left politically volatile on the issue of controls: support could be had for improved nuclear capabilities with any demonstration of improved Soviet nuclear might; arms control programs, including relatively stabilizing (but expensive) new systems, could be scuttled by reference to the dollar cost, their net increase (instead of decrease) in bilateral offensive capabilities, or their lack of foolproof inspection. With the perspective of intellectual history, the SALT process may have been killed as much by a confused American public, vulnerable to critiques from both the political left and right, as by Soviet non-cooperation. The "Great Debate" on arms control in the late 1970s that led to such radical reversal of declared purposes, was not really a debate at all but an exorcism of "control" in favor of everything ranging from more virile competition to "freeze" or disarmament.[26]

There have been, in addition, three more conventional critiques of the Cambridge Approach. One holds that it was excessively technical in its thrust. Although this is to some extent true, the criticism is frequently overplayed. The Cambridge Approach represented a dramatic break with the past in its meshing of arms control and military purposes under the rubric of security policy. It signalled a de-throning of propaganda purposes in disarmament policy and a rationalizing of real and stated objectives in nuclear affairs. The history of attempts to use arms control for political purposes was littered with failure by 1958. That the first attempt to apply a more technical approach failed that year in the inconclusive Surprise Attack Conference, ought not stand as testament to the failure of the theory but of the state of the art and the accumulated suspicions regarding motives and political purposes.

A related critique is that the Cambridge Approach, by accepting the political status quo, failed to appreciate the political significance of accepting strategic parity with the Soviets.[27] To the extent that the Soviets approximated American capabilities, intra-alliance tension and the unresolved problems of extended deterrence would be exacerbated while the projection of political influence would be undermined. It has been repeatedly argued that the arms control technicians would have been well served by a better political sense.

It is certainly true that the problems of fitting extended deterrence and non-proliferation policies with the concept of an "optimum force" were not recognized or at least dealt with adequately within the broad consensus on arms control objectives. Here, a greater sensitivity to political trends might have made the approach hardier. But again, an element of truth does not make a critique necessarily convincing. On the subject of the political implications of strategic "equivalence," talk of expected or existing "parity" of one form or another had been pervasive throughout the 1950s; the Cambridge Approach simply defined the strategic meaning of this relationship and its tolerable limits, with no exact definition of desirable force ratios. The Cambridge theorists did not prescribe equivalence, they prescribed a disciplined balance.

Besides, whether a given level of force on the American side can be made a politically viable instrument with or without arms control is arguably a problem for American political leadership not arms control or defense practitioners. The Cambridge theorists assumed that the purpose of arms control was to give politicians greater freedom not to choose nuclear war under a variety of circumstances. To ask arms control policy to restore unquestioned unilateral superiority or, failing that, to prescribe the artful diplomacy suitable to a Gulliver constrained, is asking a great deal—indeed too much—of a single instrument of policy.

In fact, the constant criticism of arms control policies as institutionalizing inferiority possibly has done more damage to the political profile of American military capabilities than those policies' effects on force relations themselves. It is probable that unregulated competition, in which both sides exuded no apparent confidence in what stores of weapons they already had, would have made minor variations in strategic capabilities even less politically useful. Certainly it would have made a credible non-proliferation policy more politically difficult.

The third critique has concerned the lack of appreciation of the Soviet adversary within the Cambridge Approach. Indeed, the paucity of literature on Soviet strategic images and arms control premises and objectives was regularly acknowledged by the Cambridge theorists in the early 1960s. As years passed, some of these theorists, such as Donald Brennan, became dissenters from the Approach when convinced that the Soviets would not buy stability designs based on limiting strategic defensive capabilities.

Attempts to blame theory for not illuminating all aspects of a problem may not be justified. The Cambridge Approach was in the first instance a heuristic construct designed to describe a form of strategic stability at the systemic level; it was based on a model, not a perfect description of reality. It is true that during the 1960s, the Soviets hardly slowed their development of strategic accuracy and anti-ballistic missile capabilities or otherwise curtailed programs in accordance with the principles of stability and second-strike so integral to the Cambridge design. However, even the critics of the Cambridge Approach point out that the United States retained superiority throughout most of the 1960s. That McNamara's annual posture statements, designed in part "to provide stabilizing information" to the adversary, did not result in a slowing of Soviet programs but perhaps in their increased pace, was not surprising nor particularly contradictory to the Cambridge model. What seemed contradictory was the nature of American programs: Washington had the lead in accuracy, ABM technology, and MIRV capabilities in the early 1970s. If the American defense establishment had adopted the Cambridge Approach as uncritically as the critics have suggested, these "destabilizing" systems should not have been serious candidates for deployment.

In fact, that the Soviet Union didn't play according to the "rules" is less interesting than the fact that the United States seemed constantly agonizing over them. Even during the years of SALT negotiations (in which the Soviets engaged too), the evidence that the

Cambridge Approach had become uncritically accepted by the entire United States weapons establishment was flimsy compared to the evidence that arms control policy was becoming disjointed and incoherent. In fact, interviews conducted by this author during the late 1970s suggested that few within the Washington security community realized there was intellectual history or theoretical underpinning to their arms control ideas at all. Why should the Soviets have gambled their strategic programs on the hope or expectation that we would play precisely according to the logic of an arms control paradigm we rhetorically endorsed but inconsistently observed ourselves?

Conclusion

A detailed critique of the Cambridge Approach, or even a description of the evolution of its features through the 1960s is beyond the scope of the present analysis. It remains simply to summarize the findings regarding its intellectual ancestry.

To begin with, the analysis has shown that the primacy of stability objectives within the Cambridge Approach was not particularly revolutionary. Preoccupation with stability (as opposed to weapons reduction) objectives emerged in the earliest postwar years. This fact helps to establish a new perspective on the period. For example, it is often suggested that the Baruch era was one in which unimaginative attachment to disarmament principles jeopardized our security. On the one hand, advocates of disarmament have focussed on the "jokers" in the official plan and lamented our lack of flexibility during this critical period; on the other hand, critics of disarmament have suggested the folly of having offered to forfeit our nuclear advantage at all.[28] Whereas the first suggests we were cynical, the second suggests that we were politically naive. Although the diplomatic record renders both critiques credible, the intellectual record affords another perspective. By placing the official approach in the context of the thinking of the Acheson-Lilienthal team, the creativity which underlay the original plan and its emphasis on reducing the likelihood of war in a world of sovereign, nuclear, and competing states, is revealed.

Second, it has been demonstrated that the general stability framework of the Cambridge theorists—the concept of assured destruction— was set forth as a coherent theoretical contribution to arms control thought as early as 1954 by C.W. Sherwin and Warren Amster. These analysts used a game-theoretic approach to support their analysis in striking similarity to the later Cambridge style. A less-surprising observation is that the arms control theorists of the early 1960s were heavily influenced in their approach to stability by the work of the growing community of civilian strategists during the 1950s.

Third, the bilateral, limited approach to the process of arms control evolved in the late 1940s and early 1950s in the work of disenchanted or frustrated disarmers both in and out of the government. Included in this evolution was the notion of unilateral arms control which, in its call for rationalized arms control and defense policies, was quite similar to the notion of self-disciplined defense policy so integral to the Cambridge Approach.

Fourth, the political underpinning of the Cambridge Approach—an endorsement of the political status quo which was to lead in practice to considerable disruption in relations among western allies—was based on rejection of the earlier more explicit political angle of the Baruch era.

As we examine the past during the present sea-change in the international system, the intellectual record of nuclear arms control may help to move current debates on arms control to a more realistic level. In the flush of an apparent Cold War victory, it will be tempting but dangerous to suppose that old methods of arms control may be applied uncritically to a vastly different international context. That old approaches to stability appeared once to "work" does not mean that conceptual packages applicable to the old bipolar system will be wholly appropriate to a new political environment in which the status quo is being redefined almost on a daily basis.

As we look to the future it seems important that we not be trapped by old, revived controversies but to be informed by them. By getting inside the logic of the Cambridge Approach one can expose its weaknesses as well as its attributes more deftly and powerfully. We can also critically weigh its relevance for the future. The exercise is important even if one were not looking to borrow from the past in an effort to construct a new arms control design for a radically changing world. The changes now underway in the international system may, after all, resolve back to a bipolar contest; regional subsystems may evolve in which theories of bipolar strategic balances become relevant to the security of the participants.

In these circumstances, which imply an unhappy continuation and even extension of the nuclear and ballistic missile threats to global security, the Cambridge Approach may continue to be relevant. For example, the importance of domestic force decisions for influencing the weapons decisions of an opponent is a powerful point made by the theory; but it also reveals a critical flaw: if continued research and development is essential to a verifiable, enforceable arms control arrangement, how does each side signal peaceful, stabilizing intent while developing technologies with potentially de-stabilizing impact? How does one handle the "bargaining chip" which is risky to forfeit, to build, or even to consider seriously given the Cambridge Approach's emphasis on projected intentions? There may well be a need to develop new arms control designs, but in the effort we would do well to understand clearly where we have been.

Notes

1. See for examples, Eric Fromm, "The Case for Unilateral Disarmament"; Edward Teller, "The Feasibility of Arms Control and the Principle of Openness," in Brennan, *Arms Control*, pp. 187–198, 122–138.

2. The "deep divisions" within the Summer Study group has also been emphasized by Morton H. Halperin (personal interview June 1984). However, Donald Brennan remembered his group (personal interview February 1978) as having had differences, but not of a fundamental nature—an assessment somewhat challenged by the remarks made in his Preface to the volume, Brennan, *Arms Control*, pp. 9–10.

3. Some disarmers such as Jerome Wiesner and Bernard Feld appeared tentatively to accept this rather dramatic turn from the priority of reductions: Jerome B. Wiesner, "Comprehensive Arms-Limitation Systems, Disarmament, Arms Control, and National Security"; Bernard T. Feld, "Inspection Techniques of Arms Control," in Brennan, *Arms Control*, pp. 198–233 (esp. pp. 207–209), p. 318.

4. For examples of this approach relating to a particular arms control proposal see, Quinn and Plaskett, "Collected Papers," 202–225, 247–263. Also Wiesner, "Comprehensive Arms-Limitation Systems," in Brennan, *Arms Control*, pp. 198–233 (esp. pp. 207–209).

5. See discussion of deterrent force competition, *Collected Papers*, pp. 49–56, 65–71.

6. See Brennan, *Arms Control*, articles by Jerome Weisner, "Comprehensive Arms-Limitation Systems," pp. 198–233; Robert Bowie, "Basic Requirements of Arms Control," pp. 43–55 (esp. pp. 46–47, 50–53); Thomas Schelling, "Reciprocal Measures for Arms Stabilization," pp. 167–186 (esp. pp. 177–179) on the role of communication.

7. This is not meant to suggest that other objectives of arms control were considered unimportant. Schelling and Halperin were for example, quite concerned with the problem of limiting war once it occurred.

8. See Schelling and Halperin, *Strategy and Arms Control*, pp. 1–6.

9. Donald Brennan, *Arms Control*, pp. 239–266. The calculations of strategic stability in the case of more than two actors was discussed briefly in theoretical terms by Marvin Kalkstein, in *Collected Papers*, pp. 77–81. Apparently the implications were not discussed to any great degree by the participants.

10. See *Collected Papers*, pp. 339–344, esp. pp. 340–342. This discussion was based in part on Fred Ikle's paper, "Nth Countries and Disarmament," *Bulletin of the Atomic Scientists*, Vol. 16, (December 1960): 391–394.

11. Richard S. Leghorn, "The Pursuit of Rational World Security Arrangements," in Donald Brennan, *Arms Control*, pp. 407–422.

12. The discussion during the Summer Study turned on the paper by Dalimil Kybal which in turn was based on a paper, "Security, Arms Control and Deterrence," delivered before the Asilomar Strategy Seminar on 27 April 1960.

13. *Collected Papers*, pp. 46.

14. See Donald Brennan, "The Setting and Goals of Arms Controls," in Brennan, *Arms Control*, pp. 25–29.

15. *Collected Papers*, p. 12, 70. Estimates as to probable sizes for the force were wide-ranging.   Maximum sizes discussed were generally considered to be "a small fraction of 'One Beach' (one Beach was that level of nuclear force which would devastate world civilization—the term being derived from the movie "On the Beach"—and was estimated at 100,000,000 MT), *Ibid.*, p. 49.

16. See the discussion of deterrence in *Collected Papers*, pp. 81–92.

17. However, Feld consistently represented a position in favor of comprehensive controls aimed at reductions. He believed it essential to consider the potential for failures of deterrence and therefore to limit the *size* of arsenals on both sides to lowest possible levels.

18. *Collected Papers*, pp. 43–48; Donald Brennan, "The Setting and Goals of Arms Control," in Brennan, *Arms Control*, pp. 37–39.

19. Brennan, *Arms Control*, p. 29.

20. Brennan, *Arms Control*, p. 26.

21. Donald Brennan, "The Setting and Goals of Arms Control," in Brennan, *Arms Control*, pp. 26–27.   Here, he refers to "high explosive" conventional bombs.

22. Thomas C. Schelling and Morton H. Halperin, *Strategy and Arms Control*, pp. 131–132.

23. Ithiel de Sola Pool, "Public Opinion and the Control of Armaments," in Brennan, *Arms Control*, pp. 333–346. Manipulating public opinion for arms control purposes was a subject of some interest.   See Lewis C. Bohn, "Non-Physical Inspection Techniques," in Brennan, *Arms Control*, pp. 347–364; also *Collected Papers*, pp. 227–244.

24. *Ibid.*, p. 85. Schelling and Halperin intimated that there might even be information which governments might be willing to discuss with an adversary but not release publicly for a variety of reasons. *Ibid.*, p. 86.

25. Schelling and Halperin, *Strategy and Arms Control*, pp. 85–86.

26. The above discussion should not be interpreted to mean that all those who opposed SALT lacked understanding of its theoretical purposes; its most effective critics knew them well. However, for the most part, the public debate played to public ignorance and the many sides of the issue never joined. Exceptions included the study done under the direction of Richard Burt at the Washington Center for Foreign Policy Research, later published as an edited volume, Burt, *Arms Control and Defense*, and an article by Edward N. Luttwak, "Why Arms Control Has Failed," *Commentary*, 65 (January 1978): 19–27.

27. Luttwak, "Why Arms Control Has Failed," pp. 27–28.

28. H.A. DeWeerd, *Disarmament Failure and Weapons Limitations*, (Santa Monica: RAND Corporation, 1956), p. 896.

Selected Bibliography

Books, Papers

Acheson, Dean. *Present at the Creation. My Years in the State Department.* New York: W.W. Norton and Company, Inc., 1969.

Amster, Warren. *A Theory for the Design of a Deterrent Air Weapon System.* San Diego: Convair-General Dynamics Corp., 1955.

Aron, Raymond. *On War.* London: Secker and Warburg, 1958.

Aron, Raymond. *The Great Debate.* New York: Doubleday, 1965.

Art, Robert J., Kenneth N. Waltz, eds. *The Use of Force.* Boston: Little, Brown and Company, 1971.

Barnet, Richard J. *Who Wants Disarmament?* Boston: The Beacon Press, 1960.

Barton, John H. *The Politics of Peace, An Evaluation of Arms Control.* Stanford: Stanford University Press, 1981.

Bechhoefer, Bernard G. *Post War Negotiations for Arms Control.* Washington, D.C.: The Brookings Institution, 1961.

Blackett, P.M.S. *The Military and Political Consequences of Atomic Energy.* London: Turnstile, 1948.

Boulding, Kenneth. *Conflict and Defense, A General Theory.* New York: Harper and Row, 1962.

Brennan, Donald G., ed. *Arms Control Disarmament and National Security.* New York: George Braziller, 1961.

Brodie, Bernard. *Strategy in the Missile Age.* Princeton: Princeton University Press, 1959.

Brodie, Bernard, ed. *The Absolute Weapon.* New Haven: Yale Institute of International Studies, 1946.

Burt, Richard, ed. *Arms Control and Defense Postures in the 1980s.* Boulder: Westview Press, 1982.

Bush, Vannevar. *Pieces of the Action.* New York: William Morrow and Company, Inc., 1970.

Byrnes, James Francis. *All In One Lifetime.* New York: Harper, 1958.

Chayes, Abram and Jerome B. Weisner. *ABM An Evaluation of the Decision to Deploy an Antiballistic Missile System.* New York: The New American Library, 1969.

Conant, James B. *My Several Lives.* New York: Harper and Row, 1970.

DeWeerd, H.A.   "Disarmament Failure and Weapons Limitations."
Santa Monica: RAND Corporation, 1956.

Donovan, Robert J. *Conflict and Crisis, The Presidency of Harry S. Truman 1945-1948.* New York: W.W. Norton and Company, 1977.

Dougherty, James E. and Robert L. Pfaltzgraff, Jr. *Contending Theories of International Relations*

Dougherty, James E. *Arms Control and Disarmament, the Critical Issues.* Washington D.C.:   The Center for Strategic Studies, Georgetown University, 1966.

Dougherty, James E. and J.F. Lehman, Jr., eds. *Arms Control for the Late Sixties.* London: D. Van Nostrand Company, Ltd., 1967.

Dougherty, James E. and J.F. Lehman, Jr. *The Prospects for Arms Control.* New York: MacFadden-Bartell Corp., 1965.

Earle, Edward Meade., ed. *Makers of Modern Strategy.* New York: Atheneum, 1966.

Eisenhower, Dwight D.   *Mandate for Change, 1953-1956.* Garden City: Doubleday and Company, 1963.

Enthoven, Alain C. "The Future of American Deterrence Policy," in Harry Howe Ransom, ed. *An American Foreign Policy Reader.* New York: Thomas Y. Crowell Company, 1965.

Enthoven, Alain C. and Smith, K. Wayne. *How Much Is Enough? Shaping The Defense Program.*   New York: Harper and Row, 1971.

Etzold, Thomas H. and John Lewis Gaddis.   Eds. *Containment: Documents on American Policy and Strategy, 1945-1950.* New York: Columbia University Press, 1978.

Ford, Harold P. and Francis X. Winters, S.J.   Eds. *Ethics and Nuclear Strategy.* Maryknoll, New York: Orbis, 1977.

Franklin, H. Bruce. *Nuclear War and Science Fiction.* Unpublished paper.

Gilpin, Robert.   *American Scientists and Nuclear Weapons Policy.* Princeton: Princeton University Press, 1962.

Gompert, David, et al.   *Nuclear Weapons and World Politics: Alternatives for the Future.* New York: McGraw Hill Book Company, 1977.

Gray, Colin. *Strategic Studies and Public Policy: The American Experience.*   Unpublished manuscript. Crotin-on-Hudson (New York: Hudson Institute, 1980).

Green, Philip. *Deadly Logic, The Theory of Nuclear Deterrence.* New York: Schocken Books, 1968.

Hadley, Arthur. *The Nation's Safety and Arms Control.* New York: Viking Press Inc., 1961.

Halperin, Morton H. *Limited War in the Nuclear Age.* New York: John Wiley and Sons, 1966.

Haynes, Richard F. *The Awesome Power.* Baton Rouge: Louisiana State University Press.

Herzog, Arthur. *The War-Peace Establishment.* New York: Harper and Row, 1963.

Hewlett, Richard G. and Oscar E. Anderson, Jr. *The New World 1939/1946, Vol. 1: A History of the United States Atomic Energy Commission* (University Park: Pennsylvania State University Press, 1962) State University Press, 1962.

Hoffman, Stanley. *The State of War.* New York: Frederick A. Praeger, 1965.

Hofstadter, Richard. *The Paranoid Style In American Politics and Other Essays.* New York: Random House, 1967.

Hughes, Emmet John. *The Ordeal of Power: A Political Memoir of the Eisenhower Years.* New York: Atheneum, 1963.

Huntington, Samuel P. *The Common Defense, Strategic Programs in National Politics.* New York: Columbia University Press, 1961.

Jacobsen, Harold and Karan Stein. *Diplomats, Scientists and Politicians.* Ann Arbor: University of Michigan Press, 1966.

Jungk, Robert. *Brighter Than A Thousand Suns.* New York: Harcourt, Brace and World Inc., 1956.

Kahan, Jerome. *Security in the Nuclear Age, Developing U.S. Strategic Arms Policy.* Washington, D.C.: The Brookings Institution, 1975.

Kahn, Herman. *On Thermonuclear War.* Princeton: Princeton University Press, 1960.

Kaplan, Fred. *Wizards of Armageddon.* New York: Simon and Schuster, 1983.

Kaplan, Morton A., ed. *SALT: Problems and Prospects.* Morristown, New Jersey: General Learning Press, 1973.

Kaufmann, William W. *Military Power and National Security.* Princeton, Princeton University Press, 1956.

Kennan, George. *Memoirs 1925-1950.* Boston: Little, Brown and Company, 1967.

Kissinger, Henry. *Nuclear Weapons and Foreign Policy.* New York: Harper and Row, 1957.

La Feber Walter. *America Russia and the Cold War 1945-1971.* New York: John Wiley and Sons, Inc., 1972.

Leites, Nathan. *The Code of the Politburo*. New York: McGraw Hill, 1951.

Levine, Robert A. *The Arms Debate*. Cambridge: Harvard University Press, 1963.

Levinson, Marie. *Arms Control and International Politics 1958-1968*. Thesis No. 270. Geneva: Universite de Geneve, Institut Universitaire de Hautes Etudes Internationales, 1975.

Lilienthal, David E. *The Journals of David E. Lilienthal, Vol. II, The Atomic Energy Years 1945-1950*. New York: Harper and Row, 1964.

Luard, Evan, ed. *First Steps to Disarmament*. New York: Basic Books, Inc., 1965.

Mandelbaum, Michael. *The Nuclear Question*. Cambridge: Cambridge University Press, 1979.

Martin, Laurence. *Strategic Thought in the Nuclear Age*. Baltimore: The Johns Hopkins University Press, 1979.

Melman, Seymour, ed. *Disarmament: Its Politics and Economics*. Boston: The American Academy of Arts and Sciences, 1962.

Millis, Walter, ed. *The Forrestal Diaries*. New York: Viking Press, 1951.

Morgenthau, Hans J. *Scientific Man Versus Power Politics*. Chicago: University of Chicago Press, 1946.

Moss, Norman. *Men Who Play God*. New York: Harper and Row, 1968.

Myrdal, Alva. *The Game of Disarmament*. New York: Pantheon Books, 1976.

National Planning Association. *The Nth Country Problem and Arms Control*. Planning Pamphlet No. 108. Washington: National Planning Association, 1960.

National Planning Association, Special Project Committee on Security Through Arms Control. *1970 Without Arms Control*. Planning Pamphlet No. 104. Washington: National Planning Association, 1958.

Noel-Baker, Philip. *The Arms Race*. London: Atlantic Publishing Company, Ltd., 1958.

Ogburn, William F., ed. *Technology and International Relations*. Chicago: Chicago University Press, 1949.

Osgood, Robert E. and Robert W. Tucker. *Force Order and Justice*. Baltimore: Johns Hopkins University Press, 1967.

Pierre, Andrew and Gregg Herken. *The Winning Weapon*. New York: Alfred A. Knopf, 1980.

Quade, E.S., ed. *Analysis for Military Decisions.* Chicago: Rand McNally, 1964.

Quester, George. *Nuclear Diplomacy: The First Twenty-Five Years.* New York: Dunellen, 1970.

Ramsey, Paul. *The Just War, Force and Political Responsibility.* New York: Charles Scribner and Sons, 1968.

Ranger, Robin. *Arms and Politics, 1958-1978.* Toronto: The MacMillian Company of Canada, Ltd., 1979.

Rathjens, G.W., Abram Chayes, and J.P. Ruina. *Nuclear Arms Control Agreements: Process and Impact.* Washington D.C.: Carnegie Endowment for International Peace, 1974.

Rostow, W.W. *Open Skies: Eisenhower's Proposal of July 21, 1955.* Austin, Texas: University of Texas Press, 1982.

Schelling, Thomas C. *The Strategy Conflict.* Oxford University Press, 1963.

Schelling, Thomas C. *Surprise Attack and Disarmament.* Santa Monica: Rand Corporation, 1959.

Schelling, Thomas C. *Arms and Influence.* New Haven: Yale University Press, 1966.

Schelling, Thomas C. and Morton H. Halperin. *Strategy and Arms Control.* New York: The Twentieth Century Fund, 1961.

Singer, J. David. *Deterrence, Arms Control, and Disarmament.* Columbus: Ohio State University Press, 1962.

Smith, Alice Kimball. *A Peril and a Hope, The Scientists' Movement in America, 1945-1947.* Chicago: University of Chicago Press, 1965.

Smith, Bruce L.R. *The RAND Corporation.* Cambridge: Harvard University Press, 1966.

Smith, Bruce L.R. "Strategic Expertise and National Security Policy: A Case Study," in Morton H. Halperin and Arnold Kanter. *Readings in American Foreign Policy, A Bureaucratic Perspective.* Boston: Little, Brown and Company, 1973, 299-318.

Snyder, Glenn H. *Deterrence and Defense: Toward a Theory of National Security.* Princeton: Princeton University Press, 1961.

Sokolski, Henry. *Eisenhower's Atoms For Peace Plan: The Arms Control Connection.* Washington, D.C.: The Wilson Center International Security Studies Program, The Smithsonian Institute, 6 July 1983. Unpublished paper.

Stimson, Henry L. and McGeorge Bundy. *On Active Service in Peace and War.* New York, Harper and Brothers, 1947.

Teller, Edward. *The Legacy of Hiroshima.* Garden City: Doubleday, 1962.

Teller, Edward with Albert L. Latter. *Our Nuclear Future: Facts, Dangers and Opportunities.* New York: Criterion Books, 1958.

Thomas, Norman. *Appeal to Nations.* New York: Henry Holt and Company, 1947.

Truman, Harry S. *Memoirs, Vol. 1, Year of Decision.* Garden City: Doubleday and Company, Inc., 1955.

Vandenberg, Arthur H. Jr. *The Private Papers of Senator Vandenberg.* Boston: Houghton Mifflin Company, 1952.

Walzer, Michael. *Just and Unjust Wars.* New York: Basic Books, Inc., 1977.

Waskow, Arthur I. *The Limits of Defense.* New York: Doubleday and Company, Inc., 1962.

Wright, Quincy. *A Study of War.* New York: Appleton-Century-Crofts, 1942.

Articles

Augur, Tracy B. "The Dispersal of Cities as a Defense Measure." *Bulletin of the Atomic Scientists* Vol. 4, No. 5 (May 1948): 131–134.

Baldwin, Hanson. "Hanson Baldwin on Secrecy." *Bulletin of the Atomic Scientists* Vol. 1, No. 9 (September 1946): 6.

Barnet, Richard. "When Will We Ever Wage Peace?" *Washington Post* (26 December 1982): El.

Barron, Arthur S. "Why Do Scientists Read Science Fiction?" *Bulletin of the Atomic Scientists* Vol. 13, No. 2 (February 1957): 61.

Bateson, Gregory. "The Pattern of an Armaments Race, An Anthropological Approach: Part I" *Bulletin of the Atomic Scientists* Vol. 2, No. 5/6 (September 1946): 10–11, 26.

Bohr, Niels. "For An Open World." *Bulletin of the Atomic Scientists* Vol. 6, No. 7 (July 1950): 213–217, 219.

Brennan, Donald G. "Commentary." *International Security* Vol. 3, No. 3 (Winter 1978/1979): 193–198.

Brodie, Bernard. "Navy Dept. Thinking on the Atomic Bomb." *Bulletin of the Atomic Scientists* Vol. 3, No. 7 (July 1947): 177–199.

Brodie, Bernard. "What is the Outlook Now?" *Bulletin of the Atomic Scientists* Vol. 5, No. 10 (October 1949): 268.

Brodie, Bernard. "The Development of Nuclear Strategy." *International Security* Vol.2, No. 4 (Spring 1978): 65–83.

Brodie, Bernard. "On the Objectives of Arms Control." *International Security* Vol. 1, No. 1 (Summer 1976): 17–26.

Brodie, Bernard. "The A-Bomb as a Policy Maker." *Foreign Affairs* Vol. 27, No. 1 (October 1948): 17–33.

Brodie, Bernard. "Nuclear Weapons, Strategic or Tactical?" *Foreign Affairs* Vol. 32, No. 2 (January 1954): 217–29.

Bull, Hedley. "International Theory: The Case For a Classical Approach." *World Politics* 18 (April 1966): 361–377.

Bull, Hedley, "Arms Control and World Order." *International Security* Vol. 1, No. 1 (Summer 1976): 3–16.

"Bulletin of the Atomic Scientists" Vol. 1, No. 1 (September 1945) through Vol.14, No.1 (January 1958). All issues.

Bundy, McGeorge. "Early Thoughts on Controlling the Nuclear Race. A Report to the Secretary of State, January 1953." *International Security* Vol. 7, No. 2 (Fall 1982): 3–27.

Burns, Arthur Lee. "Disarmament or the Balance of Terror?" *World Politics* Vol. 12, No. 1 (October 1959): 132–145.

Cavers, David F. "An Interim Plan for Control." *Bulletin of the Atomic Scientists* Vol. 6, No. 1 (January 1950): 12–13.

Cavers, David F. "The Challenge of Planning Arms Control" *Foreign Affairs* Vol. 34, No. 1 (October 1955): 65–66.

Cavers, David F. "International Control of Armaments," *Annals of the American Academy of Political and Social Science* 296 (November 1954): 117–119.

Clark, Grenville. "The Practical Prospects For Disarmament and Genuine Peace." *Proceedings of the American Philosophical Society* Vol. 97, No. 6 (December 1953): 645–651.

Clark, Joseph. "The Atom Bomb: Myth and Truth." *World Politics* (April 1949): 61–67.

Condon, E.U. "Science and International Cooperation." *Bulletin of the Atomic Scientist* Vol. 1, No. 11 (May 1946): 8–11.

Condon, E.U. "An Appeal to Reason." *Bulletin of the Atomic Scientist* Vol. 1, No. 7 (March 1946): 6–7.

Cuthbert, Daniel and Arthur M. Squires, "The International Control of Safe Atomic Energy." *Bulletin of the Atomic Scientists* Vol. 3, No. 4 and 5 (April-May 1947): 111–116, 135.

Daedalus, Journal of American Academy of Arts. "Arms, Defense Policy and Arms Control." (Summer 1975) whole issue.

Eberhart, Sylvia. "How the American People Feel About the Atomic Bomb." *Bulletin of the Atomic Scientists* Vol. 3, No. 6 (June 1947): 146–147.

Ermarth, Fritz W. "Contrasts in American and Soviet Strategic Thought." *International Security* Vol. 3, No. 2 (Fall 1978): 138–155.

Fox, William T.R. "Debate on World Government or Discussion of Atomic Energy Control." *Bulletin of the Atomic Scientists* Vol. 2, No. 5/6 (September 1946): 22–23

Gavin, Major General James M. "The Tactical Use of the Atomic Bomb." *Combat Forces Journal* (January 1951). Reprinted in *Bulletin of the Atomic Scientists* Vol. 7, No. 2 (February 1951): 46.

Halperin, Morton H. "The Gaither Committee and the Policy Process." *World Politics* Vol. 13, No. 3 (April 1961): 360–384.

Hart, Hornell. "The Remedies *Versus* the Menace." *Bulletin of the Atomic Scientists* Vol. 10, No. 6 (June 1954): 197–205.

Herken, Gregg. "The Poker Game of Arms Control." *Washington Post* "Book World" (23 January 1983): 1–2, 9.

Hill, A.V. "The Moral Responsibility of Scientists." *Bulletin of the Atomic Scientists* Vol. 1, No. 7 (March 1946): 3 and 15.

Hutchins, Robert. "Unrealistic Realism." *Vital Speeches* Vol. 11 (July 1945): 601–3.

Ikle, Fred. "Nth Countries and Disarmament." *Bulletin of the Atomic Scientists* (December 1960).

Inglis, David R. "The Fourth Country Problem: Lets Stop At Three." *Bulletin of the Atomic Scientists* Vol. 15, No. 1 (January 1959): 22–25.

Inglis, David R. and Donald A. Flanders. "A Deal Before Midnight." *Bulletin of the Atomic Scientists* Vol. 7, No. 10 (October 1951): 305–306, 317.

Inglis, David R. "Ban the H-Bomb and Favor the Defense." *Bulletin of the Atomic Scientists* Vol. 10, No. 9 (November 1954): 353–356.

Inglis, David R. "Tactical Atomic Weapons and the Problem of Ultimate Control." *Bulletin of the Atomic Scientists* Vol. 8, No. 3 (March 1952): 132–134, 138.

Inglis, David R. "National Security With the Arms Race Limited." *Bulletin of the Atomic Scientists* Vol. 12, No. 6 (June 1956): 196–201.

Inglis, David R."Evasion of the H-Bomb Issue." The *New Republic* (5 November 1956): 7–8.

Kaufmann, William. "Disarmament and American Foreign Policy," *Foreign Policy Reports* (Foreign Policy Association) (1 September 1950): 90–92.

Killian, Jr., James R. and A.G. Hill. "For a Continental Defense." *The Atlantic Monthly* (November 1953).

King, James. "Nuclear Weapons and Foreign Policy: Linked Defense." *The New Republic* (1 July 1957).

King, James. "Nuclear Weapons and Foreign Policy: Limited Annihilation." *The New Republic* (15 July 1957).

King, James. "Nuclear Plenty and Limited War." *Foreign Affairs* Vol. 35, No. 2 (January 1957).

Leghorn, Richard S. "Controlling the Nuclear Threat in the Second Atomic Decade." *Bulletin of the Atomic Scientists* Vol. 12, No. 6 (June 1956): 189–195.

Lilienthal, David E. "How Can Atomic Energy Best Be Controlled?" *Bulletin of the Atomic Scientists* Vol. 2, No. 7/8 (October 1946): 14–15.

Lilienthal, David E. "Where Do We Go From Here?" *Bulletin of the Atomic Scientists* Vol. 5, No. 10 (October 1949): 294.

Luttwak, Edward, "Why Arms Control Has Failed." *Commentary* 65 (January 1978): 19–28.

May, Ernest R. "The Development of Political Military Consultation in the United States." *Political Science Quarterly* LXX (June 1955): 161–180.

Meier, R.L. "Beyond Atomic Stalemate." *Bulletin of the Atomic Scientists* Vol. 12, No. 5 (May 1956): 147–153.

Morgenthau, Hans J. "The H Bomb and After." *Bulletin of the Atomic Scientists* Vol. 6, No. 3, (March 1950): 76–79.

Morgenthau, Hans J. "On Negotiating With the Russians." *Bulletin of the Atomic Scientists* Vol. 6, No. 5 (May 1950): 146–147.

Morgenthau, Hans J. "The Conquest of the United States By Germany." *Bulletin of the Atomic Scientists* Vol. 6, No. 1 (January 1950): 21–26.

Morgenthau, Hans J. "The Political and Military Strategy of the United States." *Bulletin of the Atomic Scientists* Vol. 10, No. 8, (October 1954): 323–325.

Newman, James R. "Towards Atomic Agreement." *Bulletin of the Atomic Scientists* Vol. 10, No. 4 (April 1954). 121–122.

Niebuhr, Reinhold. "The Illusion of World Government." *Bulletin of the Atomic Scientists* Vol. 5, No. 10 (October 1949): 289.

Novak, Michael. "Needing Niebuhr Again." *Commentary* Vol. 54, No. 3 (1972): 52–62.

Oppenheimer, Robert J. "Physics in the Contemporary World." *Bulletin of the Atomic Scientists* Vol. 4, No. 3 (March 1948): 65–68, 85–86.

Oppenheimer, Robert J. "The International Control of Atomic Energy?" *Bulletin of the Atomic Scientists* Vol. 1, No. 12 (June 1946): 1–4.

Oppenheimer, Robert J. "International Control of Atomic Energy." *Foreign Affairs* (January 1948) and *Bulletin of the Atomic Scientists* Vol. 4, No. 2 (February 1948): 39–43.

Oppenheimer, Robert J."Functions of the International Control Agency in Research and Development." *Bulletin of the Atomic Scientists* Vol. 3, No. 7 (July 1947). 192–196, 197.

Rabinowitch, Eugene. "About Disarmament." *Bulletin of the Atomic Scientists* Vol. 13, No. 8 (October 1957): 277–282.

Rabinowitch, Eugene. "Secrets Will Out." *Bulletin of the Atomic Scientists* Vol. 3, No. 3, (March 1950): 67–68.

Rabinowitch, Eugene. "A Victory and an Impending Crisis." *Bulletin of the Atomic Scientists* Vol. 2, No. 3/4 (August 1946): 1, 32.

Ridenour, Louis N. "Pilot Lights of the Apocalypse." *Fortune* Vol. 33 (January 1946): 116–117.

Rowen, Henry S. "The Requirements of Deterrence: The Great Debate," U.S. Congress Joint Economic Committee Study Paper No. 18 *National Security and the American Economy in the 1960's* (30 January 1960): 2–7.

Schilling, Warner R. "The H-Bomb Decision: How to Decide Without Really Choosing." *Political Science Quarterly* (March 1961): 24–46.

Seitz, Frederick and Eugene P. Wigner. "On the Geneva Conference: A Dissenting Opinion." *Bulletin of the Atomic Scientists* Vol. 12, No. 1 (January 1956): 23–24.

Sherwin, C.W. "Securing Peace Through Military Technology." *Bulletin of the Atomic Scientists* Vol. 12, No. 5 (May 1956), 159–164.

Shils, Edward. "American Policy and the Soviet Ruling Group." *Bulletin of the Atomic Scientists* Vol. 3, No. 9 (September 1947): 237–239.

Shils Edward."The Bolshevik Elite: An Analysis of a Legend." *Bulletin of the Atomic Scientists* Vol. 7, No. 3 (March 1949): 77–80.

Shotwell, James T. "The Atomic Bomb and International Organization." *Bulletin of the Atomic Scientists* Vol. 1, No. 7, (March 1946): 8–9.

Sienkiewiez, Stanley. "SALT and Soviet Nuclear Doctrine." *International Security* Vol. 2, No. 8 (Spring 1978): 84–100.

Simpson, John A. "The Scientist as Public Educators: A Two-Year Summary." *Bulletin of the Atomic Scientists* Vol. 3, No. 9 (September 1847): 243–247.

Stimson, Henry A. "The Decision To Use the Atomic Bomb." *Harpers Magazine* (February 1947): 97–107.

Springarn, Jerome H. "The Humphrey SubCommittee: Was it Worth It?" *Bulletin of the Atomic Scientists* Vol. 13, No. 6 (June 1957): 224–227.

Szilard, Leo. "Shall We Face the Facts? For a Truce, Not a Peace." *Bulletin of the Atomic Scientists* Vol. 5, No. 5 (May 1949): 269–273.

Taylor, Glen H. (Untitled Comment) *Bulletin of the Atomic Scientists* Vol. 3, No. 9 (September 1947): 289.

Teller, Edward. "Dispersal of Cities and Industries." *Bulletin of the Atomic Scientists* Vol. 1, No. 9 (April 1946): 13–15, 20.

Teller, Edward. "How Dangerous Are Atomic Weapons?" *Bulletin of the Atomic Scientists* Vol. 3, No. 2 (February 1947): 35–36.

Urey, Harold. "An Alternative Course for the Control of Atomic Energy." *Bulletin of the Atomic Scientists* Vol. 3, No. 6 (June 1947): 139.

Utley, Clifton M. "Atomic Superiority: A Wasting Asset" *Bulletin of the Atomic Scientists* Vol. 7, No. 3 (March 1951): 75–76.

Viner, Jacob. "The Implications of the Atomic Bomb for International Relations." *Proceedings of the American Philosophical Society* Vol. 90, No. 1 (January 1946): 53–58.

Weiner, Norbert. "A Scientist Rebels." *Atlantic Monthly* (December 1946) and *Bulletin of the Atomic Scientists* Vol. 3, No.1 (January 1947): 31.

Wohlstetter, Albert. "The Delicate Balance of Terror." *Foreign Affairs* (January 1959): 211–234.

Wohlstetter, Albert. "Is There a Strategic Arms Race?" *Foreign Policy* No. 15 (Summer 1974): 3–20; No. 16 (Fall 1974): 48–81.

U.S. Government Publications

United States Arms and Disarmament Agency. *Arms Control and Disarmament Agreements.* Washington, D.C.: Government Printing Office, 1977.

United States Atomic Energy Commission. *In the Matter of J. Robert Oppenheimer*, Transcript of Hearings Before the Personal Security Board, April 12, 1954 through May 6, 1954. Washington, D.C.: Government Printing Office, 1954.

About the Author

Jennifer Sims received her B.A. from Oberlin College in June 1975 with a major in Government. In May 1978 she completed her M.A. at Johns Hopkins University School of Advanced International Studies (SAIS) with concentrations in the fields of European Politics, American Foreign Policy, and International Economics. In June 1985 she completed the PhD program in American Foreign Policy, also at SAIS. Graduate work was supported by scholarships from the Arms Control and Disarmament Agency (Hubert H. Humphrey Fellow, 1979) and from the Johns Hopkins University.

Dr. Sims has worked with the Istituto per gli Studi di Politica Internazionale (ISPI) in Rome, Italy, and as a research associate at the International Institute for Strategic Studies (IISS) in London. She is currently American Coordinator of the multinational Nuclear History Program at the University of Maryland.

Index